Landscapes of the Imagination

ANDALUCÍA

ANDALUCÍA

A CULTURAL HISTORY

John Gill

2009

OXFORD
UNIVERSITY PRESS

Oxford University Press, Inc., publishes works that further
Oxford University's objective of excellence
in research, scholarship, and education.

Oxford   New York
Auckland   Cape Town   Dar es Salaam   Hong Kong   Karachi
Kuala Lumpur   Madrid   Melbourne   Mexico City   Nairobi
New Delhi   Shanghai   Taipei   Toronto

With offices in
Argentina   Austria   Brazil   Chile   Czech Republic   France   Greece
Guatemala   Hungary   Italy   Japan   Poland   Portugal   Singapore
South Korea   Switzerland   Thailand   Turkey   Ukraine   Vietnam

Published by Oxford University Press, Inc.
198 Madison Avenue, New York, New York 10016

www.oup.com

Oxford is a registered trademark of Oxford University Press

Co-published in Great Britain by Signal Books

Library of Congress Cataloging-in-Publication Data
Gill, John (John Joseph)
Andalucía : a cultural history / John Gill.
   p.   cm.
Includes bibliographical references and index.
ISBN 978-0-19-537610-4
1. Andalusia (Spain)—History.   2. Andalusia (Spain)—Civilization.
I. Title.
DP302.A47G55   2008
946'.8—dc22   2008024530

9 8 7 6 5 4 3 2 1

Printed in the United States of America
on acid-free paper

Contents

para Alfonso y Lupe, y su hija, Natalia

Preface and Acknowledgments

As the nineteenth-century writer Richard Ford warned us, the last thing the Spanish need is another book about them by a *maldito guiri*, a damn foreigner. Yet as a journalist living and working as a guest in this culture, I found little in the existing literature that spoke to the culture and history I found myself writing about, or to the culture and history I discussed with Spanish and guiri friends. When my friend Kiko Aguilera offered me a music column in his endearingly tiny underground *Andaluz* arts magazine, *Wha?* (after the 1960s New York Beat café of that name), a magazine perhaps best described as Andalucía's post-punk equivalent to *Oz* or *International Times* (maybe even its very own *Sniffin' Glue...*), I discovered a world, a culture, and an attitude, that had not been given voice in any of the literature, English or Spanish. It spoke to a culture left out of English language histories that slam shut at Picasso and the Civil War, and also to a post-Franco reading of a much older Spanish cultural history that is only now being reconsidered by the Spanish historians I quote here.

It is also a history that (with the exception of that estimable cabal of English specialists on the Civil War) either eludes or discomfits the majority of English authors of earlier histories on the region. I am wildly biased, with enthusiasms and blind spots, but wrote this for the people I fell in love with here, to reclaim a version of Andaluz history at risk of being lost forever. Lost, at least, in those vanilla guide-book versions of Andaluz history...

Many people helped make this book possible. Above all I must thank my unwitting mentor Miguel Ruiz Trigueros for his friendship, enthusiasm and generosity with the contents of his library. Other friends helped perhaps without realizing it (*hola* Eduardo!), giving their time, advice, inspiration, ideas, the loan of books and music, meals, lifts and the odd beer. They are:

Kiko Aguilera, Geoff Andrew, Issie Barratt, Markus Bauer, Juan Bonilla, Alastair Boyd, Linda Cooke, Luis Miguel Coronel Vallejo (*sin quién...*), John Costello, Kirsten Cowie, Rachel Dring,

Alfonso Fernández Montenegro Barragán, Michael Fletcher and Julia Vezza, Anthony Fraser, Francisco Javier García González, Antonia González Flores, Eduardo Hojman, Tom Leader, Hans Leuenberger, Stefan Lipka and Talib Syed, Bill, Maxine, Nick and the Limbo barflies (the two Andrews, Jésus, both Miguels, Nordine, Pår, Wes), Anahid Nazeli, Richard Nother, Zoë Palmer, Georgina Richmond and David Seaton, Patricia Storms, Cleo Sylvestre, Mark Thompson, Curro Troya, Marga and Peter Wessel, Rosa Zubiaur.

I must also acknowledge two long-term debts of very special thanks: *a mi pareja*, Graham, *y mi profesor*, Alan Palmer. Alan, *disculpe, voy atrasado con mis deberes...*

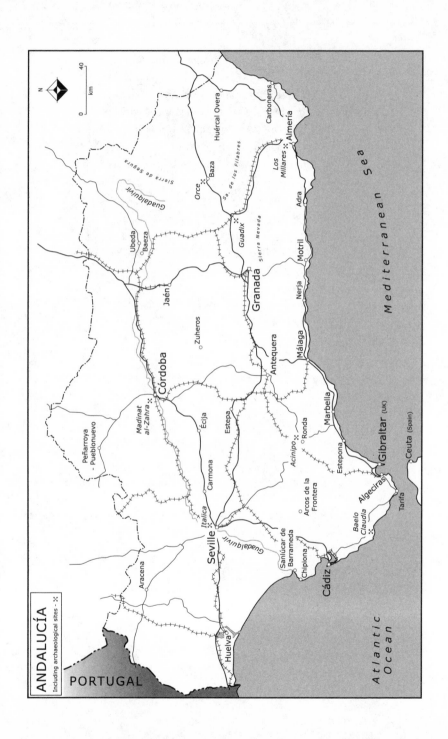

Introduction

THE GARDEN OF EARTHLY DELIGHTS: EXCAVATING THE PAST IN ANDALUCÍA

There is no other place in Europe that contains and embodies the idea of Europe as much as Andalucía. Nor indeed is there any other place in Spain that contains and embodies the idea of Spain as much as Andalucía. Europe—and Spain—were invented here, long before there was either a Europe or a Spain. Adventurous migrants from Africa first settled in Andalucía 1.8 million years ago, before moving north to settle the rest of Europe. In its more recent history, specifically the past five hundred years, Andalucía has become emblematic of Spain itself: land of flamenco, land of bullfighting, land of gypsies and poets, land of heroes and adventurers. In the millennia before those five hundred years, Andalucía *was* Spain, except it did not call itself either Andalucía or Spain. Those two places were only invented and named after 1492.

Much of what makes Andalucía unique has been due to its landscape, a landscape transformed by almost every wave of settlers over the past 15,000 years or so. Phoenicians and Greeks brought vines, olives and other crops that still underpin its modern economy. The olive groves of Jaén alone, visible from space, are the largest concentration of olive trees anywhere on the planet. Similarly, the cork oaks of the Alcornocales forest, among the *pueblos blancos* or white villages of the west, dominate the world's two billion euro cork industry. The *pueblos blancos* themselves, straggling from Vejer near the Atlantic to Setenil near Ronda, are just the most visible reminder of a cultural history stretching back millennia. Most of these villages are named after the Muslim families who introduced a sophisticated agriculture to Andalucía in the eighth century—and more besides.

If we are looking for a deeper thread running through Andalucía, from its prehistory to the modern day, it is of a place as an open, indeed at some points empty, space where numerous cultures found room to thrive, expand or simply flee from trouble elsewhere. It is a contested territory where civilizations have written themselves, been erased and rewritten by others. In its art it is frequently represented as a garden, as much for the ambitions of the waves of peoples who settled here as for its combination of landscapes and climates. Like the original "Garden of Earthly Delights", the Hieronymus Bosch triptych now housed in the Prado museum in Madrid, its history also represents hell as well as heaven, paradise lost and found, dystopia and utopia.

It has been the site of various utopias, real, imagined, proposed, failed: from the Atlantis myth that resonates in the story of the lost civilization of Tartessos, through the cosmology of Arabic gardens and architecture, to the political utopias of the two Republics, the socialist idealism of Blas Infante's *Andalucismo* movement, and even today's alternative communities in the Alpujarras, the Serranía de Ronda and elsewhere. It has played host to most western cultures, religions and languages—west, that is, of Nineveh, Babylon and Ur. It sits at the point where the more temperate northern Mediterranean littoral meets the Atlantic, where the crops first planted in the thirteenth-century BCE "fertile crescent" in what is now the Middle East found a hospitable zone at the other end of this inland sea. It is also where the earliest Phoenician and Greek explorers and traders would have tacked to starboard below the great rock outcrop at the mouth of the inland sea and headed north to meet traffic coming south down the Iberian Atlantic coast.

Then and now, it was a porous border at this busy corner of Europe. Early man arrived here from northern Africa and the eastern Mediterranean hundreds of thousands of years ago, hominids one and a half million years earlier. Hunter-gatherers began using its caves as refuges and ritual sites 100-50,000 years ago, leaving cave art at sites such as the Cueva de la Pileta in Málaga province that compare with the caves at Altamira and even Lascaux. The mysterious itinerant Beaker People left their mark in the form of their idiosyncratic pottery, and the Chalcolithic (Copper, i.e. pre-Bronze) Age vestiges at Los Millares in Almería are among the best preserved in Europe. The *Tartesios* built a fantastic city on the estuary of the Guadalquivir river 12,000 years ago that has been claimed for the Atlantis myth and which has only begun yielding archaeological evidence over the past century. Jonah, of the Biblical whale legend, was one of its visitors.

Phoenicians and Greeks helped build Andalucía's trade, in agriculture and minerals, from around 11,000 years ago. Under the Roman empire, it was *Baetica*, under the Vandals and Visigoths, *Hispania*, and during 781 years of Islamic rule by various north African cultures, erroneously dubbed "Berbers" and, worse, "Moors", it was *al-Andalus*. After 781 years of war, it became Andalucía, and would later be joined with Aragon and Castile in "Spain".

Throughout these millennia its margins flexed and shifted, and when the Spanish came to mark it on their map, the act of finally fixing Andalucía in place was so remarkable they often gave notable settlements on its perimeter the suffix "de la Frontera", of or at the frontier, as though just to make sure, like a road sign or a Keep Out notice for anyone thinking of stepping over the border and into it.

BEYOND THE BORDER

Behind *la frontera*, one of modern Europe's greatest cultures flourished for five hundred years, and barring the odd hiccup or interruption, has continued to do so. These past five hundred years formed the Andalucía, and the Spain (for the two are inextricably intertwined), we know today. This Andalucía, however, and this Spain, were both shaped, marked, altered, named and coloured by the cultures that came before them. Those cultures gave them a voice in a language that begins to unravel and run towards all horizons when you trace its origins back more than a few hundred years. Its art, its literature, its traditions, the signs that make up its culture, all follow arcs back into those earlier cultures. These can take the strangest forms. You clean your teeth every morning with something imported into Spain from Persia two thousand years ago. Whenever you switch on a radio or play a CD, you are likely to hear music played on a wooden string instrument that probably originated in Mesopotamia five thousand years ago and also arrived in Spain (Córdoba, to be precise) about the same time as toothpaste. You sit down to dinner at tables laid out and decorated in the manner of the same people who imported toothpaste. These examples multiply as you forage back in this culture, equally amusing as the bizarre history of toothpaste and the tablecloth, and pleasing to the *nomada* (nomad) mentality that might be said to mark the postmodern twenty-first-century sensibility.

These people imported the sciences, medicine, politics, philosophy, religion, arts, humanities, languages, architecture, agriculture, business and trade, navigation, armaments, drugs, alcohol, and even, although both modern Spanish and British critics might disagree, the novel. They even introduced, also via Islamic Spain, the astronomical equivalent of the hand-held GPS locator, the astrolabe. Their histories are studded with the stories of impossible over-achievers; to take one random example, notable because his brief Visigothic age produced little else, San Isidoro of Seville (560-636), bishop, philosopher, diplomat, ecumenist, polyglot, polymath and the author of the twenty-volume *Etymologiae*, an encyclopaedia so comprehensive for its time (c. 630) that its earlier sources were abandoned shortly afterwards. Canonized as a saint in 1598, he was made unofficial patron saint of the Internet in 2003.

Even the Andalucían landscape, a landscape you see from aeroplanes, trains, cars, on foot, boat or horse, has been marked and altered by these cultures. This landscape, which cries out for the adjective "immutable", has been under alteration ever since the Tartessians laid their first stones, and since the Greeks planted their first vines. Even the Camargue-like delta wetlands of the Coto Doñana National Park, the largest protected wilderness in Europe, are defined by scientists as "man-made". Essentially, everything below the tree-line (or the Sierra Nevada's winter snow-line) has been put there and altered by agriculture. It may appear wild, even eerie, but you are rarely a (perhaps longish) walk from a warm bed for the night in this man-made landscape.

The landscape has also, of course, been mediated by painters, writers, composers, philosophers and ideologues of numerous political shades, many of them now unwitting hostages of the tourism racket. Still others either contributed to or were co-opted into the mythologizing of Andalucía, from the peripatetic Cervantes to self-exiled *Malagueño* Pablo Picasso. El Greco and Goya found a mooring here alongside natives such as Velázquez, Murillo, Zurburán and Leal. Its liberal *burguéses*, bourgeoisie, bred writers from Luis de Góngora to Antonio Machado to Lorca, although by the time of Lorca's last night on earth, in a friend's house that is now a hotel in Granada's tourist district, most artists were fleeing Andalucía, and the troops of Francisco Franco Bahamonde, who launched his dictatorship from Seville (having set off from Morocco) in October 1936 with a surprise raid as successful as that of Tariq ibn-Ziyad's on Gibraltar in 711. *Extranjero* authors from Ford and

Irving to Brenan and Lee and even J. G. Ballard were also complicit in mythifying Andalucía.

Perhaps the greatest myth of Andalucía, as home of flamenco, is long overdue for dismantling. Whatever sorry mess of styles and influences might be served up to tourists and Spanish alike as "flamenco"—ancient folk forms from the eastern Mediterranean, dresses from central European Roma culture, percussion from north Africa—its spirit or *duende* is nowadays more likely to be found in Granada post-punk group Lagartija Nick, whose collaboration with Granada-born *cantaor* Enrique Morente, *Omega*, a collection of Lorca settings in the lo-fi manner of New York's Sonic Youth, gave the much-vulgarized flamenco tradition a new and original voice in the wake of the post-Franco *movida* cultural renaissance.

LANDSCAPE IN MOTION

Andalucía is a place on the move, quite literally, and quite physically, as the Instituto Andaluz de Geofísica seismology department at Granada University will happily tell you. It is also, of course, on the move on many other levels: politically, demographically, economically, and culturally. We may find ourselves in some strange places, in the company of strange people, caught up in strange events, but that is where the real Andalucía, land of toothpaste and tablecloths, lies, some way beyond and beneath the clichés.

It is a truism to say that contemporary Andalucía is both product and summation of its histories. It might, however, be interesting to consider it as an ongoing experiment but one with no written method, no list of materials and no intended or theorized outcome. Perhaps uniquely, for reasons of culture, demography, landscape and climate—a landscape known along its littoral as *la franja*, "the fringe", for reasons both geographical and economic, cultural and political—Andalucía represents in miniature form a model of processes that are under way across Europe. It is undergoing dramatic changes in population. Economic and political refugees are arriving from its east and south. Wealthy northern Europeans are retiring here in their hundreds of thousands, while more and more younger, economically and professionally mobile northern Europeans see Spain and Andalucía as an attractive place to move their economic base. Meanwhile, as industry quits the interior and agribusiness takes over the role of the *latifundio* grand estate owners, more and more young *Andaluces* are leaving rural areas for the towns and the cities, just as their grandparents and their grandparents' grandparents did. Services (commerce, health, education, transport, leisure) wither, just as the British observed in Cornwall and the Lake District in the 1980s and 1990s. Demography enters a state of flux, language bases shift, extranjeros start demanding their voting rights, and resentment and xenophobia breed in the back streets, as just one of many examples of racist graffiti attests, this written in Spanish, on a wall in one of the pueblos blancos in 1999: "Will the last Spanish leaving Jimena de la Frontera please switch off the lights?"

It is also a landscape whose "deep Mediterraneity", to quote US urban theorist Mike Davis, deserves the attentions of that great poet of water, Joan Didion. From the snowmelt torrents of the Sierra Nevada to the *marismas*, marshes, of the Guadalquivir delta and the Coto Doñana wetlands, via the temperate interior farmlands and the arid deserts of Almería, it is a landscape in action, where you can ski in the winter just a few hours' drive from the dunes where they filmed *Lawrence of Arabia* and where desertification is said to be marching north from Africa. Global warming is no mere news headline in Andalucía, but something to be watched in action as you travel through the landscape. Heat waves erupt at Christmas, unseasonal summer rains ruin vital crops, barflies joke about the fleshpots of the Costa del Sol disappearing beneath the waves and Greenpeace España produces Photoshopped visions of the day after tomorrow. As the Instituto Andaluz de Geofísica also points out, it is bisected diagonally, south-west to north-east, by a seismic fault, and both halves are moving in opposite directions, although at speeds that will rarely disturb humans.

Any survey of its cultural history should first ask us what is culture, or art. Recent media reports suggest that "art" in the Mediterranean began 82,000 years ago, although this curious dating is a median figure between the estimated age of 75,000 and 91,000 years ascribed to discoveries at a cave system at Taforalt, near Oujd and the border between Morocco and Algeria, in 2007. Specifically, archaeologists found hand-worked shells tinted with ochre, similar to shells found in South Africa, Israel and Algeria, which had been punctured, probably to make jewellery or possibly as currency, much as cowrie shells have been used as currency in some cultures. The people who produced and wore these shells also practised burial ceremonies, suggesting they had both a religious system and a belief in what Spanish historian Manuel Bendala Galán calls, drolly, the *más allá*, the "beyond", in whatever form they may have imagined it. Their burial rituals involved interment in a seated position, which suggests either an honouring of the dead or a belief in experience beyond death—or, at the very least, making their dead comfortable for whatever was coming next. These people also practised trepanning, the dangerous surgical procedure of drilling a hole into the skull, for medical, ritual or psychotropic reasons. There were several trepanning crazes in the West during the twentieth century, largely because the procedure, which releases pressure on the brain and returns the patient to a temporary state of new-born wonder, offered an entirely legal, if potentially life threatening, high similar to the effects of MDMA. It is fascinating if ultimately fruitless to wonder how these Paleolithic cave users discovered the techniques of trepanning, and the specific effect they sought in using it.

It is probable that human and hominid communities first invented culture, or art, when they grew brains big enough to respond to the environment beyond sensate reflex and started discovering tools that would help them negotiate, alter or improve the environment. In that, this book travels, briefly, some way back beyond the trepanners and necklace wearers of Taforalt, to when sentient beings first discovered that they could have an impact on the landscape around them.

More recently, and more conventionally, it also tries to consider culture, and art, in their widest meanings. The cultural history of Andalucía is not just the dead art hanging on its museum walls, however great it may be (and it is), or the magnificent monuments from its Renaissance and *al-Andalusi* epochs. Until the invention of archaeology and tourism—hardly the friendliest of bed partners—these works were either cloistered behind cathedral, monastery and castle walls, off-limits to the public, or they remained abandoned, neglected, ignored. And until archaeology put a value on it—we might date it to Schliemann's discovery of Troy in 1873—the past was just free building materials for new construction projects (witness, just one example, the columns pilfered from the Roman settlement of Itálica to decorate the outside of the Gothic stage of Seville's cathedral).

Visiting culture, then, and the even later realization that perhaps we ought to be taking better care of it, is a relatively modern notion. It belongs more to an era when, in Andalucía, you might find a living culture in the fantastic graffiti murals glimpsed from your train as you arrive at Málaga station, or the *gitano* music and oral poetry emanating from Seville's notorious Tres Mil (three thousand) ghetto, the nearest Andalucía has to a Harlem or the Bronx, or even the passion for deafening *bakalao* (Spanish for "crap techno") that young men in cars display everywhere in Spain.

There is also a more serious side to considering Andalucía's culture, not least its origins and its "ownership". In the early twenty-first century, Andalucía, and in particular la franja, is the focus of debate on the subject of borders, of fronteras. In modern Europe, this is causing many seemingly liberal democracies a great deal of distress, particularly the topic of the economic mobility of people from "elsewhere".

Barely ten miles separate the shores of *El Estrecho*, the Straits of Gibraltar, at its narrowest. If you stand on the ruined battlements at Tarifa, you can wave at Africa, and it can wave back at you. We have no trouble visiting them; they have a lot of trouble visiting us. There is a clichéd tale of houses in Tanger, Casablanca and Marrakech where the keys to a house in Ronda or Córdoba still hang over the fireplace, waiting for the owners to return to Andalucía to reclaim their property. After all these centuries, the locks probably do not work any more. Yet calls for a "new Caliphate", stretching from Baghdad to the Iberian Atlantic coast, grow shriller, if sillier, by the year. In 2007 the normally sober liberal daily *El Pais* felt the need to issue a front page warning that Islamic radicals, linked to the perhaps inevitable al-Qaeda, were plotting in the Maghreb, just as they did in 711, to launch assaults on Spain.

All this, and the grand sweep of Andalucían culture, might give us pause to consider the notions of borders, what is behind them, and what exactly they are keeping out. It might also give us pause to consider what, beyond brute force, gives anyone the right to build fronteras. The history of Andalucía, like the history of Europe, is one of emigration and immigration, assimilation, usurpation, overthrow, or, in the case of the 781 years of al-Andalus, a long period of *convivencia* among cultures and religions following the initial shock-and-awe attack that saw Tariq ibn-Ziyad's armies take the entire Iberian Peninsula in a decade. Looking back over that grand sweep of cultures, it might further give us pause to consider the possibility that, were it not for our paperwork, passports and outdated *tarjetas de residencia*, we are all nomads. We might, therefore, learn a thing or two from the people who built those cultures.

Part One

IBERIA:

FROM PREHISTORY TO THE

VISIGOTHS

"The ancient peoples of Spain do not have their own histories, or their own historians."

Manuel Bendala Gálan, historian

That post-Flintstones touch: TV aerials protrude from the ground above cave houses at Guadix

Chapter One

GARDENS OF STONE:
CAVES AND CAVE DWELLERS

It is pleasing to be able to write here, for the time being at least, that according to the latest archaeological evidence, the first known Europeans probably lived in what is nowadays Andalucía. Fragments of human and animal bone recently discovered at Orce, near Baza north-east of Granada, backed up by tests on fossilized remnants of albumin, a blood protein, along with evidence of primitive tool construction and use, suggest that hominids, specifically *Homo erectus*, were active in the Baza basin perhaps as long ago as 1.8 million years BCE.

It is even more pleasing to make a further observation about this conceptual first European: she was—of course—African. It is almost tempting to give her a name, but that privilege belongs to the palaeontologists.

The spread of hominid cultures from their origins in Africa is well known and their genetic (DNA) lineages carefully mapped. It was originally thought that they found their way north around the eastern end of what is now the Mediterranean basin, although considerations of changes in Mediterranean topography over the past two million years have led to suggestions of a prehistoric land bridge between north Africa and the Iberian peninsula. At one point in its history, the Mediterranean basin was dry (the Adriatic Sea was once covered by the vast Tethys forest). More recently, following the inundation of the Mediterranean an estimated five million years ago, there was said to be a string of islands between Africa and Europe. One, the now submerged sea mount of Spartel Island off Gibraltar, was mentioned by Plato. Unsurprisingly, this evidence has been seized by people hunting for evidence of the "real" site of Atlantis, something we will come across many more times in considering the cultural history of Andalucía. Like the fruitless search for Homer's Ithaca undertaken by William Dörpfeld, Heinrich Schliemann's assistant at the excavation of Troy, this rather ignores the point about myths such as Atlantis. Myths exist as themselves; their chief cultural function is to remain precisely that. If they are demystified, demythified, they lose their mystery, the precise reason for their existence as myths. (For the record, Homer's Ithaca was recently claimed, by means of soil testing, to be the sandy Pelekas peninsula of western Kefallonía, some way from where Dörpfeld believed it to be.)

THE FIRST EUROPEANS

It is impossible to know what caused hominids to come to Orce, beyond a long trek around the prehistoric Middle East, Turkey, Greece, Italy and France, or the shorter hop across the African-European land bridge. Climate may have played a part, the search for food, competition between different groups, or—and this is where it becomes interesting—simple inquisitiveness. The development of a brain that could do more than respond unthinkingly to basic stimuli—pleasure, pain, heat, cold, hunger, plenitude, fear, calm—is where we might site the birth of culture. The evidence is scant, not least because their numbers were so few, but a brain that could see a possible benefit to travel, beyond running away from danger or towards food, is what brought hominids to Orce. It might not be too fanciful to hazard that it was also a brain aware of its environment, which understood weather, diurnal time, maybe even noted the passage of sun, moon and stars, which lay behind the journey.

As well as negotiating their landscape, and coping with the presence of other biota, themselves and other animals, the hominids also knew how to alter it, which we might also consider another primitive cultural attribute. They used stick and crude stone implements for defence and hunting, and the bones of a wide variety of large mammals, including elephants and rhinoceros, have also been found here.

Orce today is a small pleasant town of around 1,500 inhabitants, in the *altiplano Granadino*, the semi-desert plains high above Granada. It snows here in winter. Just one bus a day connects it to Granada, 75 miles away, and the bus does not turn around. It is dominated by a handsome sixteenth-century castle, built on the remains of a sixth-century Visigothic defence, and is surrounded by ruined *atalayas*, the Arabic for watchtower. There are no hotels here, although you can stay in a series of caves, dating from more recent history, which have been "rehabilitated" in their original nineteenth-century style, but with modern services. Like other cave communities in Andalucía, such as the living "troglodyte" town of Guadix and the less famous Setenil de las Bodegas, these were lived in until quite recently (the ones at Guadix and Setenil still are), although unlike Guadix and Setenil, the Orce caves were abandoned in the 1960s, their squalor denounced by the writer Juan Goytisolo (more on whom later). Like the cave homes at Guadix and Setenil, these dwellings maintain a comfortable median temperature of 18 degrees centigrade year round.

Orce is, then, a typical sleepy Andalucían *pueblo* (town, although it can also mean people), although things livened up considerably in 1995 when an international symposium of scientists descended on it to discuss the discovery of "El Hombre de Orce", Orce Man—the lazy gendering of whom inspires the reference to the Orce finds here as "her"—and place her in the family tree of hominids. There was some initial debate about the species of bone, human or animal (possibly equine), but the albumin tests proved that the remains were human. Her, or his, skull (skulls being, as it were, gender-free; you need to find a pelvic bone to decide the gender of who you just dug up), now occupies pride of place in the town's small history museum.

She was found in the first of four excavations scattered around the outskirts of the town; Venta Micena, Fuente Nueva, Barranco del Paso Leon and the Cerro (hill) de la Virgen, all of which also revealed later human and animal finds. The digs are unprepossessing scraps of land, but the importance of the skull and accompanying shards is that they record the first (so far) known metaphorical *huella*, or footprint, of our human forebears in Europe.

The fossil record yields little more evidence of human habitation in Andalucía until much, much later, although the lack of same can be put down a variety of reasons, from migration to the several glaciation periods in the intervening time. It is known, however, from discoveries of a similar age, that these communities reached the Spanish shores of the Bay of Biscay, most famously at Altamira, but also in a dense concentration of finds along the littoral of Galicia and Basque Country. There is even evidence to suggest that localized, micro-extinction events, including large meteorite strikes, may have caused hiccups in the evolutionary curve, such as the assumed mysterious disappearance of Neanderthals from the fossil record around 40,000 years ago. A meteorite flash-over, larger than that at Tunguska in 1908, is believed to have toasted Andalucía as recently as 12,000 years ago. (Although to be strictly accurate, modern *Homo sapiens* walked out of Africa only 60,000 years ago. According to Dr. Spencer Wells, head of the National Geographic Society's Genographic Project, in an essay published in *Vanity Fair* and still on the NGS website, modern woman as a species may have been depleted to a total of just 2,000 individuals by what Darwin called a selection event, probably glaciation, coming alarmingly close to extinction. But the Orce finds prove that her ancient ancestors were out and about sightseeing 1.8m years earlier.)

Early Cave Dwellers in Andalucía

The next notable pre-human settlement discovered in Andalucía is far more recent: the Neanderthal occupation of the vast cave systems of Gibraltar, the formation of which, chiefly by limestone sedimentation, was still under way just 120,000 years ago. In evolutionary terms, *Homo sapiens* split from Neanderthal woman in the evolutionary chain when *Homo heidelbergensis* was establishing communities in the Mediterranean 500,000 years ago. Until recently, it was thought that Neanderthals died out due to the appearance of a race of superior aggressors, namely *Homo sapiens*. It is now believed that these short, stocky and prognathous-headed hunter gatherers, while suited to survive several ice ages, died out in another selection event, unable to respond to changes in landscape, climate, vegetation and food supplies.

Discoveries in 2006 at one of the largest of the Gibraltar caves, Gorham's Cave, proved, by means of carbon dating, that a colony of perhaps fifteen Neanderthals were sheltering in the cave system as recently as 24,000 years ago, undermining previous suggestions of their disappearance at an earlier date. Tools, some still sharp enough to draw blood today, found at the site suggest a developed hunting culture that not only could process the raw and the cooked (*Homo heidelbergensis* had already invented fire half a million years earlier) but also remove skins for drying and treatment for use in clothing and other domestic applications. It is also now believed that the Neanderthals had developed the skills to speak to each other in a sonic code, limited by vocal chords and epiglottis, but enough to discuss weather, food, love and sadness. Alas, whatever their homemaking skills, these were not enough to secure the Neanderthals' survival in the great Darwinian lottery.

Gibraltar, of course, has its own history, since 1704 that of a British-ruled dependency cut off by political borders from the landmass it sits on.

It reappears at various points later in our narrative. But the caves that the Neanderthals took shelter in point to a deciding factor in many major stages in Andalucía's cultural history: geology. While the sedimentation that formed its limestone caves continued until at least 100,000 years ago (and presumably continues now below the low-tide line), the rocky outcrop at the mouth of this inland sea has a geological origin dating back beyond the formation of the Mediterranean Sea to the Jurassic era, at least 144 million years ago. Geological activity in the region left it unusually rich in deposits of rare and common metals, including gold, silver, bronze, copper, lead, tin and zinc. When later cultures discovered their uses, developed the technology to work with them, and conferred fiscal value on them, they would draw invaders, settlers and traders from across the Mediterranean. First, of course, they would have to invent the boat.

Since we're here, however, we might consider modern-day Gibraltar, as its later appearances here are solely as a strategic position in other peoples' narratives, one in particular quite crucial to the birth of "Andalucía". Modern Gibraltar might also deserve prompt attention before being set aside, as the colony clearly has no desire to be considered part of Spain, let alone Andalucía, which is, for the time being at least, its right.

On any day of the year, Gibraltar is a dismal prospect once you have either crossed the border and the airport runway that lies between it and the colony, or landed at that very airport. Past Casemates Square and into its main street, called Main Street, it is a long line of British department stores, British pubs, duty free emporia and international fast food outlets. When the fleet is in, or the squaddies are out to play, it resembles nothing so much as an Essex high street in the post-war era, but one in which the outcome of the war had been rather different.

This, however, is an outsider's view, although it is one that informs much Spanish opinion of the "English" enclave. As Dominique Searle, the affable editor of its newspaper *The Gibraltar Chronicle* (the oldest newspaper in Europe; its first front page headline was the Battle of Trafalgar) will happily tell you, it actually has a rich history of accepting diasporae from elsewhere, notably from Italy, Sardinia and Malta, even if today it is known mainly as a tax-free and offshore banking and gambling haven. It even has a small but lively lesbian and gay rights movement, which is battling to persuade a conservative administration to give its community the equal rights enjoyed by their counterparts in the rest of Europe.

The reasons why the Neanderthals and their *sapiens* successors chose these particular sites to settle are uncertain, although in the case of the Gorham Cave, which would have been 300 feet higher above sea level 25,000 years ago, security and the proximity of game were prominent. As one archaeologist working on the site told the *Guardian* newspaper, "From here they could see their next meal coming."

THE CUEVA DE LA PILETA'S ALMANAC
Beyond security, no such logic explains what is perhaps Andalucía's finest cave system, the Cueva de la Pileta, outside Benaoján in the Serranía de Ronda. Unlike its larger counterpart, the Cuevas de Nerja, east of Málaga, which has been developed as a tourist attraction with modern facilities and spaces used for classical concerts and ballet, la Pileta remains just that, a cave, with a few man-made paths through the galleries, lit only by storm lamps carried by volunteers in the strictly-limited groups who are allowed in a few times a day. This may be illusory, but the lack of any commercialization makes la Pileta an ideal place to consider the culture of the people who used these caves.

Bats seem to play a key role in the discovery of Andalucía's cave systems. Teenagers hunting them discovered their nests in the Nerja caves in 1912, and a local farmer, José Bullón Lobato, discovered la Pileta in 1905 when he noticed bats flocking into an aperture high in the rocky mountainside above his farm outside Benaoján. Willoughby Verner, a retired British colonel visiting nearby Jimera de Libar, heard about the caves in 1911, wrote about them in *The Saturday Review*, and a procession of archaeologists and palaeontologists beat, and continues to beat, a path up through the rocks to the caves.

José Bullón Lobato's grandchildren now own and run the caves and take turns in guiding the groups. The resistance to commercialization may itself be an effect, but the strictness with which they preserve the caves— no touching the rocks, no flash photography—suggests they have the caves' interests at heart. Certainly, they could have made more money by installing lights, toilets, a gift shop and other tourist facilities, but they prefer to keep the caves as they are.

Several generations of academics have now visited the caves, but analysis of their contents remains speculative. But what little we can surmise from the contents and *arte rupestre* (cave art) is itself a minor marvel.

Like the Gorham and Nerja caves, those at la Pileta were used from around 30000 BCE. They sit high on the north flank of the steep sides of the Río Guadiaro valley, which cuts from east to west just north of Ronda. Formed first by the tectonic activity that thrust the *Andaluz* (Andalucían) sierras up from the sea bed, and then later by several eras of glaciation and thaw, the Río Guadiaro is today rarely more than ankle deep (I've walked across it). Yet in the twelfth century it was deep enough to have drowned men and horses among a Barcelonan raiding party fleeing Ronda and weighed down by their spoils. It is possible that in earlier times the Guadiaro was even deeper, but not enough to explain that the Pileta is a good few hundred feet above its riverbed.

The presence of freshwater pools formed by rain seeping through porous limestone in la Pileta—the name means bowl, sink or pool—may have eliminated the need to live near a water supply. And a suspiciously flat area of land 300 feet below the cave (an oddity in this rugged limestone landscape and probably formed by glaciation) offers itself as an excellent terrain for hunting or even, interestingly, pastoral farming. A lot more becomes apparent once you get inside the caves.

La Pileta is famous for its ambiguous cave painting of a large, possibly pregnant, fish, a symbol that is now the logo for the Junta de Andalucía government administration, most frequently seen on the t-shirts worn by its manual staff. It is just one of a number of enigmatic decorations distributed throughout the cave, all executed with a red ferrous oxide, charcoal, or chalk. The arte rupestre in la Pileta describes animals—horses, goats, perhaps antelopes, deer and prehistoric ancestors to cattle, possibly even more exotic creatures such as giraffes—as well as people. There are also calendars inscribed on the walls, both lunar and annual, and calendars clearly linked to the gestation periods of cattle and goats. There are trees and stars (or perhaps the sun and suns, suggesting a calendar reference) and people wearing horns, either as a sign of a notable hunting success, or adornment marking social status. Symbols and representations of female fecundity abound, including what has been interpreted as a fairly unambiguous image of a vagina, lending themselves to the suggestion that these people had constructed a belief system structured around a female divinity or divinities who held sway over nature. They had also developed crude but notable burial processes, suggesting a belief in Manuel Bendala Galán's más allá, the "beyond".

Although blackened walls in the first galleries suggest that fires, probably using animal fats, were used to light and perhaps even warm the caves, it is now believed that they were not dormitory spaces. Their most likely use was as a burial area, with other ritual, social and perhaps even intellectual uses. While some of the wall art has been ascribed to hypothesized hunters recovering from injuries inside the caves, it seems unlikely that the rows of crossed lines here are the primordial equivalent of someone keeping a tally of their incarceration in a prison cell. The information on these walls, with drawings of the animals and events they refer to, might be considered as news journalism ("I killed this!"), social history ("He killed that, which is why he's wearing the horns!"), or even a library of useful information ("this animal takes nine months to gestate"; "the full moon returns every twenty-eight days"). It might even refer to a form of magic. Some have suggested that the cave drawings were part of a petition to an unknown deity to help the hunter catch that particular species of animal. Furthermore, what were once thought to be pretty representations of turtles, still common along the riverbanks, are now believed to be diagrams of complex pens for either capturing or corralling game.

The equally enigmatic siting of some of the images, hidden in deep niches, visible now as then only with the aid of man-made light, proves that these were not mere interior décor. José Bullón Lobato's grandchildren say that these were probably icons of protecting domestic deities, or animal spirits that also featured in the cave users' cosmology. At the least, the images speak of their need to map, name and describe their environment, and by doing so exert a semblance of order or control over it. Teetering on the edge of shared, formalized language systems, they had studied their environment, had an inkling of how larger systems (climate, season, weather) affected it, and had intuited that there might be such abstract notions as deities at work in their landscape, ones who, if offered the proper votive offerings, might help them in the greatest intellectual abstraction of all, the más allá.

As one friend, a tour guide, suggested on one of our visits to the Pileta, while lacking language, paper, and the benisons of electricity, these people were not so very different from the *Homo sapiens* plodding through la Pileta today.

THE BEAKER PEOPLE SITES OF ALMERÍA

The Chalcolithic, or copper-working, culture discovered at Los Millares at Santa Fé de Mondújar, just north of Almería (in fact on the same rail line that links Granada and Almería, via Guadix, discussed below) in 1891 have been dated back to at least 3000 BCE, and represent one of the finest preservations of copper-age culture in Europe. Here, other factors also come into play, not least the role geology played in the development of these cultures, but also the geographical origin of the people who introduced these technologies, and the cultural baggage they were already carrying when they arrived. While their main industry may have been copper, and, later, iron, they are commonly known as the Beaker People, from the inverted bell shape of the pottery they left behind. They were originally believed to have been from the Iberian Peninsula, but some of the oldest finds have been in the Rhine delta. Beaker remains have been found across Europe, as far west as Britain and Ireland, and as far east as Austria and Hungary. The diffusion of Beaker culture has been ascribed to a shared "package" of technological skills, mobile in several directions criss-crossing prehistoric Europe, and not linked to any one ethnic group. As well as producing artefacts and architecture, they too practised burial rituals, with the familiar seated burial position for the dearly departed, suggesting again a complicated intellectual notion of preparing them for the beyond.

Almería's mineral wealth attracted settlers, invaders and dealers right up until recent decades. Visit Almería, the city, today, and you will find its port dominated by the impressive if rusting remains of El Cable Inglés, a tall elevated railhead (British built in 1902-4) that passes through the city and juts out over the port, where it would have offloaded tin from mines in the hinterland into waiting cargo ships as recently as 1994. (It also happens to sit alongside a newer, quite poignant, sculptural memorial to the 142 Almerienses who died in the Nazi concentration camp at Mauthausen in Austria. Another complex aspect of modern Andaluz, and Spanish, history, in which thousands of fleeing Republicans, as well as diaspora Spanish Sephardic Jews, were imprisoned, many killed, in the gulag of Franco's Nazi friends.) El Cable Inglés has been claimed as part of Spain's industrial heritage and is now a protected monument. A similar mineral commerce operated, and still operates today, in diminished form, on the Rio Tinto river north of Huelva, on Andalucía's Atlantic coast. Here Spanish tourists titter at the British suburban architecture of the Bella Vista

Barrio Inglés, a feature of the industrial theme park that now occupies part of the Rio Tinto mine-works here, and whose operational arm let loose a vast toxic spill into the neighbouring Coto Doñana wetlands reserve in 1988.

That the site at Los Millares, a large complex of vestigial settlements and some eighty megalithic burial structures, nowadays stranded in the unwelcoming moonscape north of Almería (near the Tabernas desert, backdrop for parts of *Lawrence of Arabia* and any number of paella westerns), is one of the best surviving examples of Beaker culture is simply an accident of history. What it tells us, though, with its defensive walls and the artefacts of what seems to have been a highly stratified and unequal society, is that these early Almerienses were part of an aggressive warrior culture, ruthless in the way they constructed their communities—and that they certainly did not come from Almería. As another, parallel, history unfolding at this time, considered in the following chapters, suggests, their presence in Almería should give us pause to consider the origins of the gene pool of modern Andalucía, and "Spain", just as it should in any other European country or, indeed, any other country in the world.

While there is documented evidence that the caves of Guadix were occupied at least as far back as the Muslim era, it is probable that some of the caves were occupied as early as the Paleolithic period, possibly as long ago as 12000 BCE. Guadix is one of the oldest towns in Spain, with finds dating back to the Stone Age. The use and cultural interest of the caves is rather more modern; when the Catholic armies arrived in Guadix in 1489, they found the caves inhabited and with a developed domestic habitation stretching back centuries. Today an estimated 10,000 people, half of the population, are thought to live in over 2,000 cave dwellings around this bleak and dusty town in the mountains east of Granada. (That is not to be rude to the people of Guadix: bleak and dusty describes many Spanish towns that don't feature in the tourist guides. That is where the Spanish live.)

There's a busy market in cave homes in Guadix, which today sell from between €40,000 for a wreck, and around €120,000 for a fully modernized three-bedroom property with all mod cons. The chief point of these cave dwellings was, and is, their resistance to the wild temperature swings here in the mountains. Apart from a massive cathedral designed by Diego de Siloé, responsible for parts of the cathedrals at both Granada and

Palaeolithic with all mod cons: a cave house outside Guadix

Almería, and a chic cave hotel, there is very little else to draw the visitor to Guadix, although the television aerials protruding from the ground here and at neighbouring Purullena do add to the area's surreal post-Flintstones ambience. It might be said, however, that Guadix, like prettier Setenil de las Bodegas near Ronda, maintains a link, however modernized, and however tenuous, with Andalucía's original gardens of stone.

Chapter Two

TARTESSOS: LAND OF IVORY, APES AND PEACOCKS

Geology was also responsible for the first of at least three truly fabulous cultures founded in Andalucía. Depending on your take on history and historians, it is also the Andaluz civilization that invites speculative links with the Atlantis myth, links that are still being proposed, by serious historians and writers, in the twenty-first century.

Fittingly, the (largely) lost city and empire of Tartessos, now believed to have been developed around its capital somewhere in the Guadalquivir delta near Sanlúcar de Barrameda, sits on the twilight side of historicity, where the setting sun of Greek legend only partly illuminates the facts and shadows the fictions. It was probably founded in the early ninth century BCE. Its destruction, either by envious Carthaginians or a cataclysm in the manner of Santorini (a seismological possibility in this quake-prone region, and music to the Atlantisists' ears), is dated somewhere in the sixth century BCE.

A sober and no-nonsense historian such as Manuel Bendala Galán, in his oft-reprinted *Tartesios, Iberos y Celtas* (2000), sees Tartessos as a heavily mythified tale of what is in fact a largely explicable collision of cultures and technologies in this very busy corner of the prehistoric Mediterranean. Another, even more cautious, historian, José Manuel Cuenca Toribio, in his weighty *Andalucía, historia de un pueblo* (1984), sees the peninsula at the start of the first millennium BCE as the site of a "fevered" search for minerals by prospectors from Tyre, Sidon and Biblos—in effect, a gold-rush. Yet another—more, shall we say, imaginative—historian, José Manuel Paredes Grosso, in his *El Jardín de las Hespérides: Los Origenes de Andalucía en los Mitos y Leyendas de la Antiguedad* (1985) sees it not only as the setting for the fabled civilization of Tartessos, but also as a probable site for the Atlantis myth, and even makes a brave stab at hitching the *Odyssey* legend to Tartessos as well. Paredes Grosso does in fact have myth on his side (so long as we keep the dictionary definition of the word close

There but not there: the Coto Doñana marshes, likely site of Tartessos and, quiza, Atlantis…

to hand, for ballast) as Greek myth did indeed site the Garden of the Hesperides, and Hades, the land of the dead, at the end of the earth, *finis terrae*, commonly taken to mean the modern Straits of Gibraltar, where Homer's sun would sink every night into the Ocean. Perhaps taking his cue from the German historian Adolf Schulten, who aspired to be to Tartessos what Schliemann was to Troy, Paredes Grosso gives a citation-heavy if perhaps overly literal reading of texts from Plato, Hesiod, Strabo, Ovid, Pliny and many others to support his theories. But the regular appearances of the word *quiza*, perhaps or maybe, in his text (and a word count would probably find hundreds, quiza thousands…) park it firmly in the realm of speculation. It should be noted, however, that Paredes Grosso's book is an extremely erudite work, steeped in mythology and literature, perhaps best considered as creative literary investigation (it is in fact a diversion from his long career as a high-flying educationalist and politician).

Yet even the normally unexcitable Manuel Bendala Galán seems to think himself on safe ground when he describes Tartessos as "a kind of ancient Eldorado of the western Mediterranean". He and Paredes Grosso even share similar literary sources, not least Homer, although Bendala Galán cautiously reminds us that while myths have a social function, they should not be taken as historical fact.

The facts, as Manuel Bendala Galán is able to establish them—he says very early on in his book that the *Tartesios*, the Spanish for the people of Tartessos, did not write their own history, nor did they have historians— are quite workaday, if complicated, although they are attended by some tantalizing myths and archaeological discoveries, some of which you can walk up to and look at today.

The Greeks and Phoenicians had already sailed beyond the mouth of the Mediterranean when Tartessos was founded (the Phoenicians had founded the fledgling settlement of Gades, or Gadir, later Cádiz, in 1100 BCE). Bendala Galán and Cuenca Toribio both cite the sailor Kolaios of Samos as the first Greek adventurer to reach Tartessos, the latter calling him the "Colón [Columbus] of antiquity", and Kolaios returned home a rich man, no doubt ready to spread the news about what he found. Cuenca Toribio describes the interaction between these cultures as a "symbiosis", adding that these visitors did not arrive empty-handed. If anything—and as would be the case with even more munificent Muslim arrivals, aboard boats packed with agricultural grafts that underpin Andalucía's economy today—they were about to transform prehistoric Spain's culture, landscape, agriculture and economy. Moreover, as Cuenca Toribio explains, and you sense he is *making a point* here, the colonists were peaceable and tolerant towards the Iberians, whereas the Ibero-Celtic tribes of central and northern Spain were inveterate fighters, apt to descend like a wolf on the fold at the drop of a pikestaff.

At this stage of its prehistory, the Iberian Peninsula was home to many differently named pueblos, peoples or cultures. A map of the post-Tartessos (sixth-century BCE) peninsula in *Tartesios, Iberos y Celtas* has more than fifty different pueblos, in varying degrees of concentration. The *Lusitanos* (Lusitanians) occupied what is modern Portugal (itself, we should remember, a largely British invention). Northern Spain was peopled by dozens of different communities, while the south had fewer: just three cultures, the *Turdetanos*, direct successors to the *Tartesios*, the *Libiofenicios* (Libyan-Phoenicians) and *Bastetanos* (after their capital, Basti, nowadays Baza in Granada province) occupied the area that is modern Andalucía. The size of these communities can, as Bendala Galán says, be taken as a measure of their achievement and stability. While the Phoenician explorers (Phoenicia covered what is modern-day Lebanon, Syria and northern Israel) predated the Greek arrivals, Greek culture was the most influential cultural import into the region. Both brought with them their domestic culture—notably the grape and the olive (two of the star exports of the eastern "Fertile Crescent", which Jared Diamond dates back to the thirteenth century BCE), and also the science of astronavigation, which enabled them to reach the Spanish Atlantic littoral—as well as a common tongue, *koiné*, a form of early classical Greek spoken by the Sea Peoples, the Mediterranean maritime cultures; they also brought religion, where Greek mythology intermingled with indigenous myth, and social structure. Given the lack of physical or written evidence, Bendala Galán says that it is almost impossible to determine which innovations were local, and which colonial. It is known, however, that the indigenous Iberians were already mining gold, silver and more common metals in both the Sierra Morena, north of Seville, and around the Rio Tinto north of Huelva, the primary reason the Greeks and Phoenicians came shopping. The two most famous artefacts from the era are the Tesoro (treasure) of Carambolo, an array of fantastic jewellery found at Carambolo, just outside Seville, and now housed in that city's Museo Arqueológico, and the dazzling gold candelabras excavated from the riverbed at Lebrija, between Seville and Cádiz on the Guadalquivir, and nowadays to be found in their rather gloomy home in the Museo Arqueológico Nacional in Madrid.

Tartessos gave its name to the culture, its people, its capital and its river, now assumed to be the Guadalquivir (in Arabic, *Wadi al-Kabir*, "Great River"), which flows from the mountains of Cazorla, north-east of Jaén, 400 miles to Sanlúcar de Barrameda, where it debouches into the Atlantic. Speculation on the physical nature of the capital borrows heavily from Plato's description of Atlantis, which is the source of all later Atlantis myths, of a city around two-thirds of a mile wide constructed of three or more concentric rings of land protected by surrounding moat-like waterways. Aerial photography of the Coto Doñana wetlands, one of the largest nature reserves in Europe, has revealed enigmatic rectangular outlines visible beneath the marshland, possibly the outline of the floor-plans of man-made structures, but these do not fit Plato's description. The Doñana wetlands, declared a protected national park in 1969 and a UNESCO World Heritage site in 1984, are an ever-shifting landscape of dunes, sandbanks and marshes, stretching from the tacky seaside resort of Matalascañas south of Huelva, to the northern banks of the Guadalquivir estuary opposite Sanlúcar de Barrameda, and east to the outskirts of Seville. Far from being a wilderness, they are defined by scientists as man-made, having been altered over the centuries by agriculture, fishing and salt panning, and were even used as royal hunting grounds in the thirteenth century and afterwards. Today, access is strictly controlled, with small groups allowed in each day for guided tours around a limited area of the park. The rest is left to the few remaining wild lynxes, foxes, the occasional rumour of a boar and the millions of birds that migrate, flock, nest or live here year round. Not much elbow room there, then, for archaeologists foraging for a lost civilization…

But then, half way through its writing in the summer of 2007, this chapter was rear-ended by a report in *El Pais*, and then parts of the international media, that German historian Rainer Kühne had found a set of concentric circular structures buried in the Marisma (marsh) de Hinojo, seven or eight miles inland from the aforementioned bucket and spade resort of Matalascañas. (The problem here being that, short of breaking the law and then wading for hours through a swamp, there is no access from Matalascañas.) Kühne was working with satellite photographs first discovered by another academic, Werner Wickboldt, who had been scanning images of the Mediterranean looking for topography that matched the terrain described by Plato in his *Critias* and *Timaeus* dialogues.

At the time of writing, Kühne, Wickboldt and scientists from Spain's Consejo Superior de Investigaciones Científicas (CSIC), have identified two concentric rings and two rectangles that might be the remains of temples to Poseidon and his wife Cleito. The next step will be to take deep soil samples from the Marisma de Hinojo site to ascertain the nature of the terrain (sand would suggest it was once dry; mud would suggest it was, well, wet, and not suitable for the construction of lost civilizations) and then to date whatever can be retrieved from the original layer.

Doctor Kühne is based in Braunschweig, Lower Saxony, where he stays in contact with the six-strong team of archaeologists from the CSIC, which is continuing its exploration of the Marisma de Hinojo. It was an article by Kühne in the archeological journal *Antiquity* in 2004 that first sparked the CSIC survey. He says that the survey site covers an area of two and a half square miles, inside which the CSIC team has found shards of pottery so far dating back to the Muslim period, probably nearer the (post-711 CE) beginning of their presence in Andalucía. The CSIC team is still investigating a total of five large arcs or rings (which lend themselves to Plato's rings) and four large rectangular forms, the largest of which is 750 by 525 feet. If this is the ground plan of a single structure, Kühne's posited "silver temple of Poseidon" would be vast, its contents, if any remain, befitting Manuel Bendala Galán's "Eldorado of the western Mediterranean", on a par, at the very least, with the Tesoro de Carambolo and the Lebrija candelabras. If he has "found" Atlantis, or even "just" Tartessos, this is a discovery to rival Schliemann at Troy, and certainly to silence the sceptics.

Whatever is down there—Tartessos, some other Tartesio settlement, or maybe even Atlantis (and some academics still argue that to search for Atlantis is to miss Plato's point, which they see as myth, possibly borrowing details from the eruption on Santorini, used to shape a metaphor about the nature of state and government)—it was destroyed in the sixth century BCE, either by invading armies from Carthage, envious of Tartessos' wealth (which Bendala Galán actually discounts, suggesting subtler socioeconomic forces at work), or possibly by one or more tsunamis, sparked by a seaquake. These too are known but rare phenomena in the region; the last big one razed Lisbon in 1755 and knocked down churches as far as Seville. (The enormous volcanic eruption that blew open the caldera of Santorini in the mid-second century BCE triggered a tsunami that swamped Crete and marked the end of Minoan culture.)

Unsurprisingly, Manuel Bendala Galán resists the Hollywood block-buster version of Iberian prehistory. He explains that a sophisticated network of cultural and mercantile exchange had already developed between this corner of the Iberian Peninsula and the civilizations of the mid- and eastern Mediterranean. Greeks and Phoenicians had been living among the Tartesios prior to the founding of Tartessos itself, and the latter were probably moving towards a position where they would either sup-plant or simply subsume Tartessos into their own culture and economy. He says that the Mediterranean cultures entered an *edad oscura* or dark age after the fall of Troy (popularly dated to the eleventh century BCE), and that this and the later (mid-fifth century BCE and, thus, post-Tartesio) fall of Mycenae inspired successive waves of migration to and coloniza-tion of the western Mediterranean from Greece. He also notes that these new arrivals were joined, in the sixth century BCE, by other economic migrants, *semitas*, a word common to Bendala Galán and many other Spanish historians, and open to a polysemous interpretation as meaning either Jews (descendents of Sem, Shem, one of the sons of Noah) or anyone from the Middle East. Following the disappearance of Tartessos and the appearance of later societies there was also a further influx from the Minoan diaspora, probably around the second century BCE.

Tartessos was a highly stratified society, ruled by "warrior-king-gods", famously, Argantonio (fifth century BCE) and Therón (thought to be the first Tartesio king, so presumably around the ninth century BCE). The former is said to have lived for more than 120-150 years, which Bendala Galán reads as meaning a number of successive kings in a dynasty. Therón, linked to the mythical Gerión, fought the Phoenicians at Gadir. More free-wheeling interpretations credit both with the bodies of giants, and even more fearsome aspects. While the Tartesios were skilled at mining and making exquisite gold and silver works, this was still essentially an agrar-ian society, but with the mineral wealth to build and equip powerful armies, with which they engaged in wars against rival cultures with gusto.

Bendala Galán is keen to stress, however, that this was not a slave society. Its workers were free citizens, but the upper classes controlled both the products and the means of production. Their warrior-king-gods were deified in their own lifetimes—cultures with cosmologies, religions, belief in the más allá, were commonplace by this time—and Bendala Galán sees their presence in living legend as part of the social function of myth. These societies were based on the deification of a founder, and the mythology around these deities provided both social structure and cohesion. They had yet to codify a written language, but used a structured ideogrammatic form of inscriptions with a complex agreed syntax in their symbols. Their few hypothesized texts were believed to have been laws transmitted in the form of oral poetry. Their art, music, and philosophy remain a complete mystery, although the glories of Carambolo and Lebrija might give us a measure of their likely achievements in other arts.

The heart of Tartessos was in what is called *baja* (lower) Andalucía, the area south and west of the Rio Tinto and Seville, but at its expansionist peak in the sixth to eighth centuries BCE its domain stretched as far east and north as Catalonia and the Basque Country, even to the borders of what is currently France. Tartesio and Greek artefacts, such as funerary steles, inscribed columns commemorating dead heroes, have been found throughout modern Andalucía and as far as Toledo and Alicante, as have fragments of Mycenaean pottery. War, economics and competition drove these societies, and on at least two occasions Bendala Galán cites a Darwinian selection event as the reason why some of them failed, and why some flourished. Cuenca Toribio writes that as Tartessos expanded it also fragmented, with smaller factions vying for power across the peninsula. Somewhere in the tides of cultural and economic change flowing across the peninsula, Tartessos just sank, perhaps literally.

Tartessos-qua-Atlantis

The Tartessos legend spans texts as diverse as the Bible up to the most recent novel by twenty-first-century novelist Manuel Pimentel Siles (born in Seville, nowadays a Cordobese). The Tartessos myth is frequently, indeed enthusiastically, linked with the Biblical Tarshish, referenced more than once in the Bible, but specifically in the King James version of the "Chronicles": "For the king's ships went to Tarshish with the servants of Huram: every three years once came the ships of Tarshish bringing gold, and silver, ivory, and apes, and peacocks." Tarshish was more probably Tarsus in Turkey, but the allusions to its mineral wealth still tether it to Tartessos. (The apes have been interpreted by some as a racist reference to African slaves or workers in Tartessos.) It was also directly cited by, among others, Herodotus, Strabo and Pliny.

The myth was already alive and virally active in the fourth century CE, when it was incorporated into the imagined sea voyage of the poet Avienus, the *Ora Maritima*, which would later inspire Schulten's literalist, if unsuccessful, search for Tartessos in the Coto Doñana, his theory described in his *Tartessos* (1924).

The connection with Atlantis, particularly in Spain, might equally be blamed on the great Catalan poet Jacint Verdaguer as much as on Schulten. While Verdaguer was born and lived some distance from Andalucía, his epic poem *L'Atlàntida* (1876) placed Atlantis (*Atlántida* in Spanish, and yes the accents head in different directions in Catalan and Castilian) at the heart of what we might call the Spanish creation myth. The poet-priest's epic work, which details the story of Heracles (Hercules) and the destruction of Atlantis, locating it in Andalucía, home of one of the Pillars of Hercules (Gibraltar), became a mystical text for Barcelona's wealthy religious right wing as an air of increasing millenarianism took hold in the years leading up to the nineteenth-century fin del siglo. This was a time when the Conde Eusebi Güell i Bacigalupi, the millionaire industrialist patron of architect Antoni Gaudí i Cornet, was paying teams of archaeologists to excavate the Muntaña Pelada (bald mountain), where Gaudí's failed utopian community, the Park Güell, was planned, to look for Noah's Ark there, convinced that it would be found on the slopes of the Tibidabo hill. The same millenarian fears informed Gaudí's "expiatory temple", the Sagrada Familia, which he referred to in conversation as the "cathedral", even though Barcelona had had a perfectly serviceable cathedral since 343 CE. Gaudí built his cathedral to inspire the people to atone for the sins of the modern world; the modern world, at least the working-class part of it, replied by setting fire to his cathedral (or at least some of its outbuildings), as they did to other parts of Barcelona during the Setmana Tragica uprising of 1909.

But in Verdaguer and his poem, it—quiza—seemed that Catalonia, and indeed Spain, at least those who had the luxury of worrying about such things, had found something to fill a void in their collective soul. Atlantis-qua-Tartessos, like the clumsily transplanted St. George/Santiago myth at Santiago de Compostela, anchored Spain's swelling new middle classes in a comfortable medieval, classical and religious pseudo-history, and at a time when they were understandably worrying where modernism might be taking them. Hence the Jocs Florals, the revived medieval "floral games" that were all the rage in fin del siglo Barcelona. Hence the modern-day websites where people trace their family trees "back" to the kings of Tartessos. (I am a journalist, not a psychiatrist, but it would not need a psychiatrist to suggest that these and certain other phenomena speak to the idea of a people looking for an identity and a past uncomplicated by other peoples' DNA strands.)

Verdaguer is largely guiltless, but it seems fair to say that he and Schulten (with a helping hand from none other than José Ortega y Gasset, who had his own ideas about *la Atlántida en España*) unwittingly unleashed a continuing flood of potboilers on Atlantis-in-Spain ever popular with visitors to the Barmy section of their local bookshop. This also feeds into one of the few sweeping generalizations on which this book might chance its arm; that is, the lack of a truly convincing Spanish avant-garde (which might have put a stop to all this *nostalgie de la mythologie*), and the tendency in general to hang on to the past, or at least the comfort of history and tradition, however fictional, not least in Spain's and Andalucía's curious relationship with the Roman Catholic Church, a spectacle of panoply and ecstatic devotion on the outside, a smooth hollow on the inside.

There are, however, honourable exceptions, notably the 2006 novel, *El Librero de la Atlántida* (The Bookseller of Atlantis) by the aforementioned Manuel Pimentel Siles. Pimentel Siles' novel is considered in more detail in Chapter Eighteen, but it is elegant, post-modern proof that the Atlantis-qua-Tartessos myth still resonates in Andalucía and Spain, and in this new century. It might also, in refiguring the Atlantis myth in the epoch of new millenarian fears about climate change and destruction of the environment, be seen as a timely comment on Andalucía's continuing romance with its fictionalized past.

Dr. Kühne spent the summer of 2007 waiting for permission for a further, perhaps definitive, excavation on those tantalizing buried circles and rectangles in the Marisma de Hinojo in the Coto Doñana. As the winter rains swept in from the Atlantic, he was still waiting on that all-important permit for him and the CSIC team to renew their searches. Which for the purposes of our investigation leaves Tartessos, and maybe Atlantis, hovering just below the surface, where the myth remains intact. Here we might take a leaf out of another unlikely source, the work of physicist Erwin Schrödinger, and his famous cat, the cat that inspired Stephen Hawking to say, only partly in jest, "Whenever I hear of Schrödinger's cat, I reach for my revolver." Schrödinger invented his cat as a means of explaining a quirk in his colleague Werner Heisenberg's Uncertainty Principle, which holds that we can observe a particle's position, or its trajectory, but not both. Moreover, the act of observing the particle will affect its state. To illuminate this conundrum, Schrödinger posited a cat in a box, with a phial of deadly gas that might be released if we open it. As we approach the box, the cat is theoretically both dead and alive. We only know if we open the box. Whether or not it survives is irrelevant, if harsh on cat lovers. The point is that the cat is in two states up until the moment the box is opened.

Thus with Dr. Kühne's Tartessos-qua-Atlantis, there and not there until he digs it up. And the act of digging it up will, one way or another, decide its fate as myth or historic reality. It would be churlish not to wish the good doctor *toda de buena suerte en el mundo*, all the good luck in the world, but for the time being, like Werner Heisenberg's particle, it floats between two states, there and not there, beneath the Marisma de Hinojo, perhaps the best place for a myth.

The transfixing gaze: the much-copied iconic Dama de Elche

Chapter Three

LA DAMA DE BAZA: DEITIES OF LIFE AND DEATH

She sits on a throne in the sepulchral gloom of the ground floor of the Museo Arqueológico Nacional in Madrid. The sepulchral gloom would be apt were it not for the fact that this is simply poor lighting in a museum some decades past its last refit date. She is, at least, kept company by a similar Spanish archaeological icon, La Dama de Elche, who sits alongside her, both of them contemplating the sublime gold candelabras and other Tartesio gold works from Lebrija across the room, possibly the single most powerful source of light in this gallery. (The museum is one of the most cunningly hidden in the world, un-signposted anywhere in the city, secreted behind the Biblioteca Nacional on the city's museum row, Paseo del Prado. If seeking it out, take either camping supplies for a week, or a cab.)

In fact, the sculptures form a triumvirate with the nearby La Dama del Cerro de los Santos, a trio who are said to represent the first magnificent flowering of indigenous Iberian art. The Dama de Baza might have been fashioned to offer a physical definition of the word "stolid": heavy, humourless, sour, a hint of cynicism around the lowered eyelids, tired, put-upon, a woman ready to tell you how disappointed she is in just about everything. Or perhaps this is just arrogance, or a cynical pose. Either way, the difference between her and her voluptuous neighbour from Elche is startling.

This would, however, be a rather modern reading of the fourth-century BCE Dama de Baza, who is in fact a deity, a goddess believed to hold sway over matters of life and death and fecundity in all its forms, who is thought to have served a similar deistic function as figures such as Astarte, Aphrodite, Demeter and Persephone in prehistoric, pre-Christian, Iberia.

She was only unearthed in 1971, on a hillside outside Baza, north-east of Granada, whose region includes hominid-friendly Orce. It too sits in the altiplano Granadino, but is a much larger town, with today 20,000 inhabitants, a town whose size supports over a dozen fine medieval churches and one of the best preserved Muslim *hammams* (baths) in Andalucía. It names its surrounding natural park and sits equidistant between Granada and Guadix. Contrary to what buying-a-home-abroad TV programmes tell you, it snows here in winter too.

The Dama was immediately declared one of the greatest archaeological finds in Spain, as much for her status among pre-Christian Iberian artefacts as for the remarkable condition of preservation in which she was found.

She served two functions, as a funerary relic—in fact, as a reliquary—and as religious symbol. She is assumed to represent an actual, if anonymous, individual, of the Ibero-Celt aristocracy. Her square burial chamber was discovered almost intact, now reconstructed in the Museo Arqueológico Nacional, the figure retaining much of its polychromatic colouring and surrounded by a wealth of revealing personal artefacts. As well as a variety of domestic objects—clothing, jewellery, decorated urns containing votive offerings—she was accompanied on her journey into the más allá by a large number of sword-like weapons, suggesting that the woman represented was perhaps a warrior-queen. She comes from a culture that practised cremation; a small niche in the base of the throne held an urn containing her ashes. The life-sized representation was carved from a single piece of grey limestone and then painted in blue, red, brown and black.

She is seated on a throne, and dressed in finery, most strikingly two huge cuboid earrings that look as though they weighed a ton, but also some four necklaces and a large snood-like headdress. Her hands bear large rings, and her left hand is holding the figure of a young pigeon, painted blue, a fertility symbol among Mediterranean societies who celebrated cults of the goddesses Astarte and Aphrodite. As a final touch, her throne has wings on its back, conferring on this (perhaps) warrior-queen-goddess the power of flight, possibly in life, metaphor or in the beyond. This would seem a quite logical continuation of the tradition of the warrior-king-gods of Tartessos, although with two intriguing twists, not least the gender of the figure, which invites any number of speculations about the structure of the society that revered her, and the super-human or merely magical gift of flight, which can of course operate on any number of symbolic, metaphorical or mytho-poetic levels. Considering the level of technologies extant in her era, this woman is sitting in the cockpit of her culture's equivalent to the Space Shuttle.

By the time of her deification, two centuries after the fall of Tartessos, the political map of the region had changed dramatically. The Phoenicians had settled the north African coast in the eighth century BCE, and within three centuries the city-state of Carthage (now a suburb of modern Tunis) would become one of the most powerful forces in the western Mediterranean, ready to challenge Rome in the three Punic Wars of the first millennium BCE. Tartessos had been replaced by the Turdetano culture, occupying roughly the same area as Tartessos, with the Libiofenicios settling south-western Andalucía, roughly that below the Guadalquivir, and the Bastetanos taking the area roughly east of Granada. Historians believe that the Dama was a Bastetano or, perhaps more accurately, Bastetana. Manuel Bendala Galán describes this period as a time of increasing Phoenician hegemony in the region, which, with the comfort of hindsight, can be seen as setting it in train towards a direct confrontation with Rome, and one that it would lose.

The chief cultural influence of this period was Ibero-Celtic, pressing down from the Bronze-Age Celtic cultures in northern Spain—specifically, Galicia, Asturias and Cantabria—having originated in northern Europe from what is speculated as an origin in the Balkans, from where it spread across Europe as far as Ireland, Scotland, Wales and Cornwall, all of which had been in cultural and mercantile contact with the Iberian Peninsula since the Tartesio period.

In the absence of any detailed evidence of the religions of Tartessos, which would in any case present a fusion of Greek, Phoenician and indigenous Iberian belief systems, both Bendala Galán and Cuenca Toribio describe the Dama de Baza as the first—for now—known example of specifically Iberian culture, religion, and artefact. The latter describes her as "dazzling", although perhaps figuratively in terms of the near-perfect condition in which she was found rather than in the visual sense of the drab and irascible woman sat grumpily in the Museo Arqueológico Nacional.

Wings or no, the Dama de Baza has certainly been on the move in recent years, not least in the great Iberian archaeological exhibition that travelled to Barcelona, Bonn and Paris in 1998, in the process, according to Bendala Galán, "unleashing" a phenomenon he describes as Iberomania, a new ism attended by conferences, papers and courses.

LA DAMA DE ELCHE

Her neighbour, La Dama de Elche, was discovered at a much earlier date, in 1897, outside the town of Elche, near Alicante in Valencia. It says something about the nature of archaeology at the time that a French archaeological connoisseur and collector, the amusingly surnamed Pierre Paris, was able to buy it and promptly whisk it off to the actual Paris, where it was displayed at the Louvre until the Second World War. Curiously, some histories say it was hidden from the Nazis by Louvre officials, while Manuel Bendala Galán says that it was handed back to Spain, along with certain other artefacts, in 1941. This would have been a full year after the Nazis had entered Paris. Given the Nazis' kleptomaniac attitude towards other countries' national treasures, this act of uncommon generosity on their part would seem to have been a favour arranged between those boon friends, Adolf Hitler and Francisco Franco Bahamonde, or at the very least between underlings of the Vichy government and "neutral" Spain.

The Dama de Elche dates from the same period as the Dama de Baza, and is considered by historians and curators to be an even finer example of Iberian art than the Dama de Baza. The style has its roots in Greek statuary, but its treatment here is considered to be the reified moment when indigenous Iberian art took physical form. It is a bust of her head and upper torso, although it has been suggested that it was once part of a complete tableau in the manner of the Dama de Baza. An aperture at the back of the bust also held an urn containing her ashes. She too was discovered with her polychrome colouring intact, although over the years the Dama has reverted to a light reddish limestone monochrome. At one point she was thought to be a forgery, a theory later discounted. Some still believe that she in fact represents a male, or perhaps boy-ephebe, in the act of making a votive offering to unknown gods, and it is still uncertain whether she represents a deity or a mortal, possibly both.

Manuel Bendala Galán, our keen if unwitting companion in this era, in a paper prepared for an exhibition and conference in Madrid in 1999—and perhaps part of the outbreak of "Iberomania" he describes elsewhere—has an even more intriguing thesis. He gave his paper the uncharacteristically racy, almost film noirish, title of "The Petrified

Woman". La Dama de Elche is probably a stone copy of an earlier bust, originally in wood, made as a maquette or model of how such divinities would have been dressed. A hypothesized reconstruction made for the exhibit transforms the dull bust into a, yes, dazzling upper-torso figure, clad in rich ruby-red fabrics and laden with extraordinary gold jewellery, her head clamped between two outrageous Ferris-wheel-like head adornments, almost Mayan or Aztec in aspect, her forehead beaded with jewels, her high, arched and plucked eyebrows picked out in red, her lipsticked lips the same red, her face even more a picture of icy hauteur than the one that stares back at us contemptuously in the Museo Arqueológico Nacional.

So it would seem that the Dama de Elche is a palimpsest, a series of cultural layers, which itself invites any number of speculations. If this is indeed the case, it establishes her as an archetype, or perhaps paradigm, of something the people who made this version, like the one before it, thought important enough to record. Important enough, quiza, to record the thing itself, and what you were meant to do with the thing itself. The panoply surrounding her, on its own, arrives laden with baggage about class, wealth, power, beauty, religious or social status and iconography, all sounding resonances that echo through later idealized icons of women, human or deity. But like the sphinx she almost resembles—and Bendala Galán is right when he says she transfixes you when you first glance at her—she seems likely to keep the purpose of this near-Warholian double-portrait secret to herself for some time.

La Dama del Cerro de los Santos

The third member of this triumvirate (they are accompanied in the museum by a fourth figure, the Bicha de Bazalote, but this is a bearded man-bull, resembling a small minotaur) is the Dama del Cerro de los Santos, although her full name makes her the Dama Oferente de etc., referring to the fact that this full-length standing figure is represented in the act of making a votive offering. She also comes laden with rumours of imaginative embellishment, by a local rogue dubbed the "Watchmaker of Yecla", an enterprising character who saw his fortune in "augmenting" some of the many archaeological discoveries at the Cerro (hill) de los Santos, near Albacete, south of Madrid in Castilla-La Mancha. Luckily for history, but unluckily for the watchmaker, his enterprise was soon discovered and after much academic wrangling the Dama was certified as genuine, or at least unaugmented.

She was discovered accidentally in 1871 during the felling of trees on the hill, and it was only when the authorities, in the form of the Museo Arqueológico Nacional, were notified of the unscientific mayhem unfolding on the Santos hillside that they intervened. Manuel (we have cited him so many times we're virtually on first-name terms anyway) says that the discovery is significant for its name alone, the Hill of Saints, as very few relics of such religious figures have been unearthed, and in such numbers, before or since the Cerro de los Santos find.

The wealth of statues, real or augmented, found at Cerro de los Santos was initially thought to be of Visigoth origin, but the real ones at least were later dated to the second or third centuries BCE, slightly younger than the Damas of Baza or Elche. This would place them in the time when Iberian Spain was facing a dramatic new threat, namely Rome. The Museo itself notes only that the tall, enigmatic figure from the Cerro de los Santos is hieratic, priestess-like, which confers another social function on these iconized women figures, giving them access to the inner sanctum of the priesthood, with all the authority and power that entails. Manuel, for his part, finds the Dama del Cerro an ultimately confusing figure, whose stylistic origins complicate the process of archaeological taxonomy, although she certainly adds to the variety and wealth of these images of powerful, goddess-like women adored during these centuries in prehistoric Iberia.

RITUALS OF LIFE AND DEATH

The apex of the funerary culture that idolized these women is to be found in the fourth-century BCE Bronze-Age necropolis at Toya, near Peal de Becerro between Úbeda and Cazorla, high in the mountains above Jaén, where it really snows in winter, sometimes hip-high, the Alpine vistas made all the weirder because beneath all that snow is the biggest olive-growing region on the planet. The Toya necropolis is the best-preserved example of this funerary culture. Unsurprisingly, the grandest forms of interment and celebration were reserved for the higher levels of society, although Manuel says that as these societies developed through the first millennium BCE, social structure became less vertical and more horizontal. Cremation was common among all strata of society, the size of monument depending on social status, although small and unborn children were likely to be interred without cremation below or around the family home, for sentimental or superstitious reasons. The más allá was the final destination of all levels of society, although the highest rank, such as our three Damas, in their fluid roles as aristocrats, deities and hierophants, were already, as it were, commuting between the two sides, the here and now and the beyond.

We also know something of their daily lives, thanks largely to Strabo (via Manuel), that most energetic of Greek travellers and geographers. Travelling in northern Iberia in the first century BCE, he found the natives straddling a "ferocious" savagery and a "sociability and humanity". They organized social activities among specialist or age groups, particularly sports that would lend themselves to preparing men (and women) to a level of combat-readiness, and for the health of the community. They celebrated numerous festivals with animal sacrifices, but drank wine sparingly on special occasions where dancing would be accompanied by brass and wind instruments. They did drink beer, made from barley (which would suggest an above-average strength, depending on water proportions), for its mood altering and even anaesthetic properties.

The importance of these three figures extends some way beyond what they tell us about the intellectual sophistication and artisanal skills of their time. Most obviously, all three figures are of women, and to date no comparable figures of men of a similar social or religious status have been unearthed. This would suggest that in certain ways, and whatever the quotidian experience of ordinary citizens may have been, women occupied positions of power and influence in these cultures, possibly real, possibly symbolic, and that they figured at the centre of several cosmologies, across several centuries. It is of course entirely possible that this was simply a local adaptation of earlier Greek belief systems in their manifold guises. It should, however, leave us pondering the roles ascribed to women in a Spanish history written almost entirely by men...

This also lends itself to the theory of a persistence of goddess cults throughout Iberian and even modern Spanish culture (and a countervailing suppression of these same goddess cults in some later Spanish cultures), today seen in the Marian cult of the Virgin Mary, notably in the Semana Santa processions, where every local church and *hermandad* or parish brotherhood parades their icon of the Virgin, some of them so large and elaborate they need dozens of people to carry them. None, of course, can match La Macarena, from the *barrio*, neighbourhood, of that name in

Seville, whose processions can take up to twelve hours overnight, winding through the streets and back to her church. Her appearance, in a glorious halo of candlelight, can inspire grown men to burst into tears and wrend their clothes. (True, it can also inspire others to get very drunk and fall over, but this is Semana Santa in Seville after all.)

The Marian cult is, of course, very Catholic, but it is worth noting that while the Catholics have rewritten her as a receptacle and embodiment of sadness, suffering and pain, she is also accorded an equal status as a symbol of hope and miraculous intervention: *la auxiliadora*. In Seville she is credited with saving the city from at least one earthquake and any number of plagues. She is also held responsible for untold millions of small domestic favours. This is perhaps not the place to indulge in amateur psychological analysis, but this extreme dualism, often stylized to the point where it parts company with reality, is something we will encounter in the representation of women at other points in Andaluz culture. And sometimes it gets down off the gallery walls and steps out into the street.

Chapter Four
GADIR/CÁDIZ: FIRST CITY IN
EUROPE

While all that political weather rolled back and forth across the Iberian Peninsula in the final millennium BCE, one place remained constant, and continues to do so today. Known as Gadir to its Phoenician founders (possibly from the Arabic *agadir*, "walled"), Gadeira to the Greeks, Gades to the Romans, Qādis in Arabic, Hispanicized as Cádiz, it is said to be the oldest city in Europe. The Phoenicians founded it in—quiza—1104 BCE, and today it celebrates 3,000 years of continued, if at times fraught, existence. It even claims to have the oldest continuously-occupied building in Spain, the Casa del Obispo, tucked alongside the huge cathedral looming over the Atlantic.

The Casa del Obispo is nowadays a small but fascinating museum, representing 3,000 years of *Gaditano* (the adjective for the place, the noun for the people) history, like a sedimentary side-section of layers from its Phoenician, Greek, Iberian, Roman, Muslim and Christian eras. Although the building is small, a fiendishly clever hi-tech museum has been inserted into its bricks and mortar, with glass-floored metal gantries zigzagging across and up and down its various layers of history, accompanied by multimedia displays explaining its history. The Casa del Obispo is one of the best little museums in a country profligate in its distribution of great little museums.

It can also be said that, whatever happened in the history of Andalucía, this beautiful little city Was There. As well as representing the first major trading base of the Phoenicians, its strategic and economic importance made it one of the first major targets in the Roman conquest of Spain, led by the legendary warrior Scipio Africanus, in the second century BCE. It fell to Carthage in the fifth century BCE and was the military base for Aníbal (Hannibal) in the Punic Wars. Nearby was the site of one of the key early battles between Muslims and Spanish, the 711 CE Battle of Guadalete, in which Tariq ibn-Ziyad's army defeated Visig-

First city in Europe: Cádiz, its mountainous cathedral, and, tucked behind, the
Casa del Obispo

oth King Roderic's army, killing Roderic himself. It was taken by the armies of the "Reconquest" in 1262, and in September 1493 Columbus left from Cádiz on his second journey to the Americas, this time, it might be said, knowing where he was going, and accidentally discovering the Antilles en route. It was here in 1587 that Drake famously, if apocryphally, "singéd the king of Spain's beard" by including fire-ships in the fleet that he sailed into the Bahia de Cádiz. (This was imaginatively reconstructed in one of the few landscapes by Francisco de Zurburán, *La defensa de Cádiz antes los ingléses* (1634), now hanging in the Prado.) In 1812, it was the site of the short-lived Cortes (parliament) of the liberal-progressive First Republic of Spain, a democratic anomaly promptly squashed by the monarchy.

Cádiz seems proud of its tradition of liberal-radical politics, not least the commonly held belief that Franco declined to ban its *carnaval*, the annual February carnival, as he did with carnavales elsewhere in Spain, fearing that the independent-minded Gaditanos might rise up against him. Today, it has an energetic if small university culture (staff of the philosophy faculty sometimes go jogging together in t-shirts that declare their job title with pride), which supports some of Andalucía's finest independent bookshops, and its carnaval is the wildest in Spain, perhaps on a par with Rio, Venice and Notting Hill on the global stage. Its bar and restaurant culture rivals Seville—you would be mad to leave Cádiz without eating at El Faro, either in its tapas bar or restaurant—and, one of this writer's litmus tests for a civilized city of culture, it has a modestly-sized but insouciantly visible gay community.

Curiously, and no doubt to the chagrin of its town hall authorities, Cádiz remains off the main tourist routes through Andalucía—nearly half its tourist visitors are still indigenous Spanish—partly because of its geography, partly due to its rakish reputation (until the twenty-first century, its *casco antiguo* or old town had only two hotels of any note; the sailors of earlier times would head straight for the bordellos), and partly due to the impression that it does not have as many attractions as the popular theme parks of Granada and Ronda. This means that, for the time being, its lovely squares and subtropical gardens, narrow streets, crumbling architecture, the boisterous market and its immodestly sized cathedral, whose copper dome glows golden in the afternoon Atlantic sun (and which it can do year round, even on Christmas Day), are there to be enjoyed without having to negotiate the barbarian hordes who swamp Granada and Ronda every day of the year.

The history sketched out in the Casa del Obispo is noted in detail in the city's Museo de Cádiz, which modestly houses both a museo arqueológico and museo de bellas artes in one (more) handsome building on Plaza de la Mina. Together, the Casa and the Museo present a complementary history of what might justifiably be called a unique city.

An Archipelago That Became a City

Modern Cádiz sits on a long, narrow and partly artificial peninsula, with the casco antiguo surrounded by battlements at the tip, and most of the 130,000 population living in the newer city, the Manhattan-like grid south-east of the massive Puerta de Tierra gates. But even as recently as 1100 BCE, it was still a small archipelago of islands, the passages between which either silted up or were filled in by public works, while some islands either vanished or sank beneath the waves. Much of this reshaping of the landscape was done by the fluvial action of the Río Guadelete, which debouches into the bay, and where archaeologists say the original coastline has receded by at least half a mile over the past three millennia. Some of the oldest archaeological discoveries were retrieved from the sea by the city's Centro Andaluz de Arqueológica Subacúatica, whose base is the *balneario*, a former bathing station resembling something from Victorian Brighton, which overlooks the Playa de la Caleta, the city's prehistoric harbour.

The small bay at Caleta is believed to have been home to temples to both Astarte (Aphrodite to the Greeks, Venus to the Romans) and Kronos—a stone capital unearthed at Caleta has been ascribed to the latter's temple there—while the island of Sancti Petri, inside the bay and near the suburb of San Fernando, has yielded splendid bronzes that suggest it was the site of a temple to Melqart, the Phoenician tutelary god of Tyre (a role he reprised in Gadir), later adapted by the Greeks as a temple to Herakles, or Hercules, son of Zeus, the Hercules of the twelve labours, and of the pillars at Gibraltar and Djebel Musa. The continuing excavations at Sancti Petri are described by the Museo as "without doubt, the great challenge of Spanish archaeology in the twenty-first century". The poet Avienus sited the temple of Venus on an island, now lost, in or near Caleta, which was home to one of those sad, mischievous seers of ancient

Greece, an oracle (another, older, belief being that you must be careful about what you ask of an oracle, as they have imaginative and sometimes devilish ways of parsing your request).

Cádiz is still a city under excavation, as archaeologists probe for the original topography lost to tide, time and wind, not to mention the accelerating urban development of recent centuries. Both city and its surroundings have given up Tartesio artefacts, notably the Las Cumbres site at El Puerto de Santa Maria, a half-hour ferry ride across the bay. The museo displays pottery from the Tartesio period found here, as well as artefacts from another Tartesio site near Huelva to the north, including Greek texts that mention the warrior-god-king Argantonio. El Puerto was Columbus' shipyard and is believed to have been founded by the Greek warrior Menesteo, a rather dilatory underling of Agamemnon, a sometime King of Athens, one of the many suitors of Helen and one of the conspirators inside the Trojan Horse, who was recorded by Homer as fleeing after the Trojan wars and reaching the Straits of Gibraltar and the Guadalete, where he and his troops founded a port. Menesteo named the port after himself, as you would do in these circumstances. The Muslims named it Alcante or Alcanif, "port of salt". The Christians, ever keen to wipe evidence of previous tenants off the map, gave it its current a-historical name, under Alfonso X of Castile, around 1260 CE. The place has no noticeable connection to a *santa* Maria, although the naming fits the obsession of the *Reyes Católicos*, the Catholic monarchs Isabella and Ferdinand, with renaming the universe according to their cosmology. Las Cumbres is one of the many sites currently being investigated as archaeologists reconstruct the physical history of Cádiz, retrieving stone from mud and fact from fiction.

One of the most impressive discoveries in the museo arqueológico is a pair of sarcophaguses, one male, found in 1887, and one female, only discovered in 1980, of the same size, and each carved from a single piece of marble probably dating from the early Turdetano fourth century BCE. Their style originates in Egyptian funerary design, but they are probably Greek in origin and similar to sarcophaguses found in Phoenician necropolises in Cyprus, Malta, Corsica and Sicily. These too display a new twist in funerary culture; the belief that, for the dead (presumably aristocratic) individuals to survive in the más allá, there first had to be a faithful anthropomorphic figure of them let behind in the mortal world.

According to the cautious curators of the museo, Cádiz was "definitively incorporated into the ambit of Rome" in the year 206 BCE, after the second Punic War. It was not so much defeated or taken, but signed a treaty of friendship and alliance with the new great power of the inland sea, and one that would make it "one of the most powerful and rich cities in the Roman Empire". We might imagine, however, that this alliance was implemented with a certain unambiguous leverage. As Roman Gades, its temple to Herakles became that of Hercules, and everything else changed as the second layer of the palimpsest was laid across the city. Much of the Roman city was destroyed, either by weather, war or later developments, and is only now being rediscovered. It was in this period that the Casa del Obispo acquired its first monumental edifice, having been a modest building of mud and wood for much of its Phoenician phase. The Casa acquired ingenious underground cisterns to catch and store rainwater for domestic use, a decorative patio and fountain and wall paintings, some of which survive today. The city expanded rapidly to meet its international role, which can be seen, in part, in the remains of the Roman necropolis and the fragments of the theatre.

Unusually, it does not seem to have been included in the network of the three great Andaluz Roman settlements: Itálica, outside Seville, Baelo Claudia, on the beach at Bolonia, and Acinipo, on a windswept bluff north-west of Ronda (more on each of which anon). While a wealth of domestic utensils has been discovered, particularly some beautiful glassware produced under the reign of Tiberius (42 BCE-37 CE), Gades seems to have been a working port, with none of the majestic social architecture of Baelo Claudia, just 60 miles down the coast at Bolonia. While future discoveries may change this reading, it was perhaps the Newcastle to Baelo Claudia's London. Its chief trade was fish, meat, and agriculture, and Juvenal noted that, then as now, it was more a party town than a seat of great culture. Julius Caesar declared all its citizens honorary Romans in 49 CE. Most of the finest sculptural finds displayed in the museo come from elsewhere (mainly the aforementioned Bolonia), notably a larger than life statue of the emperor Trajan, and also from the small palace inland at Medina Sidonia.

While we consider Baetica, or Roman Andalucía, in the next chapter, it is worth bearing in mind that this was the first wholesale transplant of an external culture into Andalucía, and into the Iberian Peninsula. Much of the culture we see in Roman Andalucía—its architecture, art, design, the fragments of daily lives of both citizens and aristocracy—can be seen anywhere else Rome transported its imperial culture, much of it still bearing the traces of earlier Greek culture. (In fact, José Manuel Cuenca Toribio says that Andalucía's "romanization" was so thorough that it reached a point of saturation, *saciedad*. Moreover, he adds that the *convivencia*, a word we will see many times again, between the indigenous people and the Romans would profoundly alter the psychology of the indigenous population.) The chief change was linguistic, with Latin becoming the, ah, *lingua franca*, and one that would remain for centuries after Rome fell. Cuenca Toribio sees Latin as a higher linguistic skill that enabled the Andaluces to both communicate with other cultures and also engage with abstract concepts beyond the reach of earlier, cruder, indigenous languages. Above all, he credits the Andaluces with a natural—or perhaps learned— art of assimilation—both of, and with, others.

One thing does stand out from the era of Roman Gades, though; the until this point almost unconsidered art of urban design, and communications between cities and towns—not to mention the feats of civic engineering that would make places such as Itálica, Baelo Claudia and Acinipo in many ways more sophisticated than some of the domestic structures that stand near them today.

Little remains of Visigothic Cádiz, for reasons still open to speculation. The Casa del Obispo was largely destroyed in the fourth century CE, perhaps due to an earthquake affecting much of the city, perhaps due to the sacking of the city by the invaders, a particularly punitive treatment of an important naval and commercial port. Visigothic Andalucía, like much of Visigothic Spain (the Visigothic capital of Toledo being a notable exception), would leave little mark beyond its architecture, although inland at Seville it would provide a seat for two remarkable things: the hyperdulia Christian cult of the Virgin Mary, and, in its archbishop (and in 1598 saint) Isidoro (560-636 CE), one of the intellectual giants of Spain, and indeed Europe, of the entire first millennium CE.

Things became interestingly complex again after Cádiz entered its Muslim epoch, shortly after the Battle of Guadalete, near what is now Barbate (de Franco, in full, but they are trying to play down the reputation as El Caudillo's favourite beach haunt), in 711 CE, shortly after Tariq ibn-Ziyad, then governor of Tangier, and his army had taken *Jabal Tariq*,

"Tariq's rock", later Anglicized to Gibraltar. The battle took place on, we are assured, Sunday 19 July 711 CE. With the battle won and the Visigothic King Roderic dead on the field, it was only a short march to what the Visigoths had left of Cádiz. Cádiz, still then a cluster of islands off a promontory in the bay, was renamed Yazirat Qādis, isle of Qādis, and would again become a powerful and wealthy trading and naval port, reaching its apogee during the eleventh century CE Almoravid and Almohad dynasties. While the intellectual life of the numerous dynasties remained in a tight orbit around the palaces of Córdoba, Seville and Granada, Yazirat Qādis, as it continues to be excavated today, reveals similar religious, military, public and domestic architecture and design to that found in the greater Muslim Andaluz centres. The mosque stood next to the Casa del Obispo, its minaret an adaptation of a ruined Roman building. The city was quickly walled, against the "Reconquest" that began barely a year later (Cádiz would fall to the Christians in 1262). Inside the walls the Muslims rebuilt the Roman theatre and constructed other civic buildings besides, the shape of the walled city being severely limited by its uncertain, indeed flexible, littoral. Archaeologists describe it as a small market city-port, comparable today to Ceuta or Tunis, but a vital hub in land, sea and river communications, and one the Christians would have been eager to take.

CÁDIZ AFTER THE "RECONQUEST"
At the fall of Granada in 1492, Cádiz entered two grand narratives; that of Christian Spain, which continues today, and the even livelier one of maritime Spain, which does not. As well as seeing Columbus off on his second voyage, it received an immense political and economic fillip in the seventeenth century when the gradual silting of the Guadalquivir below Seville rendered the city's river port unusable, causing a shift in business to Cádiz, which was only too happy to take in these mercantile orphans. This wealth underwrote the architecture, the city planning, the grand squares, the monumental gates and battlements, the cathedral, the churches, museums, and even the purchase of those giant sub-tropical *ficus* trees that decorate the parks, of the past three or so hundred years. It underwrote a university, as well as the Oratorio de San Felipe Neri and later the Gran Teatro Falla, named after a favoured son, composer Manuel de Falla. It might, indeed, have underwritten, directly or indirectly, the education of that favoured son and a few outlying ones, too, such as the poet

Juan Ramón Jiménez, later one of Spain's four literary Nobel laureates (and the only Andaluz), born and today celebrated in Moguer, on the Rio Tinto east of Huelva.

Does it serve anything to repeat where this wealth came from? Maybe it still does. This wealth certainly built the later additions and alterations to the spectacular cathedral in Seville. Some visitors see the fantastical retablos adorned in gold and silver and jewels, perhaps even the iconic, but undated, portrait of San Isidoro of Seville by Murillo. Other visitors, including this writer, see Meso-American blood cascading down the interior walls.

A short time before the year 1812—well, in fact, 24 September, 1810—this wealthy, liberal city became the refuge for Spain's parliament, the Cortes, in flight from the ravages of the Napoleonic Wars. Cádiz was just one of only three places not overrun by the French during that war, the others being Tarifa and, unsurprisingly, Gibraltar. This home-away for the Spanish parliament was the site for the signing of a new constitution, a document popularly known as *La Pepa* after the saint's day on it which it was adopted. After more than three centuries of absolute monarchy the constitution of 1812 promised Spain its first modern democratic government. It lasted just two years, when in 1814 Ferdinand VII quashed it, rounding up the liberal politicians who had proposed it, and reinstated absolute monarchy.

The constitution of the first Republic may seem just another event for the history books, but it would have incalculable effects on Spain, particularly during the events of 1835 and 1874 (the first and second Carlist wars), 1923 (Rivera dictatorship), 1936-9 (civil war), 1975-6 (death of Franco and aftermath) and in fact most years, especially election years, snap or otherwise, since then. The Cádiz constitution of 1812 might have given Spain a free society on which to build; instead it sank back into the Middle Ages. Culturally, this reversal informed how Spain's artists could speak, write, paint, sing, carve, create film or dance, and until only a few decades ago. Most Andaluces, and most Spanish, of course, were more worried about staying alive and finding food than they were about artistic expression.

Three considerations make themselves immediately apparent here. One is that democracy does not guarantee great art. Another is that bland and safe cultures sometimes produce bland and safe art. Still one more is that many artists, in all fields, prefer to place themselves in opposition to the consensus to produce their art. Goya is perhaps a supreme example of this. Conversely, Murillo is not, for reasons we will see. Picasso, arguably the greatest artist of the twentieth century, felt he had no choice but to leave and not only stay away but forbid the return of "Guernica" to Spain in his lifetime. Yet the Granadino abstract expressionist Jose Guerrero chose, after a sojourn in New York, to return to Franco's Spain. More recently, would the 1980s *movida*, already simmering underground long before Franco died, have been so vibrant without state oppression, or would its art have been less weedy, old-fashioned and derivative—in comparison to pan-European counterparts—without it? Spain may have its Fassbinder-qua-Sirk in Almodóvar, and one of the world's greatest cinematic poets in Victor Erice, but where are its Godard, Fellini, Truffaut, Tarkovsky, Angelopoulos? It may, similarly, have its Sonic Youth in Granadinos Lagartija Nick, but where are its Miles Davis, Talking Heads, Kraftwerk?

An impossible debate to condense here, but its mention might serve to show how men arguing in smoky rooms and soldiers gathering on borders with armaments can affect the creativity of a country. And, for reasons outlined above, one of the many ways that Cádiz offers a small, perhaps imperfect, multi-faceted history of the culture of Andalucía, and Spain. You will find similar, and often grander, narratives in many other Spanish and Andaluz cities (although not, I would argue, in Granada, for example, nor indeed in that comparative upstart Madrid, declared the capital of Spain only in 1561) but Gadir/Cádiz seemed to deserve this short diversion from chronology unlike any other place in Andalucía this writer can think of.

Writing this chapter felt at times like a small betrayal, but as this *historia breve de Cádiz* shows, the only people it really betrays are the Got-here-firstistas, who are largely concerned with real estate prices or the exclusivity of their favourite bars and restaurants. As its history shows, Cádiz—just like Andalucía—has survived any number of waves of foreign invaders, welcome or otherwise. Any publicity will draw visitors from elsewhere, and the trick that Cádiz has to learn is to adapt its dependency on tourism to the way it would prefer to depend on tourism. Unlike parts of Greece, Andalucía has not been too clever on that score so far, although, like Greece, it may be learning its lessons. Yet as far as the present reader is concerned, if you have reached this sentence without throwing this book at a wall, or perhaps even having thrown but retrieved it, it can be safely assumed that you are the sort of visitor Cádiz would like to see more of.

Handy for the beach: the heavenly city of Roman Baelo Claudia, at
Bolonia on the Costa de la Luz

Chapter Five

THE HEAVENLY CITIES OF BAETICA: ROMAN ANDALUCÍA

Before we set foot in Roman Andalucía, we have to heed several dire warnings from even local historians. Firstly, the landscape of Andalucía in its Roman period shares little with the modern region beyond its geology. Roman agriculture would transform it, not so much by importation but by the manner in which it developed the region's economy (agriculture, minerals) into a multinational industry. (And it would be transformed, quite radically, one more time again, by the Muslims, who imported a whole ark of new agricultural species.)

The second is the impossibility, and even Stephen Hawking has conceded this, of time travel. We join the historians with our noses pressed against the window of history, unable to pass through. Even though the period produced enough texts, artefacts and written histories, it is impossible to divine exactly how these cultures operated.

Thirdly—and there are many more qualifiers, but three is probably enough to be going on with—history becomes slippery around hard objects like dates, places and events. It is pleasing to anchor cultural changes to an invasion, a battle, a birth or a death, but it is more likely that—especially in the interplay between cultures in the region at this time—far more complicated currents were flowing across the newly "modern" Mediterranean.

Certain things can be chained to fact. The Romans first arrived in Spain as a ruling force in 210 BCE, having been ceded the rule of the Iberian Peninsula by Carthage after the Second Punic War. They landed at the then Greek city of Empirion (modern-day Ampurias, near Girona north of Barcelona) and were led by Scipio Africanus, then just twenty years old. Four years later, in 206 BCE, Scipio would establish a community at the former Turdetano settlement that became Itálica, just north of modern Seville. The entire peninsula (Iberia to the Greeks, [H]Ispania to the Romans) was swiftly Romanized, as we saw in the history of Cádiz, and out of the shifting structures and nomenclature of the peninsula Baetica emerged to occupy more or less the same contours as modern Andalucía.

The Romans adapted pre-existing Iberian culture—settlements, infrastructure, industry, even, it might be said, by a happy coincidence between belief systems, religion—to their own, but on a scale unimaginable prior to their arrival. Private land-ownership was transformed into the *latifundia*, a system of vast, privately-owned estates that existed under more or less the same name until recent decades. (And it could be argued that late twentieth-century multinational agribusiness merely changed the names on the title deeds to the hated *latifundista* system that fuelled social unrest across recent centuries.) *Latifundismo* is, in fact, the sole factor responsible for the way so much of Andalucía in the twenty-first century looks more or less as it has done for the past five hundred years or more. Those endless, rolling vistas of farmland, particularly around the Guadalquivir valley, broken only by the occasional white tumbledown building, look like that—look, in fact, like one giant, improbable ECM Records album cover—because the people who worked the land were never allowed to live on it, less still own it. This does upend one common misconception, though; that latifundismo was an invention of the post-Reconquest. The Spanish were simply expanding and fine-tuning what the Romans, Turdetanos and Tartesios had done before them.

Wheat, wine, olive oil and mining became Baetica's great industries, supplying Roman economies as far away as what are now Italy, Germany, France and Britain. But this was not simply a boardroom coup in a business. Other cultures also sailed, or rode, to take part in the Roman adventure in Hispania, among them Syrians and Jews from the Middle East, Greeks, northern Europeans, north Africans and others. Some of the greatest fighters in Baetica's gladiatorial games came from, or perhaps were pressed from, Germany and Thrace, the latter delimited as the area now bordered by the Black, Aegean and Marmara seas.

While there may seem to be plenty of evidence lying around, some of it literally, to build an image of how this society worked, it is still uncertain enough for a historian such as José Manuel Cuenca Toribio to call it a "history without a face". What we do know is that the Romans used their wealth to dress their culture, as can be seen in their three great settlements in Andalucía: Acinipo, Baelo Claudia and Itálica, considered here in that (happily alphabetical) order simply because it is best to leave the most impressive until last. There are, of course, others; Corduba (Córdoba) was the capital of Baetica, and there were large settlements at Malaca (Málaga) and elsewhere, with partial discoveries hinting at former glories. These three, however, present entire, if partly ruined, settlements, Itálica the most stunning of them all.

THE LOST TREASURES OF ACINIPO

Acinipo, on its windswept bluff twelve miles north-east of Ronda, was probably a Turdetano settlement as far back as the fifth century BCE. Nowadays it is marooned in beautiful rolling ECM artwork, with only its rocky scarp slope suggesting a natural strategic defence in its day, and it is hard to imagine why anyone would build something so grand where, today at least, it can snow heavily in winter. (We might call this the Toga Factor, as it will come into play again here. It may seem whimsical, but even Gibbon in his *Decline and Fall of the Roman Empire* blamed the weather, at least in part…) Historian Pedro Aguayo de Hoyos, writing in his capacity as Professor of Prehistory and Archaeology at the University of Granada for the Andaluz cultural journal, *La Serranía*, in 2001, explains that Acinipo, probably enjoying its peak at the beginning of the first century BCE, was particularly well-served by its setting—with rich agricultural resources and quarries of flint, stone and clay for construction—to make it a powerful city with communications to Gades on the Atlantic, Malaca on the Mediterranean, Corduba to the north-east, Itálica to the west and a network of roads that connected it to Rome.

Popular myth holds that many of the treasures of Acinipo were plundered—a common occurrence when bits of history are left lying around unguarded—mainly in the nineteenth century by the British to decorate their gardens in Gibraltar, but also before and after by local people scavenging for building materials. One recent immigrant to the area tells of how he discovered a large Roman stone capital in the garden of his new home. When he informed the authorities of the discovery, which he imagined they might want to cart away to a museum, they said it was probably safer left where it was.

In fact, while Acipino features in historical record from Pliny to recent histories of Andalucía, it only fell into the care of archaeologists in the 1960s and only acquired a half-decent security fence as recently as 2005.

Stuff was still disappearing from the site in the 1990s, and even today Druids and New Age cultists are known to hop over the low fence at night with candles and other paraphernalia to borrow its monumental theatre for their celebrations.

As well as its theatre, so big it can be seen from miles around, Acinipo has so far yielded a number of structures, with much of the site still to be excavated. The first discovery was a Roman baths, or at least the vestiges of a *frigidarium* (cold water room), *tepidarium* (temperate), and *caldarium* (hot), as well as the *hipocaustum*, the subterranean furnace room that warmed the waters taken from a nearby spring. The spring, or at least a large fig tree it still waters in a landscape where figs do not normally grow, is credited in another popular myth with leading an archaeological team from Seville's university to the lost settlement.

Acinipo is also slowly revealing a structure likely to be a forum, a grid-like town plan, a necropolis and any number of individual private homes, currently just tidy piles of rock. The theatre is semi-intact, with its semi-circular seating, towering stage, backstage and underground areas, all nowadays roped off against the few day trippers who make it out here. It has been used for university productions of Greek drama and would make a stunning setting for a well-behaved music festival.

To get an idea of what daily life here on Acinipo's bluff might have been like, we have to go to the least untrustworthy source, which probably means Strabo (63BCE-34CE). The legendary Greek traveller dedicated the third book of his *Geography* to "Iberia". He dismisses the north of Iberia as "wretched"—much like certain English gentleman visitors of the nineteenth century would say of the entire peninsula—but describes Baetica as "fertile" and "marvellously blessed by nature" (at least in the H. L. Jones, Harvard University Press, translation). He describes the region as we might imagine Arcadia or Cockaigne, a land not just of but over-flowing with plenty, a, for want of a less controversial word, utopia. He describes, almost in passing, the ease of its fluvial systems and how navigators could arrive here by open sea—a sea populated by unfeasibly large sea creatures, including cuttlefish two cubits (two forearms) long, and conger eels as big as "monsters", as well as innumerable spouting cetaceans at play. He even reports on the Costa de la Luz *almadraba*, the annual spring tuna cull, which continues, bloodily, into this century, most notably at Conil de la Frontera.

He confirms that wheat, wine and olive oil were its chief agricultural industries, and notes the extraction of gold and copper, the former mined but also filtered in "gold-washeries" as it was swept down the rivers, probably from the Sierra Morena north-west of Seville. As well as cereal and pastoral farming, he records the region's pre-eminence in the production of crimson dye from the kermes beetle, and cinnabar red from red mercuric sulphide. He also praises the fabrics produced in a country of "surpassing beauty". He describes the people—perhaps the power classes—as "rich, with a life of ease". He comments that they had learned "gentleness and civility" from their exposure to Romanized Turdetania, and that many, perhaps most, had become Roman in all but name, members of the *Togati*, defined by their adoption of, well, the toga. Perhaps most interestingly for the modern reader, Strabo also describes a form of maternity leave, however brief, for pregnant women working the fields.

He does not, however, report on the climate of the time, which suggests either that the Romans and their Turdetano hosts were sturdier than modern Andaluces, or that, if it did snow then, a toga, sandals and perhaps cape were enough against the elements at Acinipo on its windy perch.

THE TEMPLES OF BAELO CLAUDIA

The Toga Factor also comes into play at Baelo Claudia, nowadays reached via one of the most popular beaches at Bolonia, which it overlooks, north of Tarifa on the Costa de la Luz. Even on a hot summer's day, standing among the pillars of its forum—for Baelo Claudia is a far grander settlement than Acinipo—and looking down over the serried ranks of sunbathers along the beach, you still wonder how its Roman colonizers or the Turdetanos might have coped when the winter rains set in, as they can do, along with the maddening Atlantic winds that are said to cause sudden surges in reported cases of suicidal depression in neighbouring Tarifa.

Just 60 miles south of Cádiz, Baelo Claudia is a surprisingly impressive, if still small, settlement compared to its northerly neighbour. The difference today is perhaps that Cádiz's Roman city was buried under successive centuries of urban development, whereas Baelo Claudia was abandoned to the countryside after several earthquakes and a tidal wave, probably triggered by a seaquake, between the third and sixth centuries CE, and where it has only begun to emerge from the undergrowth in recent decades.

While it is dominated by a semi-circular theatre, temples to Isis, Juno, Jupiter and Minerva, and its sturdy forum lacks only a roof—its eerily larger than life statue of the emperor Trajan was transported to the Museo de Cádiz, but is represented by a concrete copy that still awaits a visit from Umberto Eco—Baelo Claudia was renowned as a world-class producer of *garum*, also known as *liquamen*, a potent fish paste that was prized across the Roman empire, and which today gives its name to at least one Andaluz restaurant, on the Paseo Marítimo in Marbella. The remains of its garum factory, a series of vats and rough work areas, can be seen at the edge of the settlement, above the beach where Roman boats would have run themselves up on to the sandy beach protected by the low surrounding cliffs. Garum was valued in much the way that salt had a fiscal value, and probably cost about as much as decent caviar does today. It is surprisingly easy, if slow, to make, although a bewildering variety of recipes has somehow found its way down the centuries. It is best approached, perhaps, as a marinade, even tapenade—some recipes recommend stoned olive flesh, which would take it towards a tapenade more than the fish condiment it is meant to be—or perhaps a ceviche left out in the sun. It can take a month or two to make and, depending on the authority, can either be odourless or powerful enough to clear a large building. (The consensus supports the latter, along with a Roman law said to have forbidden domestic production of garum.)

As with all recipes, it is best to improvise. It is probably advisable to start with a small quantity, perhaps 500g/1lb of fatty fish, such as sardines, mackerel or pilchards (the smaller the better) and a flat, square or rectangular airtight container, either glass or plastic. Start with a layer of fish (whole if small, pieces if large), sprinkle the layer generously with dried herbs such as oregano, sage, fennel, celery, mint, coriander (all local herbs here, even coriander, grown fresh as leaf *cilantro*) and a souse of lemon, lime or orange juice. Salt well (try rock sea salt) and souse again with olive oil, covering the fish, and add another layer, repeating until the fish is used up, and covered. Close the container tight and perhaps double-bag it in plastic shopping bags. Leave somewhere outdoors, secure against both animals and the weather, but exposed to whatever sunshine you might hope for (an upper window ledge, say), for a week. It should be macerated, soaked, by then. If the mixture has not turned cloudy—a sign the unstable mix of raw fish, herbs and salt has gone off—continue with a gentle daily stir (or, to keep it sealed, a shake) for another three weeks minimum, the theory being the longer you leave it, the better it will be. You should then have your first batch of *garum*. Use sparingly on fish, meats or even, a Roman delicacy, on desserts (pear and honey soufflé is said to be a classic Roman *postre*). Alternatively, you can cheat, like Timo Hamalainen, owner of Garum restaurant in Marbella, admits he does, and just use pre-soaked and salted anchovies...

If climatic conditions then were the same as today, Baelo Claudia would have been blessed with a hygienic *levante* (easterly) wind for much of the day, taking whatever smells its garum factory produced out to sea. At other times, with a stronger, on-shore westerly *poniente* wind blowing, the smell would have backed up into and through the town and into the emperor Trajan's nose, either literally or later in sculptural form.

While some of Baelo Claudia's finest discoveries have been transferred to Seville's museo arqueológico, it still offers a three-dimensional sense of how the Romans and their Romanized co-habitees lived in this small but opulent settlement with its curious sideline in pungent condiments. It will shortly acquire a small and very stylish visitors' centre, resembling a low-slung Zaha Hadid structure planted among the dunes, which will reveal even more of its story.

THE HEAVENLY CITY OF ITÁLICA

Evidence of the culture of Roman Andalucía can be found elsewhere, of course, most notably in the handsome large mosaic artworks to be found in Córdoba's museo arqueológico, which also boasts exquisite statues of Aphrodite and Mithras, and also in the curiously well preserved mosaics in Córdoba's Alcazar, known mainly in history as the HQ for Ferdinand and Isabella during their campaign against Muslim Granada. These minutely worked examples of *musivaria* or mosaic art record both religious and street scenes, deities and common folk such as street actors and traders, suggesting an art addressing itself to both the sublime and the mundane, perhaps even an art that has detached itself, briefly, from its ties to power, and entering the world of reportage. The most impressive of all has to be at Itálica, a twenty-minute bus ride into the suburbs of Seville at Santiponce.

Perhaps because until a few decades ago parts of Itálica were still covered by ramshackle suburban developments, much of the original

Roman city remained intact, if not entirely undisturbed: the Roman columns that surround the cathedral in Seville were borrowed from the site some centuries back, with little sign of them being returned any time soon. This is traditional in the passage of building materials from earlier buildings to newer ones. What the excavations revealed and continue to reveal is a small city whose sophistication can take the breath away. It even had the Roman equivalent of a mini-mall.

Like Baelo Claudia and its puzzling proximity to Roman Gades, Itálica was and remains just six miles from the heart of Seville and the few remnants of its Roman self, Hispalis—today meaning mainly a section of aqueduct stranded amid roaring traffic out towards the Santa Justa RENFE station. Yet Itálica, like Hispalis, was plugged into a network of *calzadas romanas*, Roman track-ways, connecting it to Gades, Corduba, Malaca and even eventually to Rome itself. These road networks, it is said, would prove an invaluable resource in enabling the Muslims to unseat the Visig-oths a few centuries later…

Itálica was built on a gentle rise with views out over the flatlands of the Guadalquivir plain, with little in its topography to suggest a defensive setting. Today it resembles a large park—its entrance might be mistaken for a cemetery—with a path leading up into the site and straight into the amphitheatre. Its journey across two millennia to today was fraught, and on a number of occasions even perilous.

After the fall of Rome and the arrival in southern Europe of the Visig-oths from the Baltic regions, Itálica briefly became the base of the Visig-othic king Leovigildo. It even survived as a minor settlement into the Muslim era, but by 1166 the Muslim historian al-Makkari would write that "Talikah [Itálica], a city now in ruins, was once the capital of a flour-ishing region."

By the close of the Muslim era in 1492 Itálica was little more than a memory. But then, in the sixteenth century, following the random dis-covery of artefacts in the area, Spanish philosophers, writers and poets began what Itálica's archaeologists describe as "a discourse on the route towards the recuperation of the *memory* of Itálica". (Italics, as it were, theirs.) Chief among these was the Sevillano poet Rodrigo Caro (1573-1647), whose famous poem "Canción a las Ruinas de Itálica" perhaps single-handedly snatched Itálica from the maw of oblivion. Its giddy lament for the disappeared athletes and gladiators, the destroyed marbles and archways, became a rallying cry for the restoration of what became known as *Sevilla la Vieja*, "old Seville".

Unfortunately, in 1711 the local authorities had more prosaic plans for Sevilla la Vieja, that is digging it up and using it as building materials in the city itself. In 1779 the area was declared a "quarry" for the excavation of materials for a new road connecting Seville with Extremadura. It was eventually saved by the intervention of various parties over various eras, among them King Carlos III, José Bonaparte, writers such as Théophile Gautier and Richard Ford, the Hispanic Society of New York and, finally, the no-nonsense countess of nearby Lebrija, Regla Manjón Mergelina, who got the excavations under way. By the close of the nineteenth century Itálica was safe. Excavations on its amphitheatre had begun in 1861 and the monumental statue of Diana was uncovered, a terrestrial Aphrodite rising from the earth, in 1900 (and promptly transported to the museo arqueológico in Seville, where it was equally promptly forgotten about. Some day, a brave Spanish investigative journalist will write a piece about the kleptomaniac behaviour of bureaucrats who snatch artefacts from their sites—Pileta, Baza, Elche, Lebrija, Carambolo—and then bury them in dusty unlit basements where no one can see them). Itálica was eventually declared a Monumento Nacional in 1912, and a Zona Arqueológico in 1989. The restoration of the theatre only began in the 1990s.

Itálica was more than just a city—a new type of Roman city, moreover, a much larger city, more complex, multifunctional, modern than any other Roman city built before it. It represented nothing less than a sentient entity with a brain and a soul, interacting with its citizens, acting as a conduit between the people and their deities, although the tough question is, of course, whether the deities bound up inside this topographical phantom city ever interceded on behalf of the mortals who lived and worshipped inside it. We can explore this among its streets and vestigial structures, and without recourse to any New Age silliness whatsoever, although it does lend itself to the post-modern parlour game of "psycho-geography" as practised by the likes of writer Iain Sinclair in books such as *Lights Out for the Territory*. This has its own precedents in the urban theories of Michel de Certeau, Walter Benjamin's *The Arcades Project* and in the Semiotext(e) gang of Paul Virilio, Deleuze and Guattari, Derrida and even the great imp (*duende* in Spanish) himself, Jean Baudrillard, all of whom might serve as interesting if mischievous guides to teasing meaning out of Baetica's heavenly cities.

Itálica's archaeologists describe it as a city that is cleverly laid out across its grid to both reflect its social structures (class, profession, military or academic affiliation, public or hieratic office, etc) and also in a form that presented an earthly mirror of its "heavenly hierarchy" (*jerarquia celeste*). The people lived among the mechanisms of their gods—their emperors, like the warrior-king-gods of Tartessos, were already divinities awaiting only ascension—and the city was designed to function as a moving part within the spinning orrery of the Roman cosmos, and to win favour with the deities who named this heaven-on-earth. The modern visitor can only hope that those deities were paying close attention to events on the ground.

Itálica was at its peak during the reigns of the emperors Trajan (born in Itálica in 53 CE) and Hadrian, born in Rome (76 CE) but raised in Itálica. Trajan ruled between 98-117 CE, Hadrian 117-138 CE, as Trajan's chosen successor. Hadrian, most famous in Britain for his wall between Britannia (which also gave its name to a deity he introduced to embody the nation) and Caledonia, was fictionalized in Marguerite Yourcenar's acclaimed novel, *Mémoires d'Hadrien* (1951), translated as *Memoirs of Hadrian* in English, and *Memorias de Adriano* in Spanish. Unusually frank for its time, Yourcenar's novel has Hadrian as the narrative voice, writing a letter to his successor, Marcus Aurelius. In it Hadrian muses on the "body's ecstasy" and, referring to his young male lover Antinous, declares himself "nailed to the beloved body like a slave to a cross." We will never know if Hadrian, who is said to have written an autobiography, assumed lost, would have appreciated Yourcenar's imaginative ventriloquy, and perhaps now even the late Yourcenar, herself an unabashed lesbian, might prefer her work to be regarded as art, and not polemic. Two thousand years on, it is impossible to construct a comparison between the sexual pluralism of Hadrian's era (and, since we're here, that of his uncle Trajan, also a boy lover) and modern constructions of homosexuality, but it seems safe to assume that at certain levels of Italicense society, at least, what the post-Victorian West might define as "bisexuality" was not only common, but celebrated. It would be ridiculous to claim Hadrian as "gay", or even homosexual (although the playful ambiguities of contemporary Queer Theory might leave him vulnerable to kidnapping in a drive-by raid by a carload of tooled-up North American academics), but this society had a sexual culture that the modern reader might find impossible to fathom, beyond the clichés of the saturnalia. At the time of writing, Hadrian was due to be the subject of an imaginative screen version of Yourcenar's novel, directed by the redoubtable John Boorman, with Malagueño Antonio Banderas in the title role.

The earthbound space station of Itálica underwent its first dramatic expansion under Trajan, who initiated what the archaeologists describe as "an explosion of urbanization". The total area of the walled city would be just over 220 acres, including its neighbouring necropolis, with other settlements clustered outside. The notable citizenry lived in what the archaeologists call "mansions", the lesser orders in *pisos*, apartments, in what were often multi-functional buildings. Trajan built the first of many baths here, as well as an aqueduct system bringing water from nearby springs and rivers, vast underground water tanks and a sewage system to cope with the city's waste. As well as its forum, the city had many buildings housing shops, workshops, schools, professional services and the headquarters of special interest groups and orders (religious, military, educational, sports and so on). It had squares, gardens and woodlands, as well as pasture and farmland supplying its markets.

The forum was the space station's bridge, where most of public life was led, debated and argued, where prayers were said, sacrifices made, laws laid down and the people informed of what was happening away from the bridge. Most people visited the baths daily to bathe, take saunas, exercise, massage and pursue other health and exercise regimes. They could also visit the *biblioteca* (library) to read or hear the latest works by authors from Baetica or from Rome. The theatre staged music, plays and comedy. The amphitheatre was used both as a public assizes, where criminals would be tried and executed if found guilty, and as a space for spectacles, including gladiatorial games, animal contests between an unusual variety of species (which might give us one of the slender roots for the origins of the *corrida*, bullfight), circuses based on Rome's famous Circus Maximus and what the archaeologists call the "national sport" of Romans, chariot races.

Hadrian, for his part, erected the Traianeum, a temple glorifying Trajan, and also expanded the city. He extended the aqueducts to bring water from as far as 25 miles away and widened some of the grander avenues to a width of fifty feet, wider even than the new roads at Pompeii and Herculaneum. He also sank a five-mile drainage system under the grid of roads across the city. Apart from these civic feats, he also maintained power across the Roman empire for a good twenty years, six of which (roughly 124-30 CE) were also the years of his relationship with a Greek teenager whose death in 130 would inspire the devastated emperor to erect not just statues but also temples and even cities in his lover's name.

One of the largest single structures here is La Exedra, over 40,000 square feet of shops, residential units, baths, a semi-open-air public arena (*exedra*, in architectural terminology), banqueting and meeting spaces. This has to be Spain's first shopping mall…

The art hanging (or lying) in these spaces is often typical rhythmic geometric patterning, although La Exedra hints at more complex works to be found here. Its *opus sectile* floor coverings, a common Roman collage style using marble, glass, mother of pearl and other materials in random, patterned or figuratively allusive forms hint at abstraction, and in their use of materials from elsewhere find later echoes in the shattered mosaic works of Gaudí's projects in Barcelona, perhaps even the crockery art of Julian Schnabel. Another stonework form here, the *opus signinum* pavement, heads in the opposite direction, towards journalism or myth in a curious representation of a group of pygmies hunting cranes. Itálica's archaeologists believe that La Exedra may have been the seat of an association of young hunters devoted to the cult of Nemesis, the Roman and Greek goddess of divine retribution. The proximity of La Exedra to the amphitheatre also suggests a link, physical and metaphorical, between the two structures, the cultures they promoted and the sporting pursuits in which they engaged.

The largest Roman baths, in the block of the Casa de Neptuno, occupies over 60,000 square feet and contains the largely intact remnants of a mosaic of the sea god and his retinue of fantastic sea creatures, many of them land animals—bulls, rams, mythical centaurs—but crossed with or mutated into marine biota. Already, this work is at play on any number of levels. The mosaic, believed to have been the floor to the frigidarium, also represents a walled city surrounded by towers, with only Neptune in polychrome among the monochrome fauna surrounding him. The city is believed to be the capital of the Minoan empire on Crete, as it has a labyrinth and a representation of Theseus, he of the Minotaur myth, and is accompanied by images of Bacchus, maenads (traditionally linked to the rites of Dionysius, Bacchus' Roman counterpart), satyrs, centaurs and tigers. By anyone's standards, this is a work replete in polysemy, or perhaps inter-textuality, fusing reportage with myth, fantasy with cross-cultural refer-ences, connecting, if it doesn't sound too grand, heaven and earth.

Other multi-functional edifices here such as the Casa de los Pajaros, house of birds, with its mosaic abcediary of semi-mythic bird species, and the Casa del Planetario, dedicated to the gods of the days (Mars, Mercury, Jupiter, etc), similarly contain artworks that are multi-referenced, and, in psycho-geographical terms at least, with their jerarquia celeste of symbols arranged vertically as well as horizontally—as lift attendants used to say, going up.

The invisible clockworks of the heavenly city of Itálica might lend themselves to a modern reading as fascist architecture, a by no means new criticism of Roman culture, and the structure of the society itself as in-herently fascist. This might be partly explicable by the fact that this was a society on a semi-permanent war footing, and with good reason to be on its guard. Yet it would seem that inside this fabulous stockade much effort was expended, by the poetry-writing, boy-loving emperor (said to have been a peaceable man) as much as the man who dug the drains, to main-tain the quality of life of the inhabitants, even if in later, declining times it may have become *panem et circences*: bread and circuses. Its culture may have been militaristic—men of certain social strata were expected to devote twenty years to an army career—but its militarism was tempered, for good or ill, depending on their mood, by the gods. If life for some was nasty, brutish and short, it was no more nasty, brutish and short than elsewhere.

It is, as the historians warn, impossible for the modern visitor, even armed with the level-headed analysis of Itálica's latter-day geometers, to see precisely how this society functioned. On the one hand, this was a society that considered other races suitable fodder for barbaric armed combat to the death. On the other, it was a refined culture of mathemati-cians, poets, astronomers and philosophers, at a time when the early Britons they conquered were still running around in the woods covered in woad and throwing rocks at each other. The archaeologists say that one of the grand philosophical ideas at Itálica was that, wherever the peoples of the empire were gathered, on the shores of the Nile, Euphrates or the Betis (our Guadalquivir), they would share the same social and cultural bene-fits as the metropolis, in effect "breathing the air of Rome." José Manuel Cuenca Toribio even goes as far as to say that the people of Baetica came to share a concept of national identity. By the same token, of course, the culture they shared and that we see today is the culture shared at any other preserved Roman settlement across Europe. This too is all a part of the flux of cultures and peoples across mainland Europe in these and indeed any times. If we look north and cock an ear for the sound of armies on the march, we can imagine how much worse it might have been, and indeed how very much worse it was about to get.

Chapter Six

VANDALUCIA: VISIGOTHS AND EARLY CHRISTIANITY

The Visigothic Kingdom of Spain offers scant evidence of intellectual excellence, for a wide variety of reasons. It lasted less than three hundred years, roughly from 426 to 711 CE, one of the darkest, most unstable periods in the peninsula's history, marked by wars that dragged neighbouring regions into the melee (the Visigoths had originally been heading for Africa, but were bogged down in Iberia). War and the enrichment of the Visigothic aristocracy took priority over any sense of social or cultural harmony. Considering the sum of Visigothic contributions to Andaluz and Spanish history, José Manuel Cuenca Toribio concludes rhetorically, "In which manner, with what elements, does the Visigoth experience contribute to the layering of popular memory, the genetic memory of the Andaluz people? It's certainly a decisive question, but impenetrable…"

Isidoro's see: Seville's cathedral today, its La Giralda tower a cross-section of *Andaluz* history

The slow decline of the Roman Empire left Baetica and the wider Hispania rudderless and virtually defenceless. The Vandals, thought to have originated in eastern Germany or Poland, invaded in 409, taking much of the north of the peninsula. The Alans, a migratory people believed to have come from the Far East but then occupying what is now Iran, invaded shortly afterwards. They were defeated by the Visigoths, neighbours and former allies of the Vandals, in 426, in an uneasy alliance with the western Roman Emperor Flavius Honorius (384-423), who would be damned in history for presiding over the final collapse of the western Roman Empire. The Vandals held on to their part of Spain for barely a quarter century before being expelled. The Visigoths held on longer.

The key cultural change in this period was religious. Christianity was being preached throughout the Mediterranean during the early centuries of the millennium, and there is evidence of wealthy Christian enclaves in Roman cities such as Corduba at this time. Among the first Christians to be martyred for their belief were the saints Justa (who does indeed name the Seville rail station built for Expo 92) and Rufina, two Christian women from the ceramics barrio of Triana in Seville whose public objections to pagan rituals in the city cost them their lives in 287 CE. This, however, is where the religious history of the peninsula grows murky. Far greater authorities than this journalist now question the story of St. James—Santiago—and his miraculous visitation by the Virgin Mary on the banks of the Ebro in the year 40 CE. They also doubt the claims that his remains are interred at Santiago de Compostela, destination for one of the world's greatest pilgrimages over the centuries. Historian Richard Fletcher, in his *Moorish Spain* (1998), dismisses the St. James/Santiago legend as a fiction some centuries out of date. (Chaucer, who visited Spain, probably as a spy, places that serial husband collector the Wife of Bath at Santiago—"In Galice at Seint-Jame"—on an earlier "pilgrymage" in the early fourteenth century.) Further doubts are thrown on the presence of James' *Siete Varones Apostólicos*, his seven apostles, in Spain at that time.

This is doubly unfortunate given that Santiago remains the patron saint of Spain today, and was given further mythic status when he was symbolically disinterred as the *matamoro*, "Moor-killer", during the long campaign against the Muslims by the Reyes Católicos. The Roman Catholic Church has maintained a delicate silence on the matter, but with tens of thousands of pilgrims still converging on this rainy Galician city every year, perhaps the myth can, like earlier mythologies, be said to serve a social function, particularly in a time when millions prefer to take their mysticism from bestselling paperback thrillers and movies than from actual religion.

The Visigoths imported a different form of Christianity, Arianism, which held that Jesus was mortal and therefore inferior to the other members of the trinity, a belief declared a heresy by the Council of Nicea in 325 CE. The Visigoths only converted to an accepted form of Christianity in 589, under King Reccared. Their chief artistic gift to the history of Spain was architecture, and specifically ecclesiastical architecture, notably in their capital, Toledo, in particular the church of Santa Maria de Melque, but also in the Paleochristian basilica of Vega del Mar, near San Pedro de Alcántara, equidistant between Marbella and Estepona on the Costa del Sol. Nowadays surrounded quite surreally by an *urbanización* (housing estate) of beach-side holiday homes, the Vega del Mar basilica was discovered by accident during the planting of a eucalyptus wood in the early twentieth century, and revealed a chapel outline with a baptismal font, and the remains of some 180 early Christians in its surrounding necropolis.

SAN ISIDORO'S ENCYCLOPAEDIA

It is perhaps fitting then that one of the greatest intellectual stars of the entire millennium should have been a religious figure, Archbishop Isidoro of Seville (560-636), priest, philosopher, polyglot, polymath, author of the *Etymologiae* encyclopaedia and a major force in promoting Greek thought in Spain, more than five hundred years prior to Averroës of Córdoba. But even San Isidoro, possibly the most unlikely pin-up for a non-believer to have sitting on his iMac desktop, comes with problematic baggage.

Isidoro's twenty-volume *Etymologiae* was recently dismissed in part as "unconditional eyewash" by the *Daily Telegraph*. Perhaps the *Telegraph* does have a point, not least when we consider some interpretations of Isidoro's work that suggest he believed the world is—ahem—flat. In fact, while his famous T-O Map (or O-T, *orbis terrae*) of the world suggests it was disc-like, his writings describe the world as a "globe". (The idea of a spherical world dates as far back as Aristotle, one of the Greek thinkers Isidoro championed as night stole over Dark Age Europe, and would have been in the first Christian encyclopaedia, Cassiodorus' *Institutiones* (560 CE), a likely inspiration for the *Etymologiae*.) Isidoro also believed, in theory, that people lived in the antipodes, the diametrical opposite point to where we are on the globe (*antipodes*: late Latin via the classical Greek *antipous*; having feet opposite to where ours are).

It also has to be admitted that Isidoro's star has waned among Spanish historians in recent times. Some consider him "overvalued" in intellectual merit. José Manuel Cuenca Toribio sees *la era isidoriana* as a cultural movement to unite the Goth nation under Roman Catholicism and to strengthen the links between the Greco-Roman legacy and Catholicism. While Cuenca Toribio suspects that Isidoro's concept of a united Spanish national identity may have verged on the "messianic", he also credits him as one of the "first and most beautiful singers" of that particular tune.

As for some of the eccentric interpretations of the workings of the universe to be found in the *Etymologiae*—among them that the universe is a vast sphere of fire, with the stars fixed in constant position in their constellations—we have to consider the availability of information in his era, the tendency among compilers, which would persist for a goodly thousand years or more, of ascribing natural phenomena to supernatural agencies and the fact that even in the twentieth century respected encyclopaedias including the *Britannica* were still passing off highly amusing unscientific theories as knowable fact. Although he thought that Aristotle's element Air was populated by birds and "demons", for his era Isidoro's intellectual scope was astounding, even if his reach sometimes delivered him to the oddest conclusions.

His name means "gift of god" and he was the youngest of four siblings who, with immodest piety, all became saints. His eldest brother, Leandro, has a similar claim on a position in Spanish history, as the man who coaxed the Visigoth King Recarred into converting himself and his people to Roman Catholicism. Legend has it that Leandro was perhaps by necessity a bully: forced into parenting his siblings by the early death of both parents, he so scared his youngest brother that Isidoro ran away from home. Captured, he was locked indoors, and sent into religious education shortly afterwards. The middle brother, Fulgencio, became Archbishop of Écija, south-east of Seville, and then archbishop at the family's original home town, Cartagena, in Murcia. Their one sister, Florentina, was an abbess at Écija and at Talavera de la Reina, in Toledo province, and founded forty other convents under the guidance of Leandro, then Archbishop of Seville, a role in which he was succeeded on his death in 600 by Isidoro. Together they are known as the Four Saints of Cartagena.

Educated at the cathedral school in Seville, Isidoro excelled at Hebrew, Latin and Greek, although one twentieth-century translator, Ernest Brehaut, in his introduction to the 1912 Columbia University edition, questions Isidoro's grasp of Greek, suggesting he worked mainly from translations. Isidoro rose swiftly through the Church hierarchy, developing a strong link with the monasteries—this, we might assume from his later career, because the monasteries were not only a repository of learning, but also a bulwark against the crude anti-intellectualism of the Visigoths. In 619, as Archbishop of Seville, he declared Anathema against anyone threatening the monasteries. (Anathema is capped here because in Catholic theology it means more than it usually does in the OED; nothing less than excommunication. Anathema apparently comes in three varieties, from simple excommunication for communicating with someone who has been excommunicated, to major excommunication, which involves the presence of the pope, in an amice (oblong sacerdotal vestment), violet stole, cope (mantle or perhaps frock) and mitre, twelve priests and a sufficiency of candles.)

Elder brother Leandro had already converted Riccared and the Visigoths to Roman Catholicism eleven years before Isidoro ascended to the archbishop's throne in Seville accompanied, intriguingly, by swarms of friendly bees. Bees are one of the religious symbols that accompany Isidoro in many of his painterly representations, often buzzing around an equally symbolic pen. He is alleged to have said "Bees are generated from decomposed veal." Life is, mercifully, far too short to search the entire twenty volumes of the *Etymologiae* to source that particular quote, although you can, apparently, buy a t-shirt with it on it (just Google for his name and add the word "bees" and you'll be there in a trice). Another, more sober, Roman Catholic authority suggests that the bees symbolize oratorical eloquence.

He did, however, continue Leandro's ecumenical work, not least in the Synod of Seville and at the Council of Toledo, which established Roman Catholicism as the state religion of Visigothic Spain. He wrote twelve books, the greatest of which is the *Etymologiae*, produced as a manuscript some time before his death but only published in 1472. Its twenty volumes address grammar, rhetoric, dialectics, mathematics, geometry, music, astronomy, medicine, law, chronology, God, angels, saints, religion, philosophy, languages, geography, beasts and birds, physics, atoms, the elements, architecture, metals, geology, agriculture, navigation, food, tools, furniture and much, much more.

Read today it might be a sister publication to the mysterious encyclopaedia of an imaginary world in Jorge Luis Borges' story "Tlön, Uqbar, Orbis Tertius", or perhaps something invented by the mischief-makers of Alfred Jarry's pataphysics movement, which included Raymond Queneau, Georges Perec, the composer Gavin Bryars and others from the literary pranksters' group, Oulipo. Typically for his age, Isidoro did not put much store in empirical evidence; thus, the plague is, not entirely unscientifically, "a corruption of the air". His intention in compassing the known universe was to make it accord to Catholic theology. His mathematics, at least in his *Liber Numerorum*, sought to reconcile science with the mystical signification of numbers in the scriptures, and his astronomy saw most astronomical objects as motionless and lit only by the light from our sun. (That noted, it would be another nine hundred years before Copernicus upended this idea, and still another century before the Inquisition forced Galileo to recant his belief in Copernicus.) Much of the material is either direct quotation from or his gloss on more than 150 earlier writers such as Ambrose, Aristotle, Augustine, Cassiodorus, Justinius, Lucretius, Pliny the Elder, Suetonius, Tertullian and others. Such was its popularity among the libraries and universities of medieval Europe (it would later inspire Liebniz and Roget, among others) that some of his source texts disappeared in published form, abandoned as redundant in the wake of the *Etymologiae*. Conversely, as Europe slid into the Dark Age, his *Etymologiae* kept the work of these writers in the public domain, however fanciful his, or indeed their, interpretations of the natural world might be. It would also, as said before, be half a millennium before Averroës rehabilitated Aristotle and the other Greek philosophers in the great flowering of intellectual enquiry in Muslim al-Andalus.

If, as L. P. Hartley wrote, "The past is a foreign country, they do things differently there," we might still make a number of safe assumptions about Isidoro and his *Etymologiae*. He wrote it to anchor the universe, or at least as much of it as was within his knowledge, to a specific Catholic cosmology, with a definite political and theological agenda. He saw Catholicism, but one that would accommodate and continue the Greco-Roman tradition, as a means of uniting and perhaps even pacifying Iberia. He addressed it to the then reigning Visigoth King Sisebut, or Sisebur, who ruled from 610-21, a man who would appear to have been both a willing student and also a friend; the king dedicated a poem on astronomy, "Carmen de Luna", or "Praefatio de Libro Rotarum", to a "friend" believed to have been Isidoro. Isidoro would also have written it with the intention of upstaging all previous writers on these matters, however modest his own improvisations on their original themes may have been (commentators such as Brehaut dismiss many of his extrapolations as at best workmanlike, at other times so off course as to be over the horizon). During its writing, he would have probably considered the project as a holding action against the barbarism of the age—although the enthusiastic response from King Sisebut should make us reconsider the Visigoth reputation as mere cultural vandals, in either lower or upper case. He must also have wagered that the *Etymologiae* would be around for much longer than its author. It is interesting—to this writer, at least—to pause and consider also that however much Isidoro's intellect might have been able to scope in the visible and invisible universe, he was still working in the pre-Gutenberg world; the first "book" version of the *Etymologiae* was only printed in 1472, in Augsburg, Germany, just seventeen years after the publication of Gutenberg's Bible. Its first full English translation only appeared in 2006, more than thirteen hundred years after his death. Some of the original manuscripts of the *Etymologiae* are preserved in the Biblioteca Nacional in Madrid, and in other antiquarian collections elsewhere.

Towards the end of his life, when failing health would have given him fair warning that his work would indeed be surviving him, he is said to have spent six months giving away everything he owned to the poor. He then, at least according to Catholic hagiography, retired to his modest room to expire peacefully after four days.

He was canonized as a saint in 1598, and declared a Doctor of the Church in 1722. The most famous portrait of him, curiously free of bees, was painted at an unspecified date between 1628 and 1682 by the great Seville school painter Bartolomé Murillo. The minor brouhaha over his proposal as the patron saint of the internet in 2003 remains unresolved; six Italian religious figures beat Isidoro into the list of finalists in a vote, and the position is still open, although Isidoro is unofficially regarded as the patron saint of the world wide web. He would very probably consider it the work of those demons he believed occupied the upper air along with the birds.

By the time Bartolomé Murillo got around to painting him, San Isidoro had been dead a thousand years. While he spared the saint the Vaseline-on-the-lens effect he brought to his multitudinous portraits of the Virgin Mary, Murillo portrayed Isidoro as a grave and sage greybeard nearing the end of his life, the weight of time and wisdom as heavy on his shoulders as the hefty tome he balances with his left hand. Beyond his bishop's mitre, vestments and crook, there is no explicit symbolism apart from a small pile of books at his shoulder. Clearly, the portrait is meant to convey the gravitas of a scholarly bishop's standing, his life, and his undertaking as both encyclopaedist and ecumenist. Even though his thinking was trammelled by theology, the scale of his imagination was nothing less than awesome, something which, demons and fiery universes aside, it is easy to underestimate in the information-soaked modern world.

While scientifically flawed, Isidoro's intellectual achievement for his time was akin to that of a modern brain such as Albert Einstein, or Richard Feynman, perhaps a Stephen Jay Gould or a Michel Foucault. While the classical Greek thinkers he championed would have been independently re-discovered by figures such as Averroës and Maimonides half a millennium later, his work, particularly the *Etymologiae*, was in effect a time capsule of the sum of human knowledge that might—did—get lost in the uncertain near future. In that, it is worth comparing to the modern-day, and eminently Googleable, Long Now Foundation, with its 10,000-year clock, and its plans for a Nevadan desert mountain depository of a library of human knowledge for the distant future.

It is also likely that San Isidoro considered himself a man charged with a mission, nothing less than the salvation of (Christianized) mankind. Yet he was not without humour, or a sense of the everyday, although these traits would not have been discernible in his public persona as Murillo's grave and sage greybeard. Consider the light, dry humour of this cultural observation from the *Etymologiae*: "The walking stick (*baculus*) is said to have been invented by Bacchus, the discoverer of the grape vine, so that people affected by wine might be supported by it."

Part Two

AL-ANDALUS:
FROM INVASION TO THE FALL OF
GRANADA

"al-Andalus… a meeting place of strangers in the project of building human culture…"

Mahmoud Darwish, poet

Night over Africa: Jabal Tariq, "Tariq's Rock", birthplace of *al-Andalus*, with Africa on the horizon

Chapter Seven

TARIQ'S ROCK:
THE CREATION OF AL-ANDALUS

"First Persia, Syria, and Egypt, then Turkey, then North Africa fell to the Muslim armies; in the eighth and ninth centuries Spain, Sicily, and parts of France were conquered. By the thirteenth and fourteenth centuries Islam ruled as far east as India, Indonesia, and China. And to this extraordinary assault Europe could respond with very little except fear and a kind of awe."

Edward Said, *Orientalism*

The Muslim invasion of Europe began on the sunny morning of 29 April, 711 CE. We can surmise that it was a sunny morning from a report in the *History of the Conquest of Spain,* by ninth-century historian Ibn Abd-el-Hakem which tells us that the invaders were able to camouflage their ships in among the busy daily commercial traffic between north Africa and Iberia as they transported an estimated 7,000 soldiers from Tangier to the Iberian Peninsula. And good sailing weather in el estrecho in late April usually means sunshine. They, like the traders they sailed among, would have needed good weather to land on the shores of the Roca de Calpe, as the Phoenicians had named the huge limestone mount at the mouth of the inland sea. That afternoon the mount would be renamed after the governor of Tangier who led the troops, Tariq ibn-Ziyad, who claimed it symbolically as his own: *Jabal Tariq,* "Tariq's Rock", from which we derive the modern "Gibraltar".

"The Muslim invasion of Europe" is in fact this author's figurative flourish, for the events of April 711 were, again, part of a far more complex cultural and political flux already at play in this busy corner of Europe. According to Ángel Luis Encinas Moral in his exhaustive *Cronología Histórica de al-Andalus* (2005), an earlier landing party of 400 Moroccan troops had already stepped on to the Roca de Calpe the previous summer, in July 710, and were busy creating background interference among warring Visigoth factions. On the death of the Visigoth King Wittiza, various figures contested the throne and one, Roderic, backed by various clans, claimed it. Unfortunately, Roderic was also alleged to have raped the daughter of the general of Ceuta, on the north African coast. The general was an ally of Tariq, and gladly supplied both the boats and tactical know-how for Tariq's expedition. Other histories suggest that factions actually invited the north Africans to "invade", or that they perhaps had the support of Jewish groups angered by the rise of anti-Semitism in Visigothic Spain (a stain that had begun to spread through late Roman Baetica). It is equally possible that the populace welcomed the new arrivals just as they had done the Romans, Greeks and Phoenicians before.

It seems that neither the *History of the Conquest of Spain* nor the anonymous *Chronicle of 754*, both written some time after the events, are entirely trustworthy, but it is accepted that Roderic was killed at the historic Battle of Guadalete, east of Barbate (in fact inland from Baelo Claudia and its garum factory) on 19 July that summer, a battle that created not one but two cultural icons. The taking of the Roca de Calpe made Tariq a Muslim icon, and his victory over Roderic made him and his governor Musa ibn Nusayr famous for decisively ending Visigoth rule in Iberia. The battle is even recorded, somewhat belated, by the nineteenth-century Valencian painter Salvador Martinez Cubells in his popular if ponderously titled "The Battle of Guadalete, detail of the escape of the Goths from the command of King Roderic in the presence of the Muslim cavalry of Tarik Ibn Ziyad, 711 AD". The painting, undated but probably contemporary to his more famous "La educación de Principe Juan" of 1877, is a curious impressionistic melee of horses and flags, painted perhaps under the sign of Goya, whose Black Paintings Cubells would bring to light in his day job as chief restorer at the Prado. The title, like the painting itself, perhaps gives a measure of the factual contortions necessary for some Spanish artists when addressing less sunny moments in their national history.

The second, and perhaps even greater, icon produced by the battle is a man who names uncounted numbers of thoroughfares across Spain, Pelayo (Pelayu in his native *Asturiano*), a Visigothic nobleman and ally of Roderic who survived and escaped the Battle of Guadalete, founded the Christian kingdom of Asturia and led a Christian army to victory at the equally historic Battle of Covadonga in 722. The Battle of Covadonga is generally accepted as the start of the "Reconquest", although Cuenca

Toribio comments, with uncommon asperity, that the idea of the "loss" of a Hispano-Gothic Iberia was a necessary myth if there was to be a reconquest of that same mythic Hispano-Gothic Iberia. He further says that Tariq and his army did not so much "conquer" Iberia as "occupy" it, and that these two things are rather different. With an equally uncommon drollery, Toribio adds that "In the history of Islamic Spain, two and two aren't always four."

A United Iberia

If the chief cultural change in Visigothic Spain was religious, the chief cultural change in Islamic Spain—*al-Andalus*, to finally give it is Islamic title—was linguistic. Everything that the Muslims introduced into al-Andalus—arts, sciences, philosophy, economics, even agriculture and more—would be led by language. In fact, this would involve a double linguistic change: while Arabic was soon the common tongue, much of the great literature of this period was written in Hebrew by members of a newly thriving Jewish community, producing works that are spoken of alongside Homer, Chaucer and Boccaccio in terms of the history of world literature.

Before we consider that in detail, we might dally with a resonant comment from, again, Toribio, who points out that the Muslim occupiers, who had taken most of the peninsula within a matter of a decade, managed in that time to achieve what the Visigoths had failed to do over the space of three centuries: unite Iberia. The speed with which the Muslims took the peninsula was extraordinary; the first firm resistance their sweep north met was when they were repelled at the battle of Tours/Poitiers, in 732, which set the northern frontier of al-Andalus just two hundred miles south of Paris, from where it would ripple back south towards the outline of the kingdom of Granada and its fall in 1492. The "macro-historical" relevance of the Battle of Tours is still debated 1300 years on, and would later inspire historian Edward Gibbon to pen his famous *pensée* that if this dramatic event in world history had had a different outcome, "perhaps the interpretation of the Koran would now be taught in the schools of Oxford, and her pulpits might demonstrate to a circumcised people the sanctity and truth of the revelation of Mahomet."

As had happened under the Roman occupation, most of the population arrived at some form of accommodation with the Muslim occupiers.

British historian Richard Fletcher, in *Moorish Spain*, writes of a "curve of conversion" to Islam that saw 75 per cent of al-Andalus converted by the year 1000. The remainder, keeping to their Christian or Jewish faiths, would have been protected as *dhimmi*, "peoples of the book", under Quranic law. In the brief and still hotly disputed alternative "Golden Age" of the tenth and eleventh centuries, all three faiths and cultures coexisted, if at times problematically, in la convivencia, which means rather more than "co-existence" in Spanish. As we shall see, la convivencia, nowhere better observed than in its dazzling apogee in the caliphate at Córdoba, was a pragmatic experiment in multiculturalism (based largely on a thriving economy) that might be said to have offered a glimpse of heaven on earth. The meaning of la convivencia has, unsurprisingly, become hostage to quite bitter political argument over the centuries, so it is best to let the facts—the buildings, the poetry, the philosophy, the science, and, yes, even the landscape, utterly transformed by the Muslims—speak for themselves.

Before we consider what the venerable Spanish historian Juan Vernet has called "Islamic Spain's gift to Europe", we should sketch out a few basic historical facts. Tariq's arrival on his rock did not represent one single Muslim front, wave, invasion or occupation during the 781 years of Muslim rule in al-Andalus (781 years that still outstrip the 500-plus years of post-1492 *Castellano*, Castilian, rule, and will continue to do so until the year 2273…). It was the first of many. He and his successors lived through the Umayyad dynasty, the first dynasty of the Muslim caliphate (660-750). They and their successors would live through centuries of local dispute and periods of accord and discord with the ruling dynasties in Baghdad. They would be succeeded by the Almoravid, Almohad and Marinid dynasties, and the Nasrid dynasty of the kingdom of Granada. With the exception of the Nasrids, responsible for the glories of the Alhambra, these successive waves of arrivals from various points across the southern Mediterranean might best be typified by their increasing fundamentalism and their increasingly harsh reaction against the multicultural liberalism of la convivencia at its dizzying peak. While held together by the overarching philosophy of their ur-text, the Quran, Muslims have been disagreeing over their readings of the Prophet's words since his death in 632. The enmity between Sunni and Shi'ite Muslims, still depressingly playing out across the Middle East today, dates from a disagreement over theological interpretation in the year 658.

As their diverse origins might suggest, this also explains why they cannot be lumped together as "Berbers", less still "Moors", with all the dubious etymology that accrues to both words. Simply put, the people these words describe would not use these words to describe themselves. Thus, when possible, this book uses the words they would prefer to use to describe themselves.

The picture becomes even more complicated when we consider their interactions with other cultures, not simply their 770-year-long, post-Covadonga battle with the Visigothic rump, but with other cultures elsewhere in Europe, not least with the rarely mentioned (in Andaluz histories, at least) Mediterranean power-in-waiting, Venice, which was trading with Granada for as long as Granada had the power to trade.

The title of Juan Vernet's book on Islamic Spain is in fact *Lo que Europa debe al Islam de España*, literally, "That which Europe owes Islam in Spain". A more accurate translation, in keeping with the spirit of his book, would be to reverse his title into "Islamic Spain's gift to Europe". Born in Barcelona in 1923, Vernet has spent almost his entire career as a professor of Arabic language and literature at its university, and is the author of, among other titles, Spanish translations of the Quran and the *1001 Nights*, as well as histories of astronomy in Renaissance Spain, a general history of science in Spain, a life of Mohammed and several collaborations on studies of Islamic culture in Spain, as well as *Lo que Europa debe al Islam de España*, published in 1999.

Vernet says that the first century of Muslim occupation was culturally barren, something echoed by Richard Fletcher when he writes, "The eighth century was probably the bleakest in the entire recorded history of the Iberian peninsula." It was only with the arrival of Abd ar-Rahman (the First) in 755 as self-appointed emir, based in the capital, Córdoba, that al-Andalus began to stabilize and grow. While much of his work was taken up building infrastructure, Abd ar-Rahman oversaw the start of work on Córdoba's magnificent Mezquita (mosque) in 786. Constructed on the site of an earlier Visigothic church (itself built on the site of a Roman temple), it was the second largest mosque in the world. Part of Abd ar-Rahman's plan was to supplant Baghdad and make al-Andalus, and Córdoba, the centre of the Islamic world. Tellingly, ar-Rahman's emirate practised a pragmatic religious tolerance towards Christians and Jews.

Juan Vernet describes his book as an "inventory" of Islamic achievements in Spain. While the first intellectual flowering of al-Andalus occurred under ar-Rahman's son and successor, Abd ar-Rahman II, Córdoba and other centres of Islamic culture, such as Seville and Toledo, began to attract not just Muslim intellectuals but Jewish and Christian intellectuals from elsewhere in Europe as well.

As had been the case in Baghdad and Damascus, libraries and mosques (Córdoba was said to have a thousand at one point) began to fill with classical Arabic and Greek texts on the arts and sciences. Córdoba was the home to the anonymous author of the earliest book written on Islamic Spain, the aforementioned *Chronicle of 754*, and also Ibn Abd-el-Hakem, author of *The History of the Conquest of Spain*. Toledo (which fell quite early in the Reconquest, in 1085) became a centre for translations, both from Greek into Arabic but also from Greek and Arabic into Latin. Their legions of translators also translated from Sanskrit, Syrian, Coptic and Pahlevi/Aramaic languages. As al-Andalus began to flex its muscles, so other aspects of Islamic culture began to emerge. Education, based on the Roman *quadrivium* of arithmetic, geometry, astronomy and music, could extend until a student was twenty-five years old. The medical works of Dioscorides, Hippocrates and Galen were translated to back a medical system far more advanced than anywhere else in Europe. The later *Canon* of Persian polymath Abu Ali al-Husayn ibn Abd Alla ibn Sina, latinized as Avicenna, collected five volumes of information on anatomy, physiology, pathology, hygiene, pharmacology, a list of some 760 proprietary medications, bacterial and viral infections, epidemics and quarantine, sexually transmitted diseases, nervous disorders, psychiatry and even psychosomatic ailments. This would appear to compare favourably with, say, a British medical system that in the late nineteenth century was still prescribing a gallon of brandy a day to no doubt cheery but doomed members of its royal family.

Córdoba's astronomers remained unsurpassed in some areas until the twentieth century. Galileo, Copernicus, Kepler and Brahe, among many others, all acknowledged their debt to astronomers working with primitive but innovative instruments before the invention of the telescope. The astronomers of al-Andalus brought the astrolabe, that medieval GPS positioning device, to Europe. Abū Ishāq Ibrāhīm al-Zarqālī, Latinized as Arzachel, also invented the *equitorium*, which was used to plot the positions of the sun, our moon and the planets for mathematical, astronomical and also astrological purposes. Using classic works including Ptolemy's *Almagest*, astronomers such as al-Zarqālī, Alhacen, Maslama al-Mayriti ("of Madrid") and others improved on their mentors' work, fine-tuning their measurements of the universe, and in the case of Alhacen's *Book of Optics*, ranked alongside Newton's *Principia Mathematica* as one of the most influential books on physics ever written, addressing issues such as the speed of light and particle theory that would still be puzzling Einstein and the pioneers of quantum mechanics in the twentieth century.

Other sciences also flourished in Córdoba and other seats of learning, including mathematics, geology, horology, cartography, and, for the modern reader the perhaps unusual adjunct to astronomy, astrology. Most caliphs had their own personal astrologers, some of whom would also have practised (that is, attempted...) alchemy. This, Vernet comments, quoting the English mystic and scientist Roger Bacon, could be taken literally in the pursuit of producing gold from base metals, or metaphorically in the production of elixirs or, with the Arabic invention of the alembic (still), producing the by-product ethanol which served particularly well in displays of "magic" in the form of smoke, explosions and fire to convince gullible audiences of their unearthly powers.

In the field of the arts, the difference between the Muslims and their predecessors can be observed, quite physically and with some force, on a visit to the upper floor of Córdoba's beautiful Museo Arqueológico, a short stroll from the house of one of the city's many later favoured sons, the poet Luis de Góngora. The visitor seems to pass through an invisible barrier between the Visigothic artefacts and the exquisite and startlingly sophisticated Muslim art works, some salvaged from the ruins of Madinat al-Zahra, the fantastical palace-city built outside Córdoba in the tenth century by Abd ar-Rahman III (912-961), which we will also be visiting at length, using a handy dedicated bus service laid on by the ayuntamiento, later.

Vernet says that epic and lyric poetry was being composed in al-Andalus from the arrival of its Muslim occupiers. The "Berber", that is, Maghrebi tribesman, troops of Tariq ibn-Ziyad marched with poets and musicians extolling their valour in poetry and song at the back of the column, with the express aim of "intoxicating" the troops with lust for glory. In a later, more refined, form this would fuse with the troubadour and *trouvère* poets of medieval France, most obviously, those at the court of Eleanor of Aquitaine and those translated by Ezra Pound. As well as promoting the translation of Homer and the Greeks, some of the great warriors of al-Andalus, including Abd ar-Rahman, Al Hakkim II and al-Mansur, were also accomplished poets.

Contemporary texts produced by al-Andalus authors fed into the works of Chrétien de Troyes, the anonymous author(s) of "The Song of Roland" and later works besides. Vernet also believes that he has identified some intertextual looping between sections of the tenth-century *Kitab al-aghani* (Book of Songs) by Abu i-Faraj al-Isbahani, in which attackers camouflage themselves as trees to surprise their intended victims, and the Birnham Wood sequence in *Macbeth* (although it would seem to lack the crucial prerequisite of the witches' prediction that Birnham Wood would make its way to Dunsinane). This might not be as far-fetched as it might seem; Shakespeare borrowed *Hamlet* from the Danish legend of Amleth, and is thought to have used Kerkyra, Corfu, as Prospero's island in *The Tempest*. Shakespeare clearly knew his Mediterranean cultures. Vernet also identifies similarities in other texts to themes in *The Taming of the Shrew*, Cervantes' *entremés* (entr'acte) *El retablo de las maravillas* and, most notably, Dante's *Divine Comedy*, where Dante condemns the Prophet to the penultimate circle of hell, in particularly grisly, indeed *Saw*-like, circumstances, in keeping with Christian theology. The likes of Averroës also make appearances, also usually in the warmer areas of Dante's hell. (Edward Said labels this as pure orientalism—well, unvarnished racism, really.) Vernet cites various recent authors who have suggested Dante may have in fact himself borrowed directly from Muslim literary mythology, notably the *Kitab al-mi'ray* (*Libro de la escalera*) and certain verses from the Quran. Later Spanish poets and playwrights such as Góngora, Quevedo and Lope de Vega also appear to have dipped their pen in the Muslim inkwell.

We will be considering these later, too, particularly in the vast library that Abd ar-Rahman II assembled at Córdoba. Before we check into the library, however, in the sense of balance and perhaps not a little mischief, we should also consider the marvellous career of a remarkable Persian arrival in Córdoba, a man whose influences can be found in your kitchen, bathroom, bedroom, wardrobe, CD or record collection, and anywhere you sit down to eat or drink. His existence alongside all that science and literature may seem frivolous but is proof that this culture was already developed to a level of sophistication where it could afford the luxury of frivolity. This man left Susan Sontag and her famous essay "Notes on 'Camp'" idling in the driveway, more than a thousand years before she sat down to write it.

The view from Ziryab's garden: Córdoba's Roman bridge and the Mezquita beyond it

Chapter Eight

THE BLACKBIRD OF BAGHDAD:
ALI IBN-NAFI AND THE INVENTION
OF ROCK'N'ROLL

It is simply too irresistible, when considering the plethora of brilliant astronomers, philosophers, mathematicians, poets, geometers, linguists and physicians who studded Córdoba's starry intellectual firmament not to identify instead a fop, dandy, gadfly and fabric queen such as Abu i-Hasan "Ali ibn-Nafi" (789-857) as perhaps the iconic intellectual figure of Islamic Córdoba. History may record him as responsible for popularizing chess, see-through clothing and toothpaste in medieval Europe, among many other style innovations, but perhaps the point of i-Hasan, nicknamed Ziryab, black bird in Arabic, gold-hunter or gold-digger in Persian, *pájaro negro* (blackbird) in Spanish, is that this culture was sufficiently sophisticated to produce such a fabulous creature as Ziryab, superfluous to any practical social need whatsoever, and all the more fabulous for precisely that.

It is difficult and perhaps impossible at this remove to measure Ziryab's influence or impact, although he recurs in enough histories to give him some anchorage in our narrative. In attempting to fix his precise cultural role in Abd al-Rahman II's court, we might consider him some charming—only charm can have carried him through the career we are about to consider—if outlandish mixture of Oscar Wilde, Andy Warhol, Salvador Dalí, Orson Welles, Christian Dior, Phil Spector, Terence Conran and Tony Wilson. Probably the most irresistible detail in Ziryab's outrageous career is that this Persian musician, poet, cook, designer, style maven and polymath might—and we are stretching a connection to perhaps unconscionable lengths here—be credited with inventing rock'n'roll. This probably needs some explaining...

Historians still debate his actual origins. He was probably of Persian Kurdish descent, although others argue he was a liberated African slave, which would lend itself to the legend that his nickname "Blackbird" came from the colour of his skin as much as his musical ability. He came to prominence as a student of the revered composer and musician Ishaq al-Mawsili at the Abbasid court in Baghdad. He left the court, either because of rivalry or because he had surpassed his teacher, and travelled to Córdoba, where his reputation won him a place as court composer and poet at Abd al-Rahman II's court, with a generous monthly stipend and a house across the Roman bridge over the Guadalquivir.

Ziryab turned Córdoba into a centre of musical excellence, building a school for his music students—possibly the first in Europe—particularly students of the lute-like *oud* (or *ud*). Archaeologists have uncovered images of the oud in Mesopotamia from as long ago as the fifth century BCE. Today, perhaps the finest performer still recording on the instrument is the gifted Moroccan musician Anouar Brahem, who has recorded some ten CDs in various group settings for our friends ECM Records, including orchestral pieces, and trios with the likes of Jan Garbarek and John Surman.

Ziryab is credited with the invention of a school nowadays known as "Andalucían classical music", an African-based "early music" form that was enhanced by exposure to Muslim and Sephardic Jewish cultures. He is also credited with developing the *nuba* or *nauba* suite form, a form still performed by north African "Andalucían classical music" ensembles today, based on a series of modes, and is said to have created a system of 24 nuba forms linked to the hours of the day. (Today in Morocco, only eleven nuba are said to survive.) He also transformed the instrument's repertoire by adding a controversial fifth string to the oud, giving the instrument, a precursor of the guitar (the word comes from the Spanish *guitarra*, itself derived from the Greek *kithara*), greater range and subtlety, and also replaced the traditional wooden guitar pick with a flexible plectrum fashioned from either an eagle's talon or a quill. The instrument's history has roots in the Indian sitar and also in the Roman cithara, but the link between Ziryab's oud and the modern guitar is indisputable, if still complex. Essentially, in his music school at Córdoba, Ziryab was inventing the instrument that James Marshall Hendrix played on "Crosstown Traffic"…

The several histories of Ziryab's career nowadays amount to a particularly heady myth, best consumed *con un pizca de sal* (a pinch of salt).

One history claims that Abd al-Rahman hired him as his court musician unheard, on the strength of his reputation, and was prepared to pay him so much that Ziryab became extremely wealthy—as he would need to be to allow him to pursue the lifestyle we are about to explore. In effect, he became al-Rahman's minister of culture at a time when al-Andalus was inventing itself amid the remains of the Visigoth nation. He is alleged to have memorized the lyrics and music to 10,000 songs or pieces, which should also be taken with another pinch of salt. But enough historians of music have concurred that he invented a musical form that would influence medieval music across Europe, and leave a legacy that can be teased out in the instrumentation and musical structures of popular music today.

His music influenced troubadours and *trouvères* (the former being the southerly Languedoc poets beloved of Eleanor of Aquitaine, the latter their northern French counterparts) or, strictly speaking, their *jongleurs*, musicians, who in turn informed much later folk music across Europe (although it has to be acknowledged that other regions would contribute their own indigenous forms to the mix).

In the ebb and flow of musical forms across Europe, his music also fed into what would later be named flamenco. We will be addressing the history of flamenco later, but for the meantime suffice to say that some histories track flamenco back beyond its baptism in nineteenth-century Andalucía to Roman, Greek and even Phoenician times. Its origins in *gitano* (gypsy, or Roma to give them their preferred self-definition) culture are undoubted, although the evidence is rather thin on the ground today. That great *Andalucista*, Blas Infante, posits an apocryphal etymology of the word in the Hispano-Arabic word *fellamenghu*, said to mean "expelled peasant" and referring to the peoples expelled after 1492.

And while post-troubadour folk and Spanish flamenco were developing, so in Africa a whole constellation of folk forms from across the continent were developing into types of music that would take ship to the Americas, against their will, when music, like poetry, was the only baggage that slaves could carry with them—in their heads. To take just one example, which can be visited today via a complicated series of connecting flights via Lisbon, the Cape Verde archipelago, 375 miles off the coast of Senegal, became in the era of slavery a way-station for cultures cross-pollinating between Africa, Europe and the Americas. The many and glorious mansions of Cape Verde music display influences from Scottish sea shanties, Portuguese folk forms, Central American and Caribbean dance and music from South America. Most recently, they blessed us with the sublime Cesarea Evora; alas, we sent them Tavares in exchange. (This is where the wheels start to come off the "world music" fad; the great Nigerian juju and high-life star King "Sunny" Adé, real name Sunday Adeniyi, once told this writer in interview that his first formative musical experience was hearing Chubby Checker's "The Twist", played to him in a childhood music lesson given by white North American missionaries.)

Few rock historians will disagree that African folk forms laid the basis for the earliest African-American music that begat gospel, the blues and "jass" or "jasz" (both words being slang verbs for, well, fucking), later christened jazz. Crossbred with the new, we might say "European", popular American song forms of composers such as Stephen Foster, these hybrids were responsible for what we now know as popular music. It could—well, is about to be—claimed that all these strands converged, metaphorically at least, at University Recording Studios at 111 East Ontario, Chicago, on 2 March 1955, where Bo Diddley recorded the "first" rock'n'roll single, "Bo Diddley/I'm a Man", a record, a guitarist, and a style with more than an echo (albeit electrified) of Ziryab's plucked oud.

ZIRYAB'S LEGACY

As if unwittingly planting the seeds for the soundtrack of late twentieth-century teenage angst and rebellion were not enough, Ziryab set about transforming everyday al-Andalus—or to adopt its true adjectival, *Andalusi*—culture in ways that would later spread to every household in the West, and beyond. He was also a gifted cook, and imported many recipes from Baghdad, some of which you can still find, in hybrid form but often bearing his name, in restaurants in Córdoba, Zaragoza and elsewhere. Some histories call him a *gourmand*; others say that calling him "someone who eats to excess" is just rude (the word is, of course, *gourmet*). He imported the idea of using glass and crystal glassware rather than gold or silver goblets, and wowed his guests with other innovations, among them the tablecloth and the place setting. He also set standards of etiquette around the dining table. Basically, if you have ever been to a dinner party, or indeed thrown one, Ziryab was there in spirit checking both your table laying and your manners. He also appears to have invented the concept of the three-course meal, from starter to main course to dessert. Few histories fail to thank him for rescuing asparagus from the status of weed and promoting it to the level of a delicate starter, although the hollandaise is probably someone else's idea.

Away from the dining room, he also made leather furnishings de rigueur, pioneered the idea of wearing white in summer and found time to introduce both see-through clothing and pinstripes into a Europe clearly in need of a visit from this one-Persian lifestyle makeover reality TV show. He set a calendar for seasonal fashions, and introduced *Andalusi* women to fringes, or bangs, perfume, powders, shampoo and depilatory and skin-toning treatments, their men to shaving and particularly zippy hairdos that, daringly, revealed the nape of the neck. Both genders were gifted the Persian invention of toothpaste, presumable a cream blended with medicinal herbs, and taught that a salt solution was better for laundering clothes than mere scented rosewater.

He is also credited with popularizing chess, Indian and Chinese in its origin, but credited to Persia and al-Andalus in its appearance in Spain, as well as polo, which in its origin form was also a Persian sport, although the form of polo known in Europe today is a British import from India during the days of Empire.

The point of this boggling inventory of homebody hints and tips is not that one person could be responsible for this giddying list of fashion do's and don't's, but that the society in which he, and they, flourished actually had the time and wherewithal to consider these quotidian matters worth addressing in the first place. It has been said that Abd al-Rahman welcomed Ziryab because he offered the precise sort of refining influences that the emir believed this "wild west of the Muslim world" needed. It also has to be said that, while the hagiographies claim, as they always do, that Ziryab was adored by all, someone who was that fussy about table manners, etiquette and dress sense might have been a nightmare to be around, let alone live with, although he raised a family of gifted children who followed him into careers in music, poetry and dance.

His gift to us here in these pages, however, is his appearance at a relatively early point in the timeline of al-Andalus. Ziryab arrived in Córdoba in 822, barely a hundred years after it became the capital of al-Andalus. We might look on his homemaker skills as whimsy, but for a medieval society to have aspired to, and achieved, that level of sophistication says as much about this civilization as its libraries and architecture. His position in the history of world music, while given a little playful rock crit treatment here, is undoubted, and hopefully some time soon archaeological work will begin on his music. It has already begun, in part, with groups such as Al-Andalus, the augmented duet of Julia Banzi and Tarik, who are excavating medieval Andaluz music in their concerts and recordings, discussed here in a later chapter. As to his sartorial sense, he would no doubt concur with Susan Sontag, quoting Oscar Wilde in her famous essay "Notes on 'Camp'", that, "One should either be a work of art, or wear a work of art."

Chapter Nine

TAMING A WILDERNESS:
MADINAT AL-ZAHRA

In Muslim al-Andalus we can see how culture could quite physically alter, transform and even imbue transcendental meaning in the landscape. And nowhere so much as the lost city of Madinat al-Zahra, which in its brief heyday might have been compared to the Hanging Gardens of Babylon in terms of sheer (and perhaps also literal) fabulousness.

The transformation can also be observed in the far more modest working landscape. It would be inaccurate to say that Andalucía was simply desert prior to its settlement in the Phoenician era, although the vast swathe east of Almería city has been stark semi-desert for millennia. As Jared Diamond observed in his monumental *Guns, Germs and Steel* (1997), settlers from the Fertile Crescent spread out through the Mediterranean basin from the thirteenth century BCE onwards, domesticating the landscape with their crops. The chief gifts of the Phoenicians and Greeks to Iberia were the olive tree, the grapevine, wheat and other cereal crops. By the reign of Abd ar-Rahman al-Nasir, or Abd al-Rahman III (911-61), the following alien crops had been introduced into al-Andalus by the Muslims: apricots, artichokes, aubergines, bananas, carrots, cotton, dates, hard wheat (for pasta), lemons, limes, oranges, parsnips, peaches, pomegranates, saffron, sorghum, spinach, sugarcane and watermelon. These things had not grown here before. They also brought words that would later be absorbed into both Spanish and English: *naranj* (*naranja*, orange); *ruzz* (*arroz*, rice); *za'affran* (*azafran*, saffron); *sukkar* (*azucar*, sugar) and others.

Figs were first introduced into al-Andalus in 840CE, and ran wild to the extent that they are now as numerous in and emblematic of the landscape as the olive and the holm and cork oak. By the eleventh century, local figs were being exported back to Baghdad. Extensive groves of mulberry trees were home to a sizeable sericulture (silkworm cultivation), and the kermes beetle was harvested for its dyes. Al-Andalus traders were be-

The shining city: some of the surviving structures of Madinat al-Zahra

ginning to source rare spices from around the globe, while perfumes or perfume bases such as civet came from as far away as Polynesia and Tibet, ambergris from a nascent Atlantic whaling industry and, by serendipity, the bitter orange-flower oil *neroli* from the oranges imported by the Muslims.

A sophisticated system copied from the irrigation network at Damascus watered Córdoba and most urban and rural/agricultural settlements. At one point, there were said to be five thousand water wheels in the lower Guadalquivir valley alone, feeding al-Andalus' breadbasket cereal farms, and watering also the countless stud farms throughout the Guadalquivir valley. Horses were still quite rare in the Iberian Peninsula at this time, and the primary beast of burden after the mule was the camel. (The wheel would be an even later arrival here.)

We can get an idea of the wealth of the region when we consider a gift given to Abd al-Rahman III in 929 by the "double vizir" Ahmad ibn Shuayd, as described by historian Richard Fletcher in his *Moorish Spain*. The gift was a "tribute", or perhaps a bribe in thanks for the gift of his powerful position, and also tells us a few other things about al-Andalus at this time.

According to Richard Fletcher, the gift included the following:

500,000 gold dinars, 400 pounds of gold bullion, 200 bags of silver ingots worth 45,000 dinars, precious wood for caskets, 30 lengths of silk, five rich heavy tunics, ten furs (seven white fox from Khorasan [the Persian hunting region]), six outfits of Iraqi silk, 100 marten furs, six tents, 4,000 pounds of spun silk and 1,000 pounds of raw silk for the royal (monopoly) manufacture of "tiraz" [embroidered fabrics, some bearing religious texts], 100 prayer rugs, 15 silken hangings, 100 horses (15 Arab and five of these complete with harness and decorated saddle), 60 slaves (40 male and 20 female) and large quantities of dressed stone and wood for the caliph's building works.

The presence of *tiraz*, opulently embellished fabrics sometimes bearing texts from the Quran and said to resemble garments worn by the Prophet, produced in factories under the royal seal, gives us a measure of the sophistication and size of this industry and the value of its product in tenth-century al-Andalus. The gold would probably have been mined in the

Sierra Morena mountains, north of the Guadalquivir valley, and around the Rio Tinto valley. The presence of slaves in the gift would suggest that al-Andalus was still either fighting wars or expanding into territories where it was able to take prisoners for slavery from non-*dhimmi* populations, people outside the protection of the "peoples of the book" (Muslim, Christian, Jew) as set out in the Quran (although this too would change later in the history of al-Andalus).

MADINAT AL-ZAHRA, THE LOST ISLAMIC WONDER

Only a culture of this remarkable wealth could have backed a project such as the aforementioned lost city of Madinat al-Zahra, five miles west of Córdoba, which, along with the Alhambra, Córdoba's Mezquita, and the *alcazares* and *alcazabas* (fortress-palaces) of the regional capitals, was one of the great wonders of al-Andalus and the Islamic world.

It has to be noted, however, that in tandem with the political and military history of al-Andalus at this time is a history also crammed with small, petty and vicious wars between rival Muslim factions, as well as incursions by pirates, Norman and Viking armies and others. Political assassinations were rife, and while the poets and philosophers in their gardens might have relaxed to the accompaniment of the new five-stringed oud, outside these charmed enclosures the general population often endured periods of famine and disease, some lasting years. History may indeed be written by the victors, but it is also written by and about the privileged, however often the Quran might remind observant Muslims of their duty to care for the less privileged.

Most guide books and histories of the region describe Madinat al-Zahra (also known by its Hispanicized name, Medina Azahara) as the whim of Abd al-Rahman III, who they say built it as a fantastic gift for a favoured concubine in his harem at Córdoba.

Well, historian Antonio Vallejo Triano, author of the official history of Madinat al-Zahra, several other works of history and today director of the archaeological site, briskly dismisses that in the second paragraph of his history of the lost city, saying that this is a fantasy "forged" (in the metallurgical sense) by westerners in the thrall of prefabricated images of monstrous oriental despots with unlimited power to indulge their "sensual pleasures". According to Vallejo Triano's readings of earlier Arabic texts, Madinat al-Zahra was a project al-Rahman embarked on to get over a bruising defeat at the battle of Simancas in 939, almost, he writes, as a "psychological cure". Perhaps unintentionally, Vallejo Triano seems to be aligning himself and the archaeologists of Madinat al-Zahra with Edward Said's criticisms of orientalist western clichés and biases in reading oriental culture. (Said, for his part, wrote in *Orientalism* that the "free-floating myth of the Orient" was an attempted "domestication of the exotic" by a West that had been programmed by centuries of literature and history to regard the Orient as inherently evil: "Not for nothing did Islam come to symbolize terror, devastation, the demonic, hordes of hated barbarians.") The likeliest reason for the construction of Madinat al-Zahra, Vallejo Triano believes, was as a symbolic act to establish Abd al-Rahman III's authority when he declared himself caliph in 929, in the face of political manoeuvering by the Fatimid caliph of Algeria and Tunis, Ubayd Allah.

Work began on Madinat al-Zahra on 19 November 936 (according to Ángel Luis Encinas Moral) under the management of the Muslim prince al-Hakam and his architect Maslama ibn Abdallah, following the instructions of Abd al-Rahman. José Manuel Cuenca Toribio estimates that as many as 10,000 workers may have been employed on a daily basis to build the "shining city" (Triano), which Toribio describes as "the pearl of Córdoba"—that is, the caliphate, not just the city.

Madinat al-Zahra took forty years to build, a timeframe spanning the life of Rahman, and that of his son and heir al-Hakam II (931-88), who ruled from 961-976 (during which time al-Hakam established the vast library at Córdoba, considered in the next chapter). His own son, Hisham II, lived there briefly, but by that time power was transferring back to Córdoba under al-Mansur ("the victor"), who wielded power over the nominal caliph Hisham II, who was made caliph at the death of his father, when Hisham was only ten years old.

The city lasted just seventy-four years. It was razed by Maghrebi mercenaries in 1010 during the second *fitna*, "strife", or more accurately civil war, between warring factions in the Muslim states of al-Andalus. At its greatest extension, the city stretched perhaps seven miles along a dramatic low spur in the foothills of the Sierra Morena mountains, just five miles west of Córdoba. Barely a tenth of the city has been excavated since the *yacimientos* began in 1911 (they continue today).

Triano describes its construction as a period of "frenetic activity" during which brief period there was still enough time for some buildings to be torn down and replaced with even grander structures. After the city was razed during the second fitna, its destruction was made almost complete on the arrival of the Almoravids, and if anything was intensified by the Almohads who followed them. While the Maghrebis may have merely smashed the place up, their successors took to the task of dismantling the city with an almost forensic detail, as though not only wreaking revenge on their predecessors but attempting to wipe Madinat al-Zahra from cultural memory. Parts still stand, almost miraculously given its violent posthumous history, but a great deal of the city's structure was carefully taken apart and distributed to, or actually sold to, the mezquita at Granada, the mezquita of al-Qarawiyyin in Fez, the mezquita at Seville (later the Giralda), the casbah of Marrakech and the tower of Hassan at Rabat, as well as a "good part" (Triano) going to the alcazares and alcazabas of the great al-Andalus and north African Muslim cities to be used as materials in public works.

By the mid-twelfth century a number of families were still living in what few structures remained, but the memory of the city was already beginning to fade. Even Arabic historians confused it with the rival seat of power built by al-Mansur on the eastern side of Córdoba, perhaps deliberately named Madinat al-Zahira. By this time, Triano writes, "the fascination and enchantment with the ruins of the city transformed it into a meeting and transit point for poets, courtesans and princes who evoked with nostalgia the splendour of a state of things disappeared, now irrecuperable." Much like the recuperation of the memory of Roman Itálica, it would take later figures, in this case a fourteenth-century monk, to begin to recuperate its memory, and a twentieth-century archaeologist to start digging the disappeared things back out of the ground.

Today, little remains of the marvels that history and myth ascribe to the lost city of Madinat al-Zahra. Certainly, within the walled confines of the city centre there seems to be little space for the parklands, gardens, lighted streets, innumerable baths, mosques, libraries and palaces some histories gift to it. Enough historians, working with near-contemporaneous Arabic histories, concur, however, that its architecture outstripped even the most imaginative definition of opulence. Most famously, the Salon of Abd al-Rahman III—one of the few structures still standing—was said to contain a huge finely-balanced bowl of mercury, which would be rocked to reflect sunlight off its walls like lightning to impress (or scare) visitors.

Legend also claims that one hall was walled with paper-thin translucent marbles; another, clad with dazzling sheets of crystal. Its zoo—actually identifiable within the precinct visible today—held a menagerie and aviary of exotic creatures from around the world, although there is little evidence of the fish ponds that were said to be so big they required 12,000 loaves a day to feed the fish they contained.

North American academic María Rosa Menocal goes even further, in her book *The Ornament of the World—How Muslims, Jews, and Christians Created a Culture of Tolerance in Medieval Spain* (2002). Ms. Menocal, director of the Whitney Humanities Centre and R. Selden Rose Professor of Spanish and Portuguese at Yale University, must, as an academic, be relying on respectable sources, and her book credits Madinat al-Zahra with, among other things, a gold and silver roofed reception hall with a giant pearl hanging, chandelier-like, in the centre; an outsized towering minaret; a moat surrounding the aforementioned zoo; "hundreds" of other pools; gardens filled with statuary, some representing human forms, in direct contradiction to the Islamic proscription against representative art; an upper, entirely private, royal space in the mosque, something also in contradiction to the democratic nature of mosque architecture; and more.

Triano says that the modern visitor, perhaps arriving on the handy ayuntamiento bus service that leaves from near the Roman bridge at the centre of Córdoba (travel tip: visit Córdoba's lovely museo arqueológico first to prime yourself), will be faced with "a conglomeration of contradictory reports, a mixture of historical dates, legends and confusions which demand extreme caution," not least because most of these histories were oral, and only written down much later.

Yet there is still evidence, some literally lying around, of the wealth that went into building Madinat al-Zahra. It used in excess of 3,400 marble columns, as well as marble, ivory, ebony, alabaster, even gold and silver used as bricks, rather than as plating or adornment. Its mosque, the Mezquita Aljama, which suffered the worst destruction in 1010, was said to have been built in a record 48 days, in either 941 or 945 (sources differ).

Madinat al-Zahra was intended to be an entirely new form of Muslim city, both physically and spiritually. It diverged from the classical Muslim urban plan of a double geometric quadrangle behind defensive walls. It also appears to have diverged from the classical practice of siting new towns and cities at points with mythological or astrological importance, as a site predicted for construction, or as one believed to hold special augury for the future. It was built to fit the undulating landscape of the Sierra Morena foothills, and to take advantage of two key geographical factors: the presence of an abandoned but usable Roman aqueduct, which had supplied water to Roman Corduba, and a nearby crossroads of three major paved roads, extending as far as Badajoz, some sixty miles north-west of Madinat al-Zahra. The site on the slopes of the Sierra Morena also enabled its builders to take advantage of earlier hydraulic systems used in agriculture and mining, and the wealth of building materials in (stone, metals) and on (wood) nearby hills.

As well as the fabulous decoration, Madinat al-Zahra was a marvel in sophisticated urban planning, while also subscribing to the religious symbolism of Islamic architecture. While some histories regard it as a rich man's folly, it had several functions in any number of levels; civic, military, symbolic, religious.

Its essentially south/south-west facing aspect would, as al-Rahman intended, present any visitors with an imposing façade stepped down a series of terraces on the slopes of the Sierra Morena foothills. Within the walled city its various sectors—public, domestic, military, royal—were laid out ergonomically, that is, in the way they could best interact with each other. Within these sectors they were also divided up into hierarchies, of power, privilege or, in the case of the caliphal court, privacy, or even perhaps divinity. In the civilian sector accommodation ranged from multi-occupancy buildings to large individual villas built around patios and fountains, with elaborate kitchen and bathroom areas. The city was plumbed to supply bathrooms, kitchens, public baths, fountains, public potable water sources, flushing public lavatories and drains to cope with domestic waste and excess rainfall. Across the city, ramps were often used between different levels, terraces and hierarchies. The military sector of the city, including barracks and a parade ground for the caliph to inspect his troops, was focused on just one gate, the Puerta Norte, an ingenious piece of design which controlled access to the city through one double-hinged gate which could be controlled, and if necessary defended, from a secure position inside the city by just a handful of soldiers. (It would not, of course, prove adequate during the second fitna.) Until its destruction, Triano says, it was an "impregnable fortress" designed to not look like one.

The central and largely private caliphal area, the site of some of

Madinat's most fantastical creations, sat at the heart of the shining city, with its own private access to the mezquita, and gardens laid out in accordance with the cardinal requirements of classical Islamic garden design: water, light, shade, colour, perfume, music (fountains, water courses) and an overall pleasing symmetry of design, itself a sign and symbol of the divine. An Islamic garden was and is something rather more than a pleasant view from indoors. The essence of water, as an agent for transforming desert, also has thematic literary links to the Quran and the Prophet's own journey to paradise and the four rivers he passed on his way. As in the case of the Roman spaceship of Itálica, the Islamic garden was a map of heaven on earth, a place where, to borrow another idea from Heisenberg's Uncertainty Principle, it might be possible to be in both places at the same time. As we will see later, the Islamic garden in al-Andalus reached its extraordinary peak at the Alcazares Reales in Sevilla, and the Generalife gardens of the Alhambra in Granada.

The grandest structure, which still stands more or less intact, was the Salon of Abd al-Rahman, the probable site of the caliph's liquid mercury lightshow and the halls of translucent marble and crystal. The splendour was designed largely to glorify the caliph—Triano uses the term *magnificar*, which does not mean "magnify" in Spanish but "exaggerate to overblown proportions"—and to either impress or simply intimidate visiting ambassadors. Its interior décor also linked architecture and design to Islamic cosmology: the walls still feature a programmatic design of repetitive vegetative patterns at the base, a central running frieze of ideograms referring to the room's function, and higher reaches and ceilings representing the starry Islamic firmament. Triano describes the surviving designs at Madinat as "one of the most singular and beautiful in the Islamic plastic arts".

When Madinat al-Zahra was finished, at least in its earliest stage, the tenth-century Arabic historian Ibn Hawqal writes that al-Rahman offered 400 *dirhemes* to every family who either built or rented a home in Madinat. So popular was the new city that a line of new houses formed along the road all the way from Madinat to Córdoba. Contemporary documents record that the administration of the caliphate was moved, office by office, from Córdoba to the new city. It was already minting its own money by 947-8, the year that the capital of al-Andalus moved from Córdoba to Madinat al-Zahra.

The Fate of the "Shining City"

Córdoba, and Madinat al-Zahra, were far from the only al-Andalus cities to suffer during the civil war that erupted in 1010, but Madinat seems to have been selected for particularly destructive treatment. It seems logical to assume that it was singled out as retribution for the hubris of al-Rahman in conceiving the project in the first place. The civil war, which signalled the fall of the Umayyad dynasty, also presaged the disintegration of al-Andalus, later into the small Taifa states, and the rise of religious fundamentalism. When, 226 years later, Córdoba fell to the Christians, Madinat was designated as a quarry for the Reyes Católicos to construct their version of Córdoba. The "battered city", as Triano calls it, was slightingly renamed as merely "the ruins of the castle of old Córdoba", the first step in its erasure from history. It would be used as a source of building materials up until the nineteenth century.

Before it vanished completely, however, a monk, Ambrosio de Morales, living in the nearby monastery of San Jerónimo at an unidentified time in the early sixteenth century, began to explore and then record the ruins and artefacts he found on the site. For centuries the abandoned site had been assumed to be part of Roman Corduba, until 1627 when a Cordobese historian, Pedro Díaz de Ribas, identified the surviving architecture and designs as Arabic in origin. It took until the mid-nineteenth century, and the birth, as Triano describes it, of modern Spanish Arabist studies, with the first translation of Madinat al-Zahra's greatest historian, al-Maggari, whose *The Breath of Perfumes*, a history of al-Andalus, was published in English in 1840 and French in 1855, for the ruins to be definitively identified as Madinat al-Zahra. Disputes with the owner of the land kept archaeologists off the site until 1911, when work began led by the architect and restorer Ricardo Velázquez Bosco, who had restored Córdoba's Mezquita. It was declared a Monumento Historico-Artistico Nacional under a royal order in 1923.

Madinat al-Zahra does not receive that many visitors these days, which is probably no bad thing. The archaeologists get on with their work, visitors only go there if they actually want to see what is there (unlike the coach loads ferried in and out of Granada and Ronda little the wiser), and the site is under little or any commercial pressure. It is probably true of most (but by no means all) of Andaluz, and Spanish, museums and heritage sites, that on the whole they seem to think that turning themselves into glorified souvenir boutiques is beneath them. At Madinat al-Zahra, you cannot even buy a copy of Antonio Vallejo Triano's history of the place, let alone a whimsical fridge magnet. There are no guides, no tourist facilities whatsoever beyond some grudgingly supplied public lavatories, and a van that sells ice cream and drinks in the car park.

Which, rather like the modest Cueva de la Pileta at Benaoján, actually serves to intensify the effect. The Maghrebi, Almoravid and Almohad vandals may have done their worst, but stand in the unadorned ruins for a while in the silence of a hot, quiet summer's afternoon and concentrate, and Abd al-Rahman the Third's shining city shimmers into view.

Field of dreams: the prayer room of Córdoba's mosque, the Mezquita, one of the ornaments of the world

Chapter Ten

THE LIBRARY OF BABEL:
CHRISTIANS, JEWS, MUSLIMS AND
LA CONVIVENCIA

The title of this chapter is stolen from Borges, but here also refers to the tower built across the Euphrates from the Hanging Gardens at Babylon—at least according to the stories and the representations of it by Breughel the Elder and Gustave Dóre. Whether or not you believe the biblical legend that says the tower was built in a foolhardy attempt to speak to God is not really the issue here. The etymology of the word *babel* simply tracks back through the Hebrew for "confusion" and the Akkadian word for "gate of God". Borges' library, if you recall, was a gothic science fiction story set in an endless library filling the universe and unintentionally overlapping with aspects of quantum theory. Here, Borges and Bible are hijacked to refer to a collection of books that represents one of the most remarkable intellectual achievements in human history, a notional building where the three great belief systems of the Middle Ages sat down and talked to each other.

During the reign of Abd al-Rahman III and his son Al-Hakam II, Córdoba's Mezquita acquired a library—whether housed in one building in the Mezquita complex or distributed among the seventy libraries said to have existed in the city at the time is unknown—that is recorded, by numerous historians, to have numbered around 400,000 "books" in its collection (some estimate it could have been 600,000). Compared to the average north European university at the time, where the average library was said to have perhaps two hundred books—Paris in the twelfth century is said to have had just 2,000—this figure is little short of astounding.

New developments in the technology of paper production had led to the establishment of paper mills along the rivers surrounding Baghdad as early as the 790s, triggering a boom in the production and consumption of books. The Muslims introduced this technology into al-Andalus, and later in the tenth or eleventh century made the town of Jativa in what is nowadays Valencia the *papeleria*, or stationery shop, of the Iberian Peninsula. At the core of the boom, of course, was the almost insatiable market for copies of the Quran. At one point Córdoba was said to have seventy copyists working on reproducing copies of the Quran alone. The boom was also in transcriptions and translations of philosophy, poetry, science and theology, although it soon expanded into copies of earlier Greek and Latin texts. These were soon joined by a third language, Hebrew, which some say was rescued from obscurity by a literary revolution of radical Judeo-Arabic poets between the ninth and the fourteenth centuries.

By the eleventh century, the libraries of al-Andalus were estimated to contain around a million individual texts. This explosion in the—it seems more accurate to say "illustrated" rather than "printed"—word fed subsidiary industries, in translation, copying, editing, publishing, paper production, bookbinding and the ancillary industries of ink, paper and pens, as well as distribution and sales. Compared to northern Europe, where the book trade had been carried out by impoverished monks whose efforts were often interrupted by war and plague and were often undermined by the lack of adequate funds, Muslim writers and publishers were flying the state-of-the-art Apple Macs of their era.

This in turn led to a no less violent explosion in the job market—information that will no doubt raise a wistful smile in anyone involved in the twenty-first-century book business—with an equally insatiable demand in the manpower, and more interestingly for the modern reader, womanpower sector, for women were employed in almost all areas of the Muslim publishing industry. It is worth noting that in al-Andalus women also worked as teachers, doctors, lawyers and in other professions. This also had a happy knock-on effect in the realm of higher education, with caliphs, emirs, viziers and lesser officials vying to lure the brightest young minds, male and female, into their employment. All in all, these were golden days for anyone toiling in the medieval Muslim equivalent of Grub Street.

The libraries also required, of course, whole battalions of those unsung heroes and heroines of the book trade: librarians, cataloguers, clerks and all the other officials required to maintain a library system coping with as many as 60,000 new titles each year (a figure roughly equivalent to the number of new titles being published each year during, say, the 1980s in Britain).

Among the texts they would be copying and cataloguing would have been the anonymous *Chronicle of 754*, detailing the Islamic takeover of the peninsula, Isidoro's *Etymologiae*, the works of al-Ghazali (1058-1111), "the Thomas Aquinas of Islam", *The Fountain of Life* by philosopher-poet Shelomo ibn Gabirol (born in Málaga, lived 1021-58), astronomer Maslama al-Mayriti's Arabic translation of Ptolemy's *Planisphere*, as well as the latter's *Almagest*, Homer, Aristotle, Dioscorides and Galen on medicine, *The Thousand and One Nights*, as well as poetry, philosophy and the new science of astronomy, which, as ever, saw the Muslims quite heretically centuries ahead of their northern European counterparts in the science of scoping the night sky.

After Córdoba fell to the Christians in 1236, many, perhaps most, of these texts fell into Christian hands, to be read and passed on to universities around Spain and the rest of Europe, some of the texts being prohibited and even expunged from the library and education system for reasons of theology, politics or, in the case of the many erotic texts produced in this period, censorship. There is also a suggestion that many texts were destroyed in the Maghrebi sack of Córdoba during the fitna of the 1020s and the final destruction of the Umayyad dynasty in 1031. The two centuries that separate the fall of the Umayyads and the triumph of the Christians were a window in al-Andalus history during which a remarkable literary culture flourished. It was also the period that gives us the idea and, yes, the myth, of la convivencia, still heatedly debated in the twenty-first century, held up by some as the true golden age in the history of the Iberian Peninsula, looked at askance by others who take a more sceptical view of just what went on in those flower-filled Cordobese courtyards and patios shared by Christian, Jewish and Muslim neighbours.

THE SPANISH MIRACLE

Still lacking a handy time machine, we might turn to no less a figure than that North American intellectual mammoth Harold Bloom for guidance on the likely nature of la convivencia, whatever you might think of his concept of the western canon. Writing in the *New York Review of Books* in June 2007, reviewing poet and translator Peter Cole's acclaimed anthology of al-Andalus Hebrew poetry, *The Dream of the Poem*, Bloom commends Cole who, "with his judicious balance, gives the best account of *convivencia* I have encountered." No skimping praise, that, coming from one of the greatest Jewish intellectuals of his era. It is, then, worth repeating, as Bloom did, the passage on la convivencia from Cole's introduction to his book that so impressed the reviewer:

> At its best, the culture gave Jews greater religious, social, economic, and intellectual freedom than they knew in any other medieval (non-Muslim) society; at its worst, it led to heavy taxation and serious oppression. When the bottom fell out of it, forced conversion, emigration and slaughter weren't long in coming. Its limitations notwithstanding, convivencia has been described as the defining issue in the history of al-Andalus, and it resulted in a major renaissance of Arabic and Hebrew literature and learning, and in an early flowering of Spanish culture.

That paragraph from Cole's twenty-page introduction to *The Dream of the Poem* seems to cover most of the bases of la convivencia: how the Jews (and, by extension, their Christian neighbours) fared under Muslim government; the pros and cons; what happened "when the bottom fell out of it"; its role in sparking "a major renaissance of Arabic and Hebrew literature and learning"; and the legacy it left to a nascent "Spanish" culture.

Peter Cole, a North American poet and translator of Arabic and Hebrew living in Jerusalem, who has also been acclaimed for individual translated anthologies of poets featured in *The Dream of the Poem*, has even more to say on the subject of convivencia, and the culture of the period in general. He begins his introductory essay to the anthology with a teasing reference to Shlomo Dov Goitein's five-volume history of Muslim Spain, *A Mediterranean Society*, as though hoping the truncated opening line "The 'Spanish Miracle' –" will make us sit up and pay attention, although the quotation marks inside the quote, and around the "Spanish Miracle", warn that Goitein was alluding to another text entirely (and in the interests of disclosure, the present author has not penetrated this textual palimpsest any deeper than Cole's footnotes). The actual quote is "then the 'Spanish Miracle' happened", but immediately Cole is off quoting other Jewish scholars on the "golden age" of Hebrew poetry in al-Andalus. But the quote serves to coax the elephant of the "Spanish Miracle" into the room and leave it standing there in the corner for us to ponder.

Cole has this to say about the poetry he has translated and anthologized in *The Dream of the Poem*: "The best of that radically new secular and religious verse produced in Muslim Andalusia and Christian Spain ranks with the finest poetry of the European Middle Ages." (Over at the *NYRB*, Harold Bloom felt a comparison with Chaucer coming on, but noted that much of this poetry actually dates from two centuries before Chaucer started writing.) The poetry of what Bloom calls Cole's "Big Seven" (see below) combined, Cole further says, "an extraordinary sensuality and intense faith that reflected contemporary understanding of the created world and its order." At the same time, it "flies in the face of our received sense of what Hebrew has done and can do, and even what Jewishness means."

Heady stuff, and it gets headier. Cole is a splendid guide to both the culture that produced this poetry and the nuances of the texts themselves. As a journeyman poet himself, he is at ease among his books, treats the poetry with respect but not undue deference, is more than happy to engage in some muscular exercise with the texts and is not averse to the occasional belly laugh. At one point, putting Bloom's Big Seven into context, Cole explains that they "were neither crumpet-munching literati in tights nor rhyme-happy rabbis with time on their hands, They were men of great learning, fierce ambition, and complex talent and spirit." Which last might be code for the likelihood that, as poets ever were, these writers were not above stabbing each other in the back at the medieval equivalent of the cocktail party. In the case of the most famous poets, Dunash, they were not above colluding in a campaign that resulted in a rival being arrested, publicly whipped, imprisoned and his home torched—because of professional enmity.

In explaining the translator's many problems negotiating the "hall of mirrors at the heart of this literature", Cole sketches out a reader-beware code for anyone approaching these texts that might serve equally well as a rough guide for anyone visiting another culture in an earlier period of history. Writing specifically about earlier translators of these poets in a brief passage that might be book-shelved alongside similar warnings against misinterpretation by the likes of Walter Benjamin, Roland Barthes and Umberto Eco, Cole says that previous translators had opted for one (or more) of four distinct approaches.

The first is the mistake of assuming a parallel between medieval Andaluz poetry and English Elizabethan and Metaphysical poetry, an approach that renders the original into a form resembling a "wax-museum-like school of translation". The second is taking a cue from Edward FitzGerald's *Ruba'iyat* or Browning's "Rabbi Ben Ezra" and turning the poem into ersatz Victorian verse. The third is immediately conceding defeat to the complexities of the text and settling for an uncontroversial prose translation of the poetry, at the risk of losing all the tensions and ambiguities of the original. The fourth, which Cole himself favours, with reservations, is "the search for a kind of Blakean vitality, seeking out Pound's 'trace of that power that implies the man'," what Cole himself describes, crisply, as "the preservation of spirit rather than a pickling of form". Above all, Cole stresses, this is a poetry that is meant to be *heard*. But not, he warns earlier, before both translator and reader have become "aware of the unconscious elements of his reading: that is, he has to consider the dynamics of orientalism in his work, and in the work on which he relies."

The Dream of the Poem contains work by some 54 different poets, including one woman, unnamed except as the Wife of Dunash, whose "Will Her Love Remember?", written at some point in the tenth century, is considered remarkable as the first full-length poem (as opposed to fragment) from this period and as the only known or surviving work of literature by a woman writer in this era. They wrote in various settings, including Andaluz-controlled Provence, between the mid-tenth century until the early sixteenth (1505), by which time the "golden age" of Hebrew literature in Andalucía had long passed; Cole dates its end to 1090 and the first invasion by the fundamentalist Almoravids, followed fifty years later by the Almohads. Cole comments bluntly, "Measures imposed by these two groups in succession would eventually bring about the destruction of Andalusian Jewry." This Jewish culture would produce its own diaspora, with people—poets among them—fleeing the new repression, into Christian Spain, France, even Africa and the Middle East.

The "big seven" that Harold Bloom identifies are Shmu'el HaNagid (933-1056), Shelomo ibn Gabirol (1021-57), Moshe ibn Ezra (1055-1138 or later), Yehuda HaLevi (1075-1141), Avraham Ibn Ezra (1093-1167), Yehuda Alharizi (1165-1225) and Todros Abulafia (1247-1300 or later). Cole himself identifies HaNagid, Gabirol, Moshe ibn Ezra and HaLevi as "the four giants of Hebrew verse in Spain". It seems likely that some of these major figures would have been represented in al-Hakam's library at Córdoba, although with the 700-years-plus war chipping away at the *frontera* of al-Andalus (that other great centre of learning and literature,

Toledo, fell to the Christians in 1085; Córdoba itself would fall in 1236) many wrote outside that golden age, and some outside the borders of al-Andalus; on Mallorca, in North Africa, some even in self-imposed exile in the Middle East.

Thanks to the skill of a sympathetic poet-translator such as Cole, many of these poems seem shockingly modern, free of the grammatical curlicues and flourishes of a Chrétien de Troyes or the archaisms of Ezra Pound's translations of the troubadour poets, and comparable, perhaps, to Robert Fagles' acclaimed translations of Homer.

Their poetry, as Coles notes in his introduction, is remarkable for simultaneously addressing the sacred and the mundane—or indeed the profane. Some are historical reportage, others ruminations on religious and culture identity, exile and deracination, and the struggle (or refusal) to reconcile belief with desire. Much of it, of course, is about love, but there are also adventure epics, such as HaNagid's "Miracle at Sea", which is a miniature "Rime of the Ancient Mariner" and offers its narrator religious redemption much as Coleridge offered it to his. HaNagid also wrote a profoundly moving poem on the nature of grief and mourning, "The Death of Isaac", which compares to contemporary texts around illness and death by a writer such as Paul Monette. The sea recurs in HaLevi's "The Heart at Sea" and others of his sea poems. There are also droll literary jokes, notably by Alharizi, whose games with palindromic poems and texts with or without certain letters predate the games of Georges Perec and the Oulipo movement by a thousand years. There are even scatological poems, also by Alharizi, but mostly they are about love, and not always the "courtly love" that they would inspire in the later French troubadour poets.

Harold Bloom, again in his four-page celebration of Cole's work in the *NYRB*, comments, casually, almost *en pasando*, that "HaNagid and many Hebrew poets who follow him seem to celebrate a bisexuality, though rather ambiguously, since social conventions govern[ed] what can be said." Cole himself, discussing the translator's role, asks rhetorically, "And what is he [the translator/reader] to make of the phenomenon itself—intensely sensuous and often homoerotic poems being written by learned and pious Jews?"

What, indeed. Of the "four giants of Hebrew verse in Spain", HaNagid, Moshe ibn Ezra and HaLevi all wrote love poems to boys or young men, while the foul-mouthed and cynical Alharizi clearly considered it an option, if, literally, damnable. And in almost every instance, these are texts where God is also present. It should also be said in balance that they also wrote love poems to girls or young women. Homoerotic—or, to be more accurate, homophilic, as only a few of these poems are explicitly sexual—texts are nothing new in Arabic literature: Abu Nuwas (Abu Nuwas al-Hasan ibn Hani al-Hakami), possibly the most infamous homosexual poet in Islamic history, still gives his name to a market square in Baghdad (a market square rebuilt in 2007 by British soldiers, no doubt unaware of the square's name's provenance). Academics were discussing this topic even before the controversy sparked in 1980 by John Boswell's book, *Christianity, Social Tolerance and Homosexuality*, a controversy that still rages in academe, and which has opened up a whole field of literature on this subject, not least Boswell's later *Same-Sex Unions in Pre-Modern Europe* as well as the widely-circulated academic essay, winningly titled "The Sodomitic Lions of Granada", by North American academic Glenn Olsen, which argues that some of the animal friezes of Madinat and the Alhambra are in fact symbolic representations of homosexual sex. This is a part of Islamic cultural history that seems to have been mislaid somewhere in more recent times…

From the evidence of these poets and these poems, it would seem that their authors lived through at least two centuries, probably at the peak of la convivencia but also before and after, when the writers, their readers and most certainly their powerful patrons would have considered such declarations of love, and at times quite unambiguous lust, commonplace, if unnamed in their communities. It is also the case, of course, that this literature was produced and consumed by and large in the educated, and privileged, sectors of that society. It is very unlikely, however, that the emotions these poets wrote about would have been limited to that same sector of society. As with their Christian counterparts, these poets appear to have arrived at an accommodation between their desires and their beliefs.

Peter Cole describes this culture as "a society where the holy and the profane merge into an indivisible and harmonious whole." While some more timorous modern translators have read these texts merely as metaphor, allusion or narrative game-playing, Cole believes that other translators, and readers, consider that these texts exist in a "charged air that might just point at penetration." Referencing an essay by Yom Tov

Assis, "Sexual Behaviour in Mediaeval Hispano-Jewish Society", in his footnotes, Cole quotes Assis as saying:

> On both sides of the ever-changing border in the Iberian peninsula, [Spanish Jews] were more deeply involved in the social, economic, cultural and political life of the land than was any other medieval Jewish community… [Hispano-Jewish society], torn between extreme and contradictory trends, found itself characterized by sexual laxity to an extent unknown elsewhere in mediaeval Jewry.

Which might just mean that we can thank the "sexual laxity" of Hispano-Jewish society in al-Andalus for the ribaldries of later writers such as Boccaccio and Chaucer, and just about anyone who followed in their footsteps, up to and including the taboo-busting twenty-first-century Andaluz novelist, Juan Bonilla, whom we'll also be meeting later.

How sexuality was perceived and represented in medieval Andalucía is no more and no less important than what the astronomers were writing about the nature of the universe in the books in the astronomy section of the library at Córdoba. Its relevance here, however, is that traditionally in histories of Islamic culture and in histories of al-Andalus and Andalucía this information has been hidden, erased, censored or denied. The insouciantly bisexual poets of al-Andalus give us a measure of the sophistication of their culture during the era of la convivencia, a time when the German nun Hroswitha of Gandersheim described Córdoba as "the brilliant ornament of the world", giving María Rosa Menocal the title for her aforementioned book on "how Muslims, Jews, and Christians created a culture of tolerance in medieval Spain" (her book also carries the imprimatur of Harold Bloom). "In the end," Menocal writes, "it would be al-Andalus's vast intellectual wealth, inseparable from its prosperity in the material realm, that made it the 'ornament of the world'."

Until, that is, the Christians turned the lights out, again.

Father of rationalism: statue of Averroës by the city walls of Córdoba

Chapter Eleven
Two Gentlemen of Córdoba: Averroës, Maimonides, and the Consolations of Philosophy

During and even after the caliphate at Córdoba, the city proved a magnet to an embarrassment of remarkable figures, drawn both by its reputation as an intellectual hot house and also by the wealth that might translate into artistic, scientific or academic patronage. Perhaps one of the most remarkable was Abbas Qasim ibn Firnas, or Ibn Firnas (810-87 CE), a near contemporary and some say acolyte of Ziryab. Born in Ronda or perhaps the nearby town of Carratraca, the polymath Firnas managed to excel as a chemist, physician, astronomer, poet, musician and inventor. Among his achievements were a unique form of water clock, a new process for processing cut crystal glass from sand and in an innovation that perhaps inspired some of the effects at Madinat al-Zahra, what is said to have been a room that generated artificial weather effects such as lightning and thunder, and in which visitors would see artificial stars and clouds (these were duly dismissed as gimmickry by his rivals).

Most notably, however, he was very probably the inventor of the first flying machine, some six hundred years before Leonardo da Vinci. In 852 he leapt off the minaret of the Mezquita in a huge cloak, which some describe as the first parachute. In 875 and aged 65, he took off from a wall on a small rise outside Córdoba in a primitive controlled winged glider that he managed to keep airborne for a few hundred yards before turning to land at his launch point, where he crashed. In designing his flying machine from his observations of birds, he had failed to include the key mechanism that birds use in landing, the tail. He was injured, but not so badly that he did not live another twelve years. His story, which spread far and wide in medieval Europe, was probably the inspiration for the eleventh-century English aviator, Eilmer of Malmesbury. Today his name lives on in a small astronomical observatory at Ronda, an airport to the north of Baghdad and a 55-mile-wide crater on the dark side of the moon.

AVERROËS AND RATIONALISM

Wander around the centre of this most agreeable of all the Andaluz cities and you will inevitably trip over statues of two of its greatest sons, the philosopher and scientist Averroës, or Ibn Rushd (1126-98), to give him his full name Abul Walid Muhammad Ibn Ahmad Ibn Rushd, and the rabbi, physician and philosopher Maimonides (1135-1204), often called the father of modern medicine, known less by his own full name, Abu Imran Mussa bin Maimun ibn Abdallah al-Qurtubi al-Israili. Although they were predated by earlier Muslim thinkers such as Ibn Bajjah (perhaps better known by his Latinized name, Avempace), Avicenna and al-Ghazali, their work on the foundations built by these three—well, in reaction to or outright refutation of their work—represents the philosophical and scientific peak of al-Andalus. María Rosa Menocal credits both men with nothing less than sharing "a basic vision that can be characterized as the defense of human freedom."

While both were born in Córdoba, Ibn Rushd was a Muslim, Maimonides a Jew, the latter fleeing Córdoba and later Spain with his family when the Almohads invaded al-Andalus in 1148, when he was thirteen. By the mid-twelfth century la convivencia was a thing of the past, and the fanatical Almohads gave the Jews of al-Andalus three options: conversion, exile or death. Both men were to die in exile, Maimonides self-exiled to Egypt, Ibn Rushd banished to Marrakech because of his heretical views.

Both men came from intellectual backgrounds. Ibn Rushd's father and grandfather were judges in Córdoba, Maimonides' father a rabbi who schooled his own son to follow him. While Maimonides' family was forced to flee, Ibn Rushd became a judge, a *qadi*, like his father and grandfather before him, holding important posts in Seville, Córdoba and later Morocco. It was only with the advent of Almohad rule that his rationalism got him into trouble with Islamic fundamentalists. Even though Ibn Rushd was the private physician to the caliph al-Mansur, he was exiled to Marrakech, and his work and reputation were only re-evaluated some time after his death. Both eastern and western historians point out that, paradoxically, Ibn Rushd is probably better known in the West than the East, where his books had little impact and are rarely read. His importance in Europe is as a champion of Aristotle, and as a (if not the) key conduit of philosophical thought between the East and the West. Better known in Spain and France than Britain, Ibn Rushd is described by our friend José Manuel Cuenca Toribio as probably the most important Spanish thinker in the history of philosophy.

Ibn Rushd's stature can be measured by the lofty company he kept, if only figuratively. In Raphael's famous painting, *The School of Athens* (1509-10), Ibn Rushd is featured reading over the shoulder of Pythagoras in a group including Heraclitus, Parmenides and Hypatia of Alexandria. In Dante's *Inferno*, he appears in Limbo alongside a group of fellow "pagan" philosophers including Euclid, Ptolemy, Hippocrates, Galen, Avicenna, "And Averroes, who made the Great Commentary." The "great commentary" was on the surviving works of Aristotle, which Ibn Rushd probably read in Arabic translation. Aristotle's works had lain largely ignored, or discredited, for centuries, and when they re-appeared, referenced in the works of al-Ghazali, it was largely as a target; for al-Ghazali and others, rationalism was incompatible with religious belief. Ibn Rushd argued, most famously in his work *The Incoherence of the Incoherence* (a rebuttal of al-Ghazali's earlier *The Incoherence of the Philosophers* and as combative as its take-no-prisoners title), that when both are fully understood then there should be no contradiction between rational thought and religious belief. His *On the Harmony of Religions and Philosophy*, written late in life, is a complex attempt to accommodate religious belief, from the creation of the universe to the day of judgment, with Aristotelian rationalism.

As well as his commentaries on the work of Aristotle, he also wrote commentaries on Plato and a number of works that directly confronted Islamic law on the matter of philosophical debate. In 1194 he published an encyclopaedia of general medicine, the *Kulliyyat*, in Latin the *Colliget*, which is considered his outstanding non-philosophical masterwork, and also works on the medical writings of Galen and Avicenna. He also wrote on logic, metaphysics, rhetoric, poetics and even psychology. In the physical sciences he wrote on astronomy—where he diverges from Ptolemy and argues for a universe constructed of concentric rings, along which the planets, and a transparent moon, toddle—and more convincingly on geography, positing the idea that a "new world" lay beyond the great Ocean. In physics, his ideas about motion and gravity, derived from Aristotle and Avempace, contained germs that would be found in Newton, and perhaps thermodynamics, maybe even entropy, centuries later.

His greatest contribution, however, underpinned by his reading of Aristotle, was the establishment of what would later (much later; around 1846) be termed "secularism", that is, philosophical thought independent of religion. Prior to the coining of the term "secularism" by the agnostic thinker George Holyoake, it was known as the "Averroist" school, or "Averroism". This in turn laid one of the foundation stones of the Enlightenment.

None of which was much help to Ibn Rushd towards the end of his life. Although he became the personal physician to the short-lived caliph al-Mansur (1160-99), who was said to have protected Ibn Rushd, his strict rationalism put him at odds with an increasingly hostile religious establishment. Al-Mansur would appear to have moved Ibn Rushd away from the heat of the debate, eventually posting him to Morocco, but he was finally banished to Marrakech and spent the last decade or so of his life concentrating on his philosophical works, and probably under some form of house arrest. These days, thanks to a trio of astronomers working at Mount Palomar observatory in 1973, his name graces a 17-mile-diameter asteroid, Asteroid 8318 Averroës, out in the asteroid belt between Mars and Jupiter, with an average fly-by periodicity of every five and a half years.

THE SECOND MOSES

The achievements of Maimonides, known by the acronymic RamBam (from "Rabbi Moshe ben Maimon") in Hebrew, are perhaps all the more remarkable when we consider that he spent much of his adult life as a fugitive, although one whose connections and skills protected him. When the Almohads issued their ultimatum to the Jews of al-Andalus in 1148, Maimonides' family chose to flee, when he was probably only thirteen. They went first to Almería, and later, around 1160, to Fez, then Acre, Jerusalem and finally Fustat, then near and now a suburb of Cairo. He was said to be a lazy student, but he wrote his first book, a treatise on logic, at the age of sixteen. His father, Maimon, was a rabbi and schooled his son in the Muslim and Greek philosophers and scientists, an education he continued at the University of Al Karaouine in Fez, where he wrote his first key theological work, the commentary on the *Mishnah,* the first written version of the "oral torah" of Judaism, including his "Thirteen principles of faith". These were considered controversial, but were later adopted as fundamental beliefs by Orthodox Jews.

Some authorities believe the family may have converted to Islam, or at least passed as Muslim, but the former seems unlikely; he remained a practising rabbi for the rest of his life, although when his brother died at sea, effectively pauperizing the family, he became a doctor. When his family settled at Fustat, his skills won him the position of personal physician to the grand vizier of Cairo, and also to the caliph, Saladin, a job which he complained kept him away from home too long and interfered with his ministrations to his community as doctor and rabbi. By this time, he had been made *nagid*, leader of the Egyptian Jewish community, a title his family held for another four generations.

It was in Fustat, during the years 1170-80, that he composed his greatest religious work, the *Mishneh Torah*, still today the only published authority on Jewish law and observance. For this, and perhaps this alone, he was and still is known as "the second Moses".

His greatest philosophical work, *Guide for the Perplexed*, in which he sought to reconcile Aristotelian logic with Jewish theology, was also written at this time. This was his most controversial work; some authorities banned it outright, others said that it should only be read by mature students with sufficient education to understand its complexities (Maimonides himself said it was only intended for a specialist audience). It was denounced and even burned in France by the Inquisition, although this was the same Inquisition that a few years later would also burn copies of the *Talmud*. Like Ibn Rushd, whose influence on Maimonides is undisputed, he argued that when considered in full there is no contradiction between Aristotelian philosophy and Judaic theology.

Despite the controversies, Maimonides was acclaimed as a brilliant thinker in his time, and on his death in 1204 the Egyptian Jewish community declared three days of mourning. He is said to be one of the most widely studied Jewish scholars even today, and certainly one of the most widely read outside Jewish scholastic circles. One Maimonides specialist quoted in *Time* magazine described him as "the most influential Jewish thinker of the Middle Ages, and quite possibly of all time." If we consider their influences on later thinkers, and the link does grow tenuous as the centuries pass, we might also conclude that together Ibn-Rushd and Maimonides indirectly influenced, among others, Locke, Hume, Spinoza, Kant, Schopenhauer, Hegel, Nietzsche, Husserl, Heidegger, Wittgenstein, Sartre, Foucault, Althusser, Derrida and more.

That both Ibn Rushd and Maimonides completed their work in exile, one banished, the other prevented from returning to his birthplace for fear of persecution, is a measure of the changes that had overtaken al-Andalus since the destruction of the caliphate at Córdoba. The region had fragmented into Taifa statelets, often at war with each other and unable to protect themselves from the united Christian armies pressing down from the north. The Almoravids and Almohads had invaded, ostensibly to support them, but swiftly assumed power for themselves. This was not enough to stave off the united armies of Castile, Aragon, Navarre and Portugal. Their victory at the Battle of Las Navas de Tolosa, just south of the Desfiladero de Despeñaperros, vividly if imaginatively depicted in nineteenth-century neoclassical painter Francisco de Paula van Halen's "Battle of Navas de Tolosa in which the Kings of Castile defeat the Almohads in 1212"—16 July, to be precise—was the turning point in the "Reconquest of Spain". Piece by piece, al-Andalus fell to the Christians. Toledo, Córdoba's twin city at the height of al-Andalus, had fallen in 1085; Córdoba itself would fall in 1236, Jaén in 1246, Seville in 1248, Cádiz in 1262, Jerez in 1264, Ronda in 1485, Málaga in 1487, Almería in 1490. The following year, from their war rooms in the Alcazar of Córdoba, the Reyes Católicos launched their eight-month siege on Granada.

The time scale for all those falling cities also frames another question, of course: what happened to al-Andalus culture between the Battle of Las Navas de Tolosa and the capitulation of the last Nasrid king, Boabdil, at Granada on 1 January 1492? Muslim and Jewish communities remained in Toledo, Córdoba and elsewhere, although under increasing pressure to either convert or flee. Islamic architecture continued to influence public buildings, notably in the Reales Alcazares at Seville, and poets, as we have already seen, continued to write, also under increasing restraints on their liberties. By 1250, the greater part of the Iberian Peninsula was under the control of Castile, Aragon and Portugal. This new Spain spoke Castilian, and Arabic began to leak from the demotic tongue (although it bubbles quietly away in the etymology of modern Castilian Spanish today). As the Almohads had offered Córdoba's Jews and Christians, the options the *reconquistadores* offered the remaining Muslims and Jews were bleak: convert, die or flee. Many Muslims chose to stay as Mudéjars, from the Arabic *mudajjan*, "those allowed to remain." The Jews, as was perhaps already apparent and as we will see next, were already living on borrowed time.

Part Three

ESPAÑA:

FROM RECONQUEST TO THE

TWENTY-FIRST CENTURY

"The myth of the 'loss' of a united Spain had to exist for it to be 're-conquered.'"

José Manuel Cuenca Toribio, historian

A machine for thinking in: part of the Alhambra complex at Granada

Chapter Twelve

1492: THE FALL OF GRANADA

The last redoubt of al-Andalus was the Nasrid "Kingdom of Granada", founded in 1238 and initially stretching from Algeciras to Almería and inland to Huéscar, near the border with modern-day Murcia, but shrinking as each Christian victory brought the frontera closer to Granada itself. While the original Alhambra (from the Arabic *qa'lat al-Hamra* or red fort, the colour of the local earth used to build its walls) was begun in the ninth century, the great edifices inside the Alhambra palace-city such as the Palacios de los Nazaries and the Patio de los Leones were built by the twenty or so Nasrid kings who reigned, problematically, during their 250-year Nasrid dynasty. Here, the aesthetic and philosophical complexities of Islamic architecture can be seen in their ultimate expression, although perhaps only because this tradition was about to be abruptly terminated. Left to their own devices, who knows what further complexities of design and semiosis their architects might have achieved? While architecture in the Mudéjar style continued here and elsewhere, some later Nasrid structures were destroyed after 1492, while others were crudely painted over, adapted to Christian use or simply vandalized and abandoned. The eminent contemporary Arabist Robert Irwin has argued, in his *The Alhambra* (2005), that much of the Alhambra we see today is a sorry mix of botched reconstructions and crazy misinterpretations of Islamic aesthetics. Visitor, beware...

THE ALHAMBRA

It is unlikely that even if you double the recommended visiting time (the authorities say it can be "done" in three hours) you will see all that there is to be seen in the Alhambra, even though it is right there in front of your eyes, and even if you are lucky enough to visit when it is not crowded. Most visitors on their first visit will find themselves stalled on, perhaps even stunned by, the scale of the architecture, and the decorative surfaces that run wild across the site (and unlike the compact alcazares and alcazabas at Seville and elsewhere, this is a large, sprawling complex, much of it outdoors).

If we can abscond briefly with the spaceship simile from Roman Itálica, the Alhambra is an alien mother-ship humming to life as it prepares for takeoff. Its circuitry (think: those endless vistas of mysterious Krell technology in the basement of Walter Pigeon's groovy space-age pad in *Forbidden Planet*), laid out in the algebraic diagrams repeating into infinity across the tiles and stucco, in patterns that defy sophisticated computer design programmes, resembles a vast and improbable mathematician's conceit, based on Pythagoras and Euclid, but intended to harmonize architecture with cosmology. Specifically, the boggling network of geometric patterns, based on Pythagoras' theory of the right-handed triangle (observable in the Sala de los Abencerrajes) and the Golden Mean (or section, or ratio) which underpins the layout of the Patio de los Leones, are here found in such stunning complexity that today it takes a computer programme—specifically a programme such as The Geometer's Sketchpad—to reproduce the level of mathematical ingenuity that went into the Alhambra designs. (The Alhambra designs are actually used as a teaching tool by professors of higher and abstract geometry.) It is difficult to discuss the signification of these designs without seeming to stray into the pseudo-mysticism of a Dan Brown, or even the mischief of Umberto Eco's novels (and both *The Name of the Rose* and *Foucault's Pendulum* were elaborate, indeed long-winded, games of pulling the reader's leg; Borges could have told the same gag in under twelve pages). It would seem that these patterns had an elaborate intellectual and philosophical resonance for the people who designed them, and the people who lived with and even inside them, which, like the mysteries of Pi and the Fibonacci series, recur in nature, from the micro to the macro, and accord with Islamic ideas of harmony, symmetry, pattern and order. They also offer a direct correlation between pure science, mathematics and an art that borders on the numinous, divine—or perhaps more accurately, was intended to represent the numinous. Robert Irwin says, simply, "The Alhambra was designed by and for intellectuals with mystical inclinations. It was a machine for thinking in."

It is unlikely that its inheritors would have had much time or inclination to ponder the subtleties of just what it was they were inheriting. Given that the Alhambra and other Islamic structures in the new "Spain" were the work of heathens, this would have been something to be dismissed, denied or even erased, as happened at the Alhambra and elsewhere where Islamic art was painted over, augmented or destroyed. Nor was this just the case at Granada. These elegant and mysterious games with geometry, proportion, symmetry and mathematics can also be observed in the stucco and tile work in Seville's (lovelier) Reales Alcazares, or the sloping water gardens and the clever Torre de Polvora echo chamber in Almería's Alcazaba, and even in the tiny water gardens of Ronda's Palacio Mondragon, a pocket-sized version of the Generalife gardens. Without exception, these and other Islamic monuments only really re-emerged from disuse and abandonment in the second half of the twentieth century, and almost all are still undergoing renovation or reconstruction. (The fountain in the Patio de los Leones was recently given an exhaustive, months-long clean, revealing, among other things, graffiti scratched into one of the lions by none other than Richard Ford, who scored his name and the date of his visit, 1831, into the fountain. It is somehow heartening to see that a titled toff like Ford could be as much a vandal as the average idiot in a hoodie armed with a wide-gauge magic marker pen.)

The worst act of Christian vandalism against the Muslim heritage took place some time after Boabdil handed over the keys to Granada to the Reyes Católicos, dressed for the occasion, bizarrely, in Arabic costume, which María Rosa Menocal reads as a tribute to the Muslims but which others might suspect to be an act of breathtaking sarcasm, not least given the wide-scale ethnic and religious cleansing that occurred mere weeks afterwards. While Córdoba had fallen in 1236, the new city authorities resisted the temptation to either demolish or alter the grand Mezquita, perhaps fearing an uprising by the remaining Mudéjars. However, in 1371 work began on the first of many alterations to the Mezquita, with the construction of the small Capilla (chapel) de Villaviciosa. Piece by piece, more and more stations of the conventional Christian church—nave, basilica plan, side chapels, altars, retables, private family chapels—were inserted in and around the mosque until, in 1523, work began on the cathedral proper. The first effect was the blocking of the light that would have streamed in from the orange courtyard into the forest of double arches inside the mosque, reducing the interior to the crepuscular gloom we see today. The second effect would be to interrupt the clean and simple music of its architecture with ornate and overblown outbursts of Christian ecclesiastical architecture. One can only guess at just what the good *burgueses* of Córdoba thought when they celebrated their mass in the shell of a Muslim mosque thronging with ghosts, metaphorical and literal. María

Rosa Menocal takes the rosier, if curious, view that the monarchs respected the Muslim heritage, although by the time the cathedral at Córdoba was completed, King Charles I felt moved to reproach the cathedral chapter, "You have destroyed something that was unique in the world."

BOABDIL HANDS OVER THE KEYS

The handover of Granada on 1 January 1492 was a stage-managed affair of the kind we are more accustomed to nowadays in the era of spin and media management. The terms of the surrender had been brokered in December, and were in any case preceded by earlier political deals and settlements with defeated Muslim enclaves in what remained of al-Andalus. Certainly, all offers, to either Boabdil or the remaining Muslim and Jewish populations, were off the table in a matter of weeks after the Reyes Católicos took the keys from Boabdil, with Genoese privateer Christopher Columbus watching admiringly in the audience at the Alhambra. Columbus was there to win favour with the new monarchs, having failed to impress the Portuguese court, and Queen Isabella was particularly keen to back his proposal to open up a sea route to the "Indies". It is difficult and perhaps impossible to underestimate the role and influence that Columbus would have in the following years and perhaps even centuries of Andaluz and Spanish culture, right up to the disastrous Spanish-American war of 1898.

Columbus left the port of Palos de la Frontera, on the Rio Tinto south of Huelva, on 3 August 1492, with three ships piloted by Juan de la Cosa and the Pinzón brothers, Martin and Vicente, all of them celebrated in the area's thriving Columbus Trail heritage industry. (While his reputation may be tarnished elsewhere, perhaps oxidized by all that sea air, Columbus and his captains are still local heroes around here, celebrated in a little nautical theme park at Rabida at the mouth of the Rio Tinto, the Pinzón brothers in their hometown of Palos de la Frontera, sites such as the interior town of Moguer, where they celebrated mass prior to weighing anchor, and elsewhere.) Columbus' first trip only got him as far as the Antilles, specifically the island of Hispaniola, then known as Ayiti to the people who lived there, but this was the beginning of Spain's great panglobal enterprise, which at its expansionist peak stretched from Manila to San Francisco, to Buenos Aires and back.

At home, however, there was still some mopping up to do. The campaign against the Jews had already begun in earnest in 1391, with the massacre of 4,000 Jews in Seville, massacres in other cities and the enforced conversion of those unable or unwilling to flee. The North American writer Robert Preston Junior writes in his deliriously bad *Dogs of War: Columbus, the Inquisition and the Defeat of the Moors* (2006) that Spain's Jews were "confined to a ghetto, forced to wear red badges identifying their lineage, to wear their beards long and uncut, to be barred from holding important governmental positions, from having their own markets and from selling food Christians ate and the clothes they wore, to cease to minister to Christians as physicians or apothecaries." Anyone who has even glanced at Victor Klemperer's three volumes of autobiography, *I Will Bear Witness* (1995), about Jewish life in Nazi Germany, will find chilling similarities between the treatment of Jews under the Catholic monarchs and their treatment under the Third Reich.

As well as dealing with its Jewish problem and coping with the fractious rump of the Mudéjars, those Muslims "allowed to stay", the Catholic monarchs had to put their new house in order. Wars of attrition lasting 781 years do not come cheap, although on the plus side there were the spoils of war to be divided among the monarchs and their allies. We should also bear in mind exactly what the Reyes Católicos were inheriting: a whole, newly unified country, with 781 years' worth of Muslim infrastructure, including their improvements on Roman communications and those earlier Tartesio latifundio land holdings. The two great kingdoms of Aragón and Castile had been unified in the dynastic marriage of their respective monarchs, Isabella and Ferdinand, in 1469, and with the fall of Granada (it had been a "vassal" or puppet state since 1236) only the northern territory of Navarre remained outside the newly christened "España", from the earlier "Hispania", until it too was absorbed in 1512.

Recent economic and academic studies, from such august sources as Harvard and MIT, suggest that Spain's exploitation of the New World may not have been the free-for-all hemispheric shoplifting spree we might imagine it to be, although its cultural impact was devastating, not least on Aztec and Inca societies, creating also the abiding mystery of the disappearance of classical Mayan civilization. Some Mexican authorities believe the Mayans may have just walked away, or vanished into the forests, in disgust. And six hundred years on, Central and South American intellectuals still complain about the eradication of their indigenous cultures by the Spanish conquistadores, starting with the native languages.

Certainly, enough wealth returned with Columbus and later explorers to transform aspects of Spanish culture, but its economy did not experience a dramatic expansion. Even the sober *Encyclopaedia Britannica* notes that, "Most of it was used for display by the court and ruling circles, to pay for Spanish imports, for the Spanish armies abroad, and to satisfy the government's German, Italian, and Netherlandish creditors. Thus Spain, with all the treasure of the New World at its command, remained a poor country."

As José Manuel Cuenca Toribio points out, however, Andalucía was better suited to survive than any other region of Spain, particularly in its agriculture and mineral wealth, and it benefited from the riches that did arrive from the Americas at its key ports of Seville and Cádiz and the smaller ports of Sanlúcar and Huelva. (In fact, the trade with the Americas transformed economies along the entire Costa de la Luz Atlantic coastline, from Tarifa to Ayamonte near the modern Portuguese border.) During the sixteenth century, starting around the 1520s, barely thirty years after the fall of Granada, the equivalent of two trillion euros in gold and silver from the Americas passed through these ports on its way to the crown's coffers, which, for a goodly part of the same century, were in Seville. Not a little of this went on the extraordinary religious, civic and private architecture of Seville, Granada, Córdoba and outlying towns, such as the wealthy seaport of Sanlúcar, and the grand mansions of Carmona and Úbeda. Some of it found its way into projects for the public good, such as universities and hospitals, and some of it must also have found its way into the hands of artists, sculptors, maybe even poets and playwrights, but these would, by and large, be dancing to a selection of tunes chosen by the rich and the powerful or equally the similarly powerful religious orders such as the Dominicans, whose commissions kept many painters out of the poorhouse. The lucky ones, of course, were those who won royal or aristocratic patronage.

Mostly, however, it went into the aggrandizement of a small elite, much as it did in any economically powerful country in sixteenth-century Europe, including England, France, Germany and Holland. But Andalucía, and Spain, would hang on to, or remain mired in, this iniquitous system long after the rest of Europe had ceded control to more democratically minded parties. It clings to life even in the twenty-first century, in orgies of criminal self-entitlement such as the Malaya scandal in Marbella, and Andalucía's jolly tradition of gangster mayors, some twenty or so of whom had their collars felt in the early 2000s for the imaginative misapplication of vast quantities of public funds to such eye-popping personal projects as pseudo-Gothic castles, neoclassical palaces and personal back-garden menageries, complete with pet lions, possibly inspired by the zoo at Madinat al-Zahra.

As for the Muslim heritage of Andalucía, it took until the eighteenth and nineteenth centuries before it was rediscovered, and until the late twentieth century before historians, academics and critics began to restore it to its proper place in Spanish history. By then—by now—it would have been comprehensively rewritten, rinsed of its complexities and ambiguities and re-branded as a safe, antiseptic and untroubling narrative, pitched at the level of a children's fairytale story and minus the heretical philosophers, mad scientists and randy bisexual poets who originally wrote it. In the hands of writers such as Prosper Mérimée and Washington Irving and artists such as Gustave Doré it started to resemble a *parque tematico*, lacking only the white knuckle rides of Seville's Isla Magica.

Modern Spain has arrived at an accommodation with its Muslim past, although that past is one normally visited accompanied by an audio guide, which imprisons the visitor in someone else's version of events, and which comes with the soothing assurance that this is the official, expert version. It might even be said to preclude, maybe even forbid, any alternative reading of that past.

Which might leave us to consider just how, five hundred years or so since they were violently expelled from their garden, their paradise, all those "Berbers" and "Moors" ten miles across el Estrecho might be feeling, as they finger those house keys that legend claims still fit doors in Córdoba and Granada, just waiting to be brought home by their rightful owners. This fanciful notion is as preposterous as the calls for a "new caliphate" stretching from Baghdad to the Atlantic, although, property rights aside, it might tell us something about how 781 years of culture can be reduced down, eventually, to the status of a souvenir fridge magnet, and what the creators of that culture might quite rightly think of that very same souvenir fridge magnet.

The dismissive gaze: statue of Velázquez outside the Prado in Madrid

Chapter Thirteen

TAKING THE GARDEN INDOORS: VELÁZQUEZ AND THE LANDSCAPE ARTISTS OF ANDALUCÍA

In his famous essay on Velázquez's "Las Meninas", the French philosopher-critic Michel Foucault carefully and cleverly decodes or dismantles just what is or might be going on in the artist's most famous painting, possibly the most famous Spanish painting ever after Picasso's "Guernica". Published as the opening essay in his *The Order of Things* (Foucault's preferred translation of its original French title, *Les mots et les choses*) in 1966, the essay established Foucault as one of the most daring, indeed intimidating, thinkers of his era, maybe even his century.

Foucault's ruminations on what Velázquez—or Diego Rodríguez de Silva y Velázquez (1599-1660), to give him his full name—was up to in "Las Meninas" are as enigmatic as the original painting. After eighteen pages of delineating the painter's play with light, sightline, spatial relationships between subjects, and the various levels of surface, Foucault declares that in fact the subject of the painting has vanished, and we are left with "representation in its purest form"—that is, minus the thing it is meant to be showing you. (He was, however, beaten to the first deconstruction of the painting by Théophile Gautier, who on seeing it in the Prado in 1846 asked, "Where, then, is the picture?")

Velázquez himself might well have surrendered, grinning and with his hands up, to Foucault's reading of "Las Meninas". His painting purports to be a group portrait of the Infanta Margarita of Austria, two of her ladies-in-waiting (the English translation of the Spanish title) and entourage, preparing either for a special event or indeed for the sitting itself. They are accompanied by a dwarf and a midget (there *is* a difference, visible here…), a dog, two court officials, the painter himself, a passing palace bigwig and, in an almost ghostly apparition, which Roland Barthes would no doubt have called the *punctum*, the detail that punctures and focuses an image,

King Philip IV and his wife Mariana, seen as though in a mirror on the back wall. On an initial glance, Velázquez appears to have created a clever conceit apparently based on a mirror reflection, or an invented point-of-view as seen by the observer, an intruder or indeed the king and queen themselves. This is only the first trip-wire that Velázquez lays for the visitor viewing "Las Meninas"—if, that is, you can get anywhere near it in the permanent scrum in front of it in the Prado...

Before we delve further into "Las Meninas" and the Spanish baroque it dominates we should first triangulate Velázquez, and also unpack the double meaning of the title to this chapter. While born in Seville in 1599 and trained under the Sevillano painter Francisco Pacheco, Velázquez pursued his adult career in Madrid, arriving there in 1622 aged just 22, with a letter of introduction to the king's chaplain, Don Juan de Fonseca, which would be his ticket into a lifelong career as a court official and painter. But he is considered as, among other things, the leader of a "triad" of the leading Sevillano painters, along with Bartolomé Esteban Murillo (1617-82) and Juan de Valdés Leal (1622-90), who exerted what Cuenca Toribio describes as the "indisputable hegemony" of the Seville School of painting. Also assisting in this hegemony over Spanish art at the time were Juan Martínez Montañés (1580-1649), Alonso Cano (1601-67), Jusepe de Ribera (1591-1652) and Francisco de Zurbarán (1598-1664). There were of course earlier Sevillano painters, notably Luis de Vargas (1505-67), considered the "first" great Sevillano painter, and Alejo Fernández (1475-1545), said to be the first painter to introduce Renaissance ideas into Spain. Similarly, Domenicos Theotocopoulos, El Greco (1541-1614), late of Crete, trained in Italy and later of Toledo, is considered a precursor and near-neighbour of the Sevillanos. There were also the undoubted precedents in Flemish and Italian painting and the considerable intellectual traffic between these cultures; Velázquez himself spent two lengthy periods in Italy, studying his contemporaries and purchasing art for the king.

While Velázquez created much of his work away from his birthplace, Seville still guards its Velázquez connection jealously, not least in the bust of Velázquez in the tiny Plaza del Duque de la Victoria, these days a small garden in the shadow of a huge Corte Inglés store that dominates it. His casa natal, the house where he was born, on Lluis Maria Llop in the city centre, is now part Velázquez museum, part gallery celebrating the work of its current owners, Andaluz couturiers Victorio and Lucchino. The city's Museo de Bellas Artes contains just one major work from his early period, the "Retrato de Don Cristóbal Suárez de Ribera", painted in 1620 when Velázquez was just 21. A year later, he was already in Madrid and painting his first portrait of the king.

Most of the art of this period was privately commissioned by royalty, aristocracy or the Church, and it stayed private. "Las Meninas" itself was hung first in a private salon of the king, then in his dining room at the Escorial palace outside Madrid, and the painting only appeared in a "public" space shortly after the opening of the Prado in 1819, more than one hundred and sixty years after it was painted in 1656. It was only properly cleaned and restored in 1984 and given pride of place in the Prado's Sala Velázquez in 1990, when, according to Gabriele Finaldi, one of the directors of the Prado and the author of a pop-up guide to the painting, it "ushered in the age of mass museum visiting" in a huge Velázquez retrospective at the Prado that same year. Nowadays the Prado will not let the painting out of its sight, or indeed site, which is why it was absent from the great overseas Velázquez shows of the early 2000s.

Rethinking the Landscape in Renaissance Spain

"Las Meninas" is the most famous of the many examples of how painters and patrons of Renaissance Spain took the garden indoors, a period when landscapes and the *bodégon* (still life) were swept aside by the religious allegorical painting and the A-list celebrity portrait, a shift in aesthetic thinking that had an unambiguously social, political and even epidemiological basis. While a few either subverted or diverged from the pattern, this was largely a closed circuit of artists producing paintings of and for powerful or wealthy patrons who hung their expensive portraits or religious allegories in private spaces where few others could see them.

It is of course arguable whether there was any true democratic access to the great art of earlier eras, although given the structure of Muslim, Roman and earlier Iberian societies, it might be imagined that their art could have been accessible beyond the confines of the commissioners' castles or monasteries. It is also the case that this was similarly true of the great art hung in the castles and monasteries of any European country in the Renaissance. No queues formed outside the Tower of London or Versailles, and it would be a good half-millennium or so before any of these locales acquired either a ticket office or a souvenir shop. (Since we are, again, here, as it were, we might also pertinently ask, from an Andaluz perspective, what exactly was being *renewed* in this renaissance?)

Nor were the tiny elites inside these castles and monasteries alone in taking their art, or their garden, "indoors". The subject matter of this commissioned art, often religious iconography or at worst representational hagiography of the rich and famous, was an entirely private business transaction between the commissioner and the commissionee. The landscape, if it featured at all, was at best a picturesque backdrop or an alien environment given its own, often malevolent, role in the picture's *mise en scène*. The landscape was frequently stylized out of all relation to reality, often for symbolic purposes, and usually played a supporting role in the representation of the figure or figures who had paid for their representation in this setting.

This curious—even fearful—relationship between painter, patron and landscape reaches its extreme in a museum such as Köln's famous Ludwig/Wallraf-Richartz Museum. Some years ago (the Wallraf-Richartz collection was recently re-housed and re-hung) it housed an entire room of quite fearsome representations of "The Temptation of St. Anthony", most famously that by David Teniers the Younger, although you will find this tension between painter, patron and landscape in other paintings contemporaneous to Velázquez elsewhere in the Prado too. Best observed in Bosch's triptych of the same title, these days hanging in the Museu Nacional de Arte Antiga in Lisbon, it is the allegorical representation of the saint's torment by squadrons of aerial monsters in a pitiless landscape seething with menace. The theme clearly has a didactic, religious function, but you are also left with the resonating impression that, while the "Temptation" may indeed have had a didactic religious function, those squadrons of aerial monsters were in fact part of the furniture of the outdoors as far as most people living at that time were concerned, and that the outdoors was not something to be trifled with but rather, indeed, avoided. Coleridge's lines about the traveller who, "having once turned round, walks on,/And turns no more his head;/Because he knows a frightful fiend/Doth close behind him tread", spring more than readily to mind in this instance.

Here be monsters, and this fear of landscape would continue up to the eighteenth century, when the landscape painter's monsters were more likely to be bandits, gypsies, or enemy armies, as we will see later, and beyond.

Given this, for the painter to represent their subject in a position of jeopardy, *outdoors*, might find its contemporary equivalent in John Carpenter's decision to send Jamie Lee Curtis down into the unlit basement in *Hallowe'en*, albeit without the narrative payoff that John Carpenter had in mind…

Whimsicality aside, the landscape, outdoors, had a very different meaning for Velázquez and his contemporaries than it does today, although the demands of the job were more likely the reason for its relegation to the background than simple fear of the dark. These brilliant hacks were being paid to represent their commissioners in their best lights, although in some cases Velázquez was either a very good judge of character or so assured of his own political position that he felt able to take risks in the form of subverting court protocols in "Las Meninas", or in his startling portrayal of Pope Innocent X. In the case of Velázquez's baleful representation of the pope in his "Retrato del papa Inocencio X" (1650), the painting that obsessed Francis Bacon throughout much of his career, Innocent *liked* his portrait so much that he hung it in his visitors' waiting room in the Vatican. Look into Innocent's eyes in that painting, eyes that you would never play poker with, and think about where the pope hung his scary publicity image (little surprise that Innocent had originally trained as a lawyer, or that his face was used to represent Satan in a painting by Guido Reni). You will either gasp or tremble at his holiness's breathtaking ploy in leaving his visitors alone in a room with this vision of a lizard-eyed Nosferatu in papal finery prior to their interview with God's priest on earth.

(Bacon, who completed his first "screaming pope", "Head VI", in 1949, produced some 23 such variations on Velázquez's portrait of Innocent, the last in 1971. His friend, the art critic David Sylvester, sourced the scream itself to the equally iconic still of the woman whose spectacles are shattered in the famous Odessa Steps sequence of Eisenstein's *Battleship Potemkin*. Paradoxically—or, all things considered, maybe not—Bacon never actually saw the painting itself, and is said to have made a point of avoiding it, preferring to use reproductions as the source for what Sylvester read as a bleak comment on the recent war.)

Velázquez was not taking as many risks with "Las Meninas" as he did with Innocent, although he was certainly flouting court protocols, depending on who was actually at the sitting or, indeed, if there was even a conventional sitting at all. Gabriele Finaldi writes that "the very informality has no precedent in Spanish royal portraiture, and seems at odds with the strict protocol of the Hapsburg court." Like Foucault, we need to track back through the production of this image to consider what might have been going on that room in the Escorial palace.

One of the factors that Foucault seems to have set aside in considering the genesis of this painting ("overlooked" seems too unlikely a word to apply to such a fierce intelligence as his) is the fourth dimension of time, possibly because Foucault assumed it was taken as given that the subjects did not stand still like that for as long as it took Velázquez to complete his painting. (And we can get a rough Time and Motion study on his work rate from reports that his first sketched portrait of the king's head took him a full day.) Foucault maps a dense net of lines, loops and crosses back and forth across the canvas that Velázquez used to position the figures in the frame (some have read cabbalistic symbolism in the placement of the figures). A diagram produced in 1972 by art historian and Velázquez specialist Bartolomé Mestre Fiol suggests that Velázquez imagined the viewer to be positioned standing by the king's right shoulder and "seeing" Velázquez's portrait of the monarchs reflected in a mirror on the far wall. In this interpretation, Infanta, *meninas*, dwarf, midget, dog and court officials are watching the king and queen having their picture painted. (It still leaves the question, however, of whether or not Velázquez was planning to include this phantom visitor from the future, the viewer, in his mirrored portrait of the monarchs. Similarly, it does not explain why we do not see Velázquez himself—that is, his back—in the mirror—or did he figure himself leaning back to stay out of the way of the investigator's gaze?—or what else apart from the heads and torsos of the monarchs was being represented on that canvas, which must be around twelve feet high.)

It is likely that while plotting (either sense) his masterwork, Velázquez may have mapped out the spatial relation between the figures before painting them into the scene, but again it would be unlikely for him to expect them to, or for them to be willing to, stand perfectly still while Velázquez committed this to oil paint on canvas—least of all the dog. Velázquez was a fast worker, thanks probably to his training with long-haired brushes under Francisco Pacheco. His genius has been analyzed as the ability to use deft brush strokes to imply greater detail than is actually there, inviting the viewer to, as it were, join up the dots. Even so, going on the Time and Motion study on his head of the king, it would have taken an unconscionable length of time to commit "Las Meninas" to canvas in the single sitting that the image implies (the passing courtesan, the nattering officials, the solicitous maids, the midget kicking the dog, Velázquez leaning back to appraise his work, and us—*is Velázquez staring at our left ear?*).

Caravaggio favoured (and, therefore, faked) mid-afternoon light that gave him his famously preferred forty-five degree angle of "natural" light. Cézanne worked simultaneously on different canvases of the same landscape seen at different times of the day. Modern painters, portraitists particularly, are often happy to work with photographs of their subjects, fabricating an agreed "sitting" with the subjects. It seems possible that Velázquez may have sketched this tableau before fleshing it out later, or, intriguingly, that he may have used an optical device, either a *camera obscura* (a darkened room turned into a pinhole camera) or a *camera lucida* (a mirror or lens employed in the manner of a modern overhead projector) to trace the models on canvas for later embellishment, resulting in a left-to-right reversal, "flipping" in newspaper speak, of the image. This is, in fact, the suspicion that feeds the curious little ritual of some visitors who sneak a small mirror into the Prado to view the painting in reverse over their shoulder, to see what Velázquez was "really" painting.

This theory got David Hockney into hot water in 2001 when he proposed, in his book *Secret Knowledge: Rediscovering the Lost Techniques of the Old Masters*, that not only was Velázquez using this technology, but that Caravaggio, Da Vinci, Hals, Holbein, Ingres, Van Eyck and others probably were as well. The idea that Velázquez might have used a *camera obscura* in preparing "Las Meninas" has in fact been around for at least a quarter century or longer, but there seemed to be quite a long queue of people with a grudge waiting to criticize David Hockney when he published his book. In preparing his book, he spent two years away from his own painting "eyeballing" the works of the old masters, his suspicions sparked by some visual anomalies in the work of Ingres, and given further impetus by further anomalies he spotted elsewhere, not least in the curious elongation of form in Velázquez's "Venus del espejo"—literally, the Venus of the mirror, better known by its English titles of either "Venus at Her Toilet" or "The Rokeby Venus", after Rokeby Park, the home of its first English buyer, John Morritt. Hockney was not declaring war on the old masters, rather he was elaborating on his fascination with the possibility that they may have used these tools in their work, but the *ad hominem* attacks on Hockney – we could probably date it back to 1967 and the antipathies sparked by his "A Bigger Splash"—echoed with the sound of old scores being settled.

In any event, "Las Meninas" was stage managed down to the most minute detail, either physically, or on the drawing board. This is nothing new, and certainly no scandal, although the hostility meted out to David Hockney showed that there are certain myths about the work of art before the age of mechanical reproduction that still need dismantling. We accept that elisions of reality are necessary in filmmaking, television and textual editing (including this one) but not, it seems, the elision of reality in which, say, it always seems to be precisely 3.30pm (and sunny outside) in the paintings of Caravaggio, or in which Velázquez took his subjects on trips through time and space to achieve his masterworks.

It is just as likely, as some commentators suggest, that "Las Meninas" was designed as a visual conundrum that would resist any final defining explication, and there is an arrogance to the painted portraitist's eyes that suggests he knows he is having the last laugh on just about everybody, not least the monarchy (Foucault complains that "we are dismissed by the gaze" of the painter). It has become a much-loved popular icon, part of a shared Spanish cultural shorthand, an image frequently detourned by Spanish newspaper cartoonists on the assumption that everyone knows the tableau being referenced. It certainly stands as a yardstick against which later artists felt they had to measure themselves: Goya made numerous etchings of it, and Salvador Dalí nuked it in his "Diego Velázquez Painting the Infanta Margarita with the Lights and Shadows of His Own Glory" (1958), placing a tiny Velázquez alongside a gigantic Infanta (as ever, with the face of Gala Dalí) in what looks like an exploding palace interior for a work he described as "atomic mysticism". Picasso clearly felt its heavy weight on his shoulders: he produced at least fifty-eight oil versions of "Las Meninas" roughly between 1957 and 1962, part in *homenaje*, but also, it would seem, as a form of exorcism, or perhaps as the Cubist scrapper squaring up to the Velázquez legend with his dukes up. It has reappeared as outdoor sculpture and as video art, notably in Eve Sussman's *89 Seconds at Alcázar*, a twelve-minute film loop in which Sussman imagines the staging of the Meninas sitting. In a droll visual conceit, even David Hockney turned his "Self-Portrait with Charlie" (2005) into a homage to Velázquez and "Las Meninas", flipping the image so that the canvas is on the right (same height, though, and same two stretchers), with his friend Charlie Scheips perched on a table at the back, and Hockney fixing either us or a mirror quizzically in the eye.

VELÁZQUEZ AT THE MOVIES

The notion of time, and the mention of film, throws up a fascinating series of coincidental connections between Velázquez, "Las Meninas", cinema, and Andalucía, which fell into the lap of this book during its writing. During the visit of the great Velázquez exhibition of 2006, a variety of complementary events were organized by the National Gallery in London, including a rare showing of Eve Sussman's film. Among these events was an illustrated lecture at the National Gallery by the film critic and head of programming at the BFI Southbank (the old National Film Theatre), Geoff Andrew (disclosure: Geoff's an old friend and colleague). Geoff prefaced his talk by saying, "I'm certainly not proposing a direct link between Velázquez's work and the films I'm about to discuss, in terms of influence, cause or effect. The distance between the artist and the filmmakers in terms of time, place and technology is too great for that," before going on to discuss a series of film clips which either coincidentally or deliberately overlap with Velázquez's relationship to realism in painting, his treatment of characters, the passage of time, point of view and the artist's presence or absence in the work, not least the disturbing tendency of the painter and some characters to stare straight into the eyes of the viewer.

Among the filmmakers he discussed were Luis Buñuel, Eric Rohmer, Orson Welles (an adopted son of Andalucía, specifically Ronda), Michael Haneke, Abbas Kiarostami, Jean-Luc Godard and Ingmar Bergman, the last two recommended to him by a Spanish filmmaker, the Vizcaya-born Victor Erice, who appears at numerous points in the talk/essay (Andaluz cinema, such as there is, is discussed in a later chapter here). Erice is Spain's greatest living poet of the cinema, comparable to the likes of Andrei Tarkovsky and Theo Angelopoulos on the world stage, more commonly compared to figures such as Kiarostami and Terrence Malick in the way he approaches filmmaking. Even though he may be Spain's greatest living film-maker, Erice only manages to produce a film around every decade, and supports his work by making corporate promotional films. His best-known work is *El espiritu de la colmenar* (The Spirit of the Beehive), released in 1973 and regarded as an international art-house classic, followed by *El sur* (The South), released in 1983, and *El sol del membrillo* (The Quince-Tree Sun), from 1992. He has also produced a small number of *cortometrajes*, short films.

El sol del membrillo, a quasi-fictional documentary portrait of the real-life "hyper-realist" painter Antonio López García (born in Ciudad Real, 1936), is two hours and twelve minutes of Erice's camera watching López Garcia attempting to paint a quince tree in his Madrid garden as the seasons pass, the quince tree fruits fall and family and friends come and go. Clearly, director and painter are in cahoots here, and the reality of López García painting his tree is obviously mediated by Erice in the cutting room. Some viewers hated the film, others were mesmerized by its pace, modesty and humour. Yet it is possibly one of the most engrossing and honest films about the mechanics of the artist's trade ever (and more besides). Geoff Andrew reveals that *El sol del membrillo* was in fact the film that Erice made when circumstances forced him to abandon a film he wanted to make about "Las Meninas". In an interview with *Cahiers du Cinéma* magazine, Erice compared López García's painterly processes to "those of the Spanish Baroque, of Velázquez. There is in the Baroque a semblance of sleep in death, the idea of the light that is extinguished, of death." In the film, Erice directly cites the process at work between painter and viewer in "Las Meninas", having López García painting by using a mirror to view his subject. It might be said that, while operating in an entirely different medium, *El sol del membrillo* is the most eloquent critical commentary on Velázquez and "Las Meninas" made so far, while remaining quite emphatically *not* about either. Anyone perplexed, amused or annoyed by Velázquez's sly play with the viewer might hunt out the DVD of *El sol del membrillo*, perhaps in a double-bill with Peter Greenaway's period-costume *después-Borges* prank, *The Draughtsman's Contract*.

The essay version of the lecture, published in *Ten Bad Dates with de Niro* (2007), lists, among others, Godard's *Pierrot le fou*, Buñuel's *Viridiana*, Rohmer's *A Winter's Tale*, Welles' *Citizen Kane*, Altman's *The Long Goodbye*, Erice's *Quince Tree Sun*, Bergman's *Summer with Monika*, Haneke's recent *Hidden* and others, all of which share Velázquez's interest in subverting the viewer's perception of just what (they think) they are looking at, not least in the figures who fix the viewer straight in the eye ("Las Meninas", "La rendición de Breda", "La Tela Real") or where figures even point out ("Príncipe Baltasar Carlos en la escuela de caballo") where the viewer should be looking. (Just 1,700 words, but it will tell you more about Velázquez than many books on the subject...)

FOREGROUNDING THE BACKGROUND

Beyond his portrait of St. Anthony and St. Paul, landscape rarely intrudes into Velázquez's work. Even "La rendición de Breda" (1634), shows the smoking city of that name as a distant detail behind the surrender (*rendición*) negotiations taking place in the foreground. It is there in the background of his portraits of chubby princes on horseback, but by the very nature of some subjects—those countless tiny princesses built like pocket battleships, whose frocks suggest that their main means of perambulation would have been by wheels or rollers, and that they would never have made it outdoors—they remained resolutely in their natural habitat, indoors. His few painterly sallies into the streets, such as "Vieja friendo huevos" (1618) or "El aguador de Sevilla" (1620) were, according to some, more exercises in displaying his facility of technique than any realist desire to represent an old woman frying eggs or an old man selling water on the streets of Seville, even though some have described these figures as simple mortals in a state of grace. Yet even here, in the detail of glass, the water-seller's shirt, the glistening eggs or the old woman's gleaming pestle and mortar, we can observe what the painter Luca Giordano described as Velázquez's founding "theology of painting".

The landscape rarely impinges in the work of his fellow Seville School indoor gardeners. It features in some of the works of Ribera, notably his "Adoración de los Pastores" (1639) and his moving and noble "El Lisiado" (1642), a dignified portrait of, as the English translation puts it, a club-footed boy, in a country setting. Both Montañés and Cano were best known as sculptors, the latter nicknamed the "Michaelangelo of Spain", although he is perhaps more famous as the artist arrested for the alleged murder of his wife, an unproven and unlikely allegation, but one which drove him to take holy orders to avoid prosecution. Leal, along with Murillo one of the "triad" of leading Seville School painters, took religious allegory to its grisly, fire-and-brimstone extreme in his diptych "Jeroglíficos de las Postrimerías" (1670-74), in English the "Hieroglyphics of the last days", portraying the triumph of death over human ambition and folly, in its second panel, "Finis Gloriae Mundi", depicting a mitred bishop decomposing in a shattered coffin. Fittingly, Leal's career was brought to a premature end by an attack of "apoplexy", which disabled him for the final decade of his life.

There in fact appear to have been two Murillos, working in tandem throughout his career. The first painted fetching and almost realistic portraits of Seville urchins and flower girls, and even managed to produce at least two passable but largely empty landscapes, as well as the famous portraits of San Isidoro and his brother, Leandro. The second became even more famous and successful for his ascending Virgin Marys wreathed in sparkling, luminous mists and accompanied by rosy-cheeked cherubs. If he were alive today, Murillo would probably be the multi-millionaire rival to Hallmark Cards. Yet his chocolate-boxy religious confections themselves connect to an interesting religious allegory.

Among Murillo's influences was his elder (by nineteen years) Francisco de Zurbarán, nicknamed the "Spanish Caravaggio", who enjoyed a decade of dizzying acclaim between 1630 and 1640 and was feted by both clergy and court; King Philip IV is said to have called him "Painter to the king, and king of the painters". A year older than, and a friend of, Velázquez, he was young enough to have seen the older Caravaggio's works and adopted his realism and use of dramatic chiaroscuro changes between darkness and light. He painted mainly religious images, but also produced bodegones in the manner, if not quite the luscious detail, of Caravaggio, and is known to have produced two landscape works, "La expulsión de los holandeses desde la isla de San Martín", said to have been destroyed in a fire, and "La defensa de Cádiz ante los ingléses" (1634), now hanging in the Prado. Zurbarán's immense skill with texture and sheen are near perfect in this; alas, his sense of perspective is catastrophic, with fore, mid and background telescoped together as though in a bizarre natural disaster, although some see this telescoping as an allegorical effect. Curiouser still, there is no prominence in or indeed anywhere near Cádiz that would have given the gentlemen in the foreground their vertiginous perspective over the background, unless Zurbarán had taken them aloft in a hot air balloon.

What Zurbarán excelled at was surfaces, skin, cloth, water, wood, porcelain and metals, but in an austere, perfectionist and almost minimalist fashion, which is what makes his paintings seem startlingly modern, startlingly, in fact, similar to a Hockney or a Tom Phillips. His depiction of physical human details and domestic settings—his way with white cloth won him a long-standing working relationship with Seville's Carthusian monastery—verges on photorealism. One of his masterpieces for the Carthusians, "La virgen de los Cartujos" (1635), depicting a group of white-robed Carthusian monks kneeling in prayer around a very down-to-earth (any sense) virgin, also teeters on the edge of unintentional homoeroticism; those tonsured monks with their five o'clock shadow and patina of perspiration look as though they just tumbled out of a gay bar on Seville's Alameda de Hercúles. This is of course our old friend the sliding signifier, and says more about changing sub-cultural trends today than monastic life in seventeenth-century Seville, although the Aldous Huxley who wrote *The Devils of Loudon* might have argued otherwise.

Zurbarán painted, otherwise free of any further hints of homoeroticism, throughout his career, including many commissions from the Carthusian friars of Seville, as well as numerous mythological and religious scenes, among them a fair number of ascensions and miraculous conceptions. He is also one of the first artists to use himself as a model in his own works, notably in his portrait of St. Luke (and starting a tradition alive today with artists such as Cindy Sherman, who has turned to the old masters for inspiration in recent years). But around 1640 his career went into freefall. The only explanation histories offer for this is a drastic change in aesthetic opinion in religious circles, or perhaps a simple commercial decision to move away from the cool, grave and unsparing visions of Zurbarán towards the softer, warmer, sexier, pinker Murillo.

Most histories, relying on just one unreliable encyclopaedia for their source, say that Zurbarán died in poverty and obscurity. His fall from fashionability certainly affected his income to the extent that he moved from Seville to Madrid to seek the help of his old friend Velázquez, who readily came to his assistance, and Zurbarán even attempted to alter his own style to paint more like Murillo—but to no avail. He continued to win commissions, from the Carthusians and from their missions in the Americas, as well as from churches in Spain, but it seems that his later life was beset with money troubles. He was also widowed twice, the second time going so far as withdrawing to a monastery to grieve, and was said to have been traumatized by the death of his son and assistant Juan from the plague in 1649, when the five-year-long Great Plague of Seville (1647-52) killed a quarter of the city's 600,000 population, taking a major role in shaping Andaluz history. (The several epidemics of the 1640s are credited by historian Maria del Valme Muñoz Rubio with contributing to the newly pious atmosphere in Seville, or at least among its arts patrons.)

It was shortly after this that Zurbarán moved to Madrid to enlist the help of his friend Velázquez, yet despite winning commissions at the court, he became embroiled in a crippling lawsuit over non-payment of fees, a recurring problem through his career, and died in poverty in 1664.

Velázquez's teacher Pacheco left Zurbarán out of his influential *Arte de la pintura* (1649), the "official" contemporary text on art and Spanish artists, and this slight seems to have lodged in the cultural memory until the twentieth century, when Zurburán's artistic recuperation began. He is well represented in the Prado, Seville's Museo de Bellas Artes and in Cádiz's Museo de Cádiz (where an ingenious lighting system follows you around the gallery, illuminating the works as you approach), yet there are few biographies or studies of him. The sudden, violent, change in fashion in religious art in the 1640s suggests a move away from the intellectual rigour and purity of a Zurbarán towards the fluffier niceties of a Murillo. If we consider these closed circuits between artists and patrons to be at least in part a public relations exercise, this might suggest a Catholic Church rebranding itself to appear more humane, or perhaps less apocalyptic, and Zurbarán's works do tend towards the severe, however beautiful they may be. In the twenty-first century, however, when Murillo seems destined to turn up on a tea towel in one of those souvenir kiosks in the back streets around Seville's cathedral, Zurbarán's star may yet reappear back over the horizon in all its dazzling glory.

Chapter Fourteen

NIGHTS IN THE GARDENS OF SPAIN: THE ROMANTIC ERA FABRICATES "ANDALUSIA"

Given the circumstances of the production and hanging of much Spanish art during the Renaissance, we might consider the idea that in fact we *are* visiting it in a time machine; it only became part of any notional public discourse on culture when it left the castles, monasteries and state buildings and entered the galleries and museums of the eighteenth century. By which time, and in which circumstance, it would—our old friend Schrödinger's cat again—have changed its nature. It was no longer the portrait or religious allegory commissioned entirely in private for the wall of a king's dining room or a monastery's chapel, but something salvaged from the garbage compactor of history, something to be venerated inside grand public architecture, and later to be protected by subdued lighting, carefully controlled environments, in some cases behind bullet-proof glass and protected also from the attentions of slashers, paint-throwers and cat burglars. It was, of course, completely out of its original context—snatched from the intimacy between artist and patron, dumped into the public domain to be misinterpreted and misread by whoever happened by—but it was Culture, although we might wonder just who was enjoying this Culture until it finally went public. Not enough people to make this anything more than great art created by and for a tiny elite, offshore from the lives lived by normal people, and Erwin would probably have declared the cat dead when we opened this particular box.

This, again, would have been exactly the case anywhere else in Europe where the cultured patronized culture. It might, however, lead us to ponder how this art is considered, not least given that Andaluz culture effectively took a nap, or at least remained offline from the mainstream, for the best part of two or more centuries (what in another context the historian James Simpson called, snappily, "the long siesta"). It might, indeed, make us re-

Landscape of the imagination: the real Cueva del Gato, fabricated by painter Manuel Barrón y Carillo

consider how this or indeed any culture is mediated, perhaps even giving us time to re-read Susan Sontag's landmark essay, "Against Interpretation", published in the book of that title in 1966, in which she inveighed against "the philistine refusal to leave the work of art alone". Essentially, Sontag was saying that criticism and art history, "the compliment that mediocrity pays to genius," gets in the way between the artist and the viewer or reader.

Art historian Rocio Izquierdo Moreno has written that the Seville School "disappeared" after the death of Murillo, although she notes that his influence persisted in Sevillano and other painters up until and including the nineteenth century. She also believes that it "reappeared" in the eighteenth century, when Seville still exerted its "hegemony" over Spanish art. While Spanish and Andaluz art was having its little nap, a number of important changes had taken place in Spanish society, not least the appearance of a visible and moneyed middle class, with their own ideas of what made good or even great art. The reign of Queen Isabella II (1830-1904) from the 1830s to the 1860s was a time of unprecedented economic growth in Spain, and the rapid expansion of a wealthy middle class called for art that would suit home and gallery rather than castle and monastery. Its arbiters were what Susan Sontag rather testily described as the "philistines" who refused to leave the work of art alone, and whose opinions form the greater part of the body of art history.

Something rather unusual had also happened to Spanish art when it started appearing in public spaces. Political and social changes had seen the emergence of Romanticism, neoclassicism, several schools with their own take on realism, history and academic reference, and the schools known as *paisajismo* (landscape), *preciosista* (precious, either in sense of cost or prettiness), and *costumbrismo*, which can mean traditionalist, folkloric or, more tellingly, capering around in period costume.

THE FICTITIOUS LANDSCAPES OF MANUEL BARRÓN Y CARILLO

The most famous of the Romantic paisajistas was the Seville painter Manuel Barrón y Carrillo (1814-84), who painted many splendid landscapes of and around Seville, some reminiscent of the bolder Turner, others the folksier Constable. He studied at the Escuela de Bellas Artes in the city and was a founding member of its Liceo Artistico, its artists' circle or union. One of his finest landscape paintings is "Emboscado de unos bandoleros en la cueva del Gato" (1860), roughly, "The ambush of some bandits in the Cave of the Cat", although with one tiny factual difference: *it isn't*. Beyond mere deconstructionist fun with famous paintings, there are some strange things going on in this purported representation of an Andaluz landscape with some figures in it.

It is hard to tell, even when "eyeballing" it up close in the Museo de Bellas Artes or blowing up an illegal download of the image on an iMac screen, just what is being represented here. A group of people, "bandits", including a woman and a child, at the entrance of a large cave are pictured in the middle of an ambush set by the Guardia Civil (the tough paramilitary force formed, in fact, to counter the bandit threat in the nineteenth-century countryside), who can be seen scrambling down rocks "into" the "cave" towards them. The woman appears to be gesticulating off canvas, seemingly alerting her companions to the approach of other Guardia Civil officers, as a companion above her takes aim with a rifle also in the same direction off canvas. The child clutching at her skirts is either terrified or guffawing with excitement as he stares straight at the viewer, or the painter (more of Velázquez's painterly *Verfremdungseffekt*, Brecht's "alienation effect").

So far, so expected, particularly from a painting that could not possibly have been posed, nor really could the scene have even been glimpsed by the painter, except at great risk to his own safety. It is clearly a work of the imagination. And the technique is fantastic; dramatic mountainscapes, dripping rocks, desperate and trapped criminals, the brave and rugged Guardia Civil scrambling across mountainous terrain to capture the criminals.

Except: this is not the Cueva del Gato. There are various possible explanations for this mystery, although they each point to the emergence of probably the most powerful and persistent theme in recent Andaluz history, its representation, its re-interpretation—even its reification—as a romanticized, fictionalized landscape and culture. Barrón y Carrillo's painting is perhaps the thin end of the wedge whose fat end is the fairytale fictions of Washington Irving and that business with the polka-dot flounced skirts, the huge hoop earrings and the castanets…

Today, the Cueva del Gato, cave of the cat, named because someone thought its entrance looked like the face of a cat (it doesn't), sits where it has sat for millions of years, a few miles down the road from the Cueva de la Pileta cave system, a ten-minute walk downhill from the town of Benaoján and a few minutes' stroll from the Estación de Benaoján RENFE railway station, one of the loveliest railway stations in Spain, perhaps in the world, where a bar the size of a wardrobe will serve you a drink while you sit on the platform surrounded by green, tree-covered mountains waiting for your train. Three passenger train services roar past the cave each day, and in high summer bathers cool off in the freezing waters draining through the cave and cascading into its outfall pool. With the right equipment and underwater caving experience, you can explore the twenty-odd caverns and subterranean lakes inside the system, although even experienced cave divers have died attempting to negotiate the route under the mountain to the Cueva del Hundidero (cave of the fallen, or perhaps cave-in) on the other side of the mountain.

Yet you could scour the mountains around Benaoján for the landscape that Manuel Barrón y Carrillo painted in his picture and never find it. It doesn't exist. The Gato end of the cave system does not look like that, nor does the Hundidero end, and there is not a view of a tall thin mountain peak through the caves, whose two entrances are perhaps three miles apart connected by a deep cave system buried under thick rock. The most logical interpretation is that the painter was working from memory, or hearsay, or simply making it all up, each of which possibility asks us the question: why? A modern road between Ronda and Benaoján would probably have been present as an unpaved track during Barrón y Carrillo's day, and he may well have passed the cave on a journey through the countryside. He may have been told of a newsworthy arrest of bandits at a dramatic setting in the Serranía de Ronda mountains. He may have decided, for his own narrative reasons, to cheerfully re-invent or fictionalize the Cueva del Gato in his painting. One thing is for certain; his Cueva del Gato does not bear the resemblance to the thing it names as is the case in another more famous, and similar mountain landscape, Turner's "Gordale Scar", which, well, actually looks like Gordale Scar.

This might be explicable, and even forgivable, given that at the time Barrón y Carrillo was painting, the landscape truly *was* a dangerous place to go, even, as his painting suggests, in broad daylight. (The good folks of Benaoján no doubt sensibly kept to their homes between sundown and sunrise.) Yet Barrón y Carrillo clearly intended his painting to be read as reportage, or adventure or legend or moral exemplar. He could equally have represented the bandits camped around a fire, or robbing upstanding

Christian travellers, but instead he chose to portray the bandits and their camp followers as they are being ambushed. (And to what end? Did they get away? Were they shot? And what happened to the mad kid? Were Barrón y Carrillo's contemporary viewers in fact looking at an oil-paints-and-canvas equivalent of an episode of *Starsky and Hutch*?)

It may seem extreme to interrogate something as seemingly harmless as a nineteenth-century landscape painting, but equally we should not let it pass unquestioned. If we look a little closer at the painting, the figures in fact seem to be dressed as either peasants or gypsies (a culture discussed later in this book), and the fact that this seems to be a family group lends credence to the latter reading. Conventionally—if we can use the word conventionally in the context of banditry—*bandoleros*, bandits, were solitary individuals, sometimes working in gangs, who did indeed rule the mountains. One such figure, the famous El Tempranillo, is apocryphally said to have claimed that "The King may rule Spain but I rule the Serranía." Others were also largely solitary figures such as the bullfighter Jose Ulloa Tragabuches (*né* Navarro), who turned to banditry after allegedly killing his lover when she was unfaithful to him, or Pasos Largos ("long strides"), the nickname of Juan Mingolla Gallardo, deriving from his remarkable height. Their daring exploits were truly legendary, their capture or killing a moral fable repeated to naughty children everywhere. These days, Tragabuches names a Michelin-starred restaurant in Ronda, Pasos Largos, wittily, a hiking club in the same town.

Our family group, however, seem to be here for a purpose, and not simply fleeing the cops. If this is not a group of bona fide gitanos, it is a group of peasants turned just as bad. What we see today as a group of colourful country folk in vibrantly *ethnic* outdoor wear, would, in the years when Barrón y Carrillo was painting, have been members of a loathed and feared underclass. In the era when Barrón y Carrillo painted his scene, the English writers George Borrow and Richard Ford were already famous for books that detailed, in part or whole, *gitano* culture in Andalucía. Their books, Borrow's *The Zincali; or, An Account of the Gypsies of Spain* (1841) and Ford's *Hand-book for Travellers in Spain* (1845) are discussed in a later chapter. The gentlemanly Ford would have had little to do with the gitanos, in any sense of the phrase, while Borrow lived among them, learned their dialects and even traded insults with them in their own languages. He had a certain respect for them, although it was more the respect a big-game fisherman might have for a man-eating shark. While he defended them and their culture, he was also willing to contemplate ex-urban myths that claimed these folk devils were ruffians, cut-throats, poisoners, baby-snatchers and even possibly cannibals.

All of which puts our group of colourful country folk in vibrantly ethnic outdoor wear in a rather different light. If the contemporary viewers of Barrón y Carrillo's painting were looking at the nineteenth-century equivalent of a modern-day police actioner, it would have been less *Starsky and Hutch* and more *The Texas Chainsaw Massacre*, or perhaps one of those North American reality TV police car-chase documentaries.

Was Barrón y Carrillo, then, wittingly or unwittingly contributing to what was already a potent mythology about gypsy culture in Spain? Neither he nor fellow Romantics and *costumbristas* such as Valeriano Becquer (1833-70), were far from alone. The Romantic obsession with Spain and specifically Andalucía had already received a massive boost in 1846 with the publication of Prosper Mérimée's novella, *Carmen*, although the Bizet opera taken from the novella would not be premiered until 1875. Mérimée (1803-70) took his torrid tale from a sordid real-life story told to him by a Spanish noblewoman of a Málaga lowlife figure who had killed his lover in a fit of rage. Mérimée imagineered the tale into that of his first-person narrator encountering the actors in a hyper-dramatized story of savage love among Andaluz gypsies, a tale tricked out, in fact, with large helpings of research borrowed, no pun intended, from none other than George Borrow. (Bizet's opera is based on just one of the four sections of the original novella, and excised many of the narrative and moral complications of the original.)

Aided by the questionable midwifery of Washington Irving (also considered later here), not to mention the art of Gustave Doré (notably, his "Dancing in a Taverna in Triana" [1802] and his illustrations for the *Quijote*) and the poetry of Théophile Gautier (1811-72), the great ur-myth of Andalucía—land of flamenco, land of bullfighting, land of gypsies and poets, land of heroes and adventurers—was born, fully-fledged and monstrous. If you hear an ominous humming noise here, perhaps a subterranean rumbling, it is the sound of the great Andaluz myth factory still churning out clichés even today enthusiastically promoted by the Spanish tourism industry, clichés that still lure people on to aeroplanes touching down at Málaga, Seville, Granada, Córdoba, Jerez and other Andaluz airports every few minutes from Britain, northern Europe, the USA, Japan and elsewhere…

As stated in the very first chapter of this book, all these things did occur here, and those people did live here, but they have become hostage to a pernicious fiction about Andalucía, and one that many Spanish people consider to be at best risible and at worst offensive. A similar fiction about, say, Britain, would be of a country represented by Morris dancers, figures from Arthurian legend, Sherlock Holmes and Winston Churchill (oh, and The Beatles). A similar North American fiction might encompass Paul Revere, George Armstrong Custer, figures from Mark Twain, Abraham Lincoln, Charles Lindbergh and JFK (oh, and The Beach Boys).

There is nothing inherently wrong or bad with any of these examples, but, as the similes might make plain, both the tourist and those who are, in the words of historian Paul Fussell, "touristed", that is visited, deserve better, and more.

Chapter Fifteen

THE PICASSO CENTURY: CUBISM, ABSTRACTION AND POST-MODERNISM IN *ANDALUZ* ART

We are already in trouble before we even begin to contemplate the life and work of self-exiled Malagueño Pablo Picasso (1881-1973), or, to give him his full name, following the Spanish tradition of combining both parental names, Pablo Diego José Francisco de Paula Juan Nepomuceno María de los Remedios Cipriano de la Santísima Trinidad Clito Ruiz y Picasso. While he was born in Málaga—his *casa natal* is now the Fundación Picasso museum in Plaza de la Merced, a square favoured by young Malagueños for their *botellones*, those otherwise good-natured all-night drinking binges that horrify parents and authorities—he spent much of his peripatetic youth away from the city where he was born.

Picasso's family left Málaga for La Coruña, Galicia, in 1891, following his art teacher father in pursuit of work. Picasso junior had already begun painting, but took formal lessons at the school where his father taught in La Coruña. Work took the family across Spain to Barcelona in 1895, where they settled, dividing the year between Barcelona and Málaga. Picasso continued his art studies, and even spent a year studying in Madrid, but illness drove him back to Barcelona.

It is a sign of his early development as a painter that by 1900, the year of his nineteenth birthday, he was already travelling between Barcelona and Paris, and had been adopted as the mascot of the artists and writers who gathered at Barcelona's legendary Els Qatre Gats (the barman's estimate of the average crowd any night of the week—four cats). Barcelona's modernistas exerted a definite influence over Picasso, and the critic Robert Hughes, citing painter Ellsworth Kelly, believes that the broken crockery *trencadis* mosaics of Gaudí's projects may have influenced the shattered planes of Cubism. Els Qatre Gats gave Picasso his first exhibition, also in 1900, and the following year its house journal, *Pèl i Ploma* (Paper and

Pen), which also acted as a forum for the modernistas, ran the first ever magazine article about him.

From here, Picasso's career took a northerly and easterly trajectory, to Paris and shortly after that to Provence where he painted what is considered his first defining Cubist work, "Les Demoiselles d'Avignon" (1907), with its drastic mixture of African masks, early Iberian sculpture and echoes of Cézanne's treatments of the female nude. Picasso spent the rest of his life in comfortable, if controversial, exile, his political opinions—still hotly debated between admirers and enemies in the twenty-first century— leading him to declare that his "Guernica" (1937) would not visit Spain until it had a Republican democracy in place. (The painting spent much of its post-war life at MOMA in New York before being returned, first to the Prado in 1981, and later to its current home at the Reina Sofía in Madrid.)

The spelling of the title of that iconic anti-war work—the francophone spelling rather than the Gernika the bus from Bilbao or San Sebastian will take you to—says something about the genesis of the painting, a work made elsewhere but referring back, to that Luftwaffe Condor Legion bombing attack on Gernika of 26 April 1937, and the first use of this war technology against civilians. It can be said, however, that although he spent the rest of his life in exile, Picasso lived, painted and died an Andaluz and Español, not least in his almost neurotic obsession with Velázquez and "Las Meninas", but also his charged reference in "Guernica" to Goya's famous earlier anti-war painting, "El Tres de Mayo" (1814), which inspired that blinding light at the centre of "Guernica" and the distressed positions of the figures (the outstretched arms, the looks of panicky dread). It can also be said that whether he was painting on the Côte d'Azur or the Costa del Sol, it was still in that Mediterranean version of what Raymond Carver called "a marine light".

Picasso's later life – the mistreated wives and mistresses, the punch-ups and rivalries, the million and one post-Freudian analyses of man and work—has been so raked over in the past half century that the most sensible thing might be to call a moratorium on any further art history gossip until a certain chronological distance provides enough space to decide if he really was only painting his dick over and over again in those paintings. It might also give us space to consider other painters trampled in the rush to lionize the dead Picasso.

A Painter in New York

Pre-eminent among these is the Granadino Abstract Expressionist José Guerrero (1914-91), whose biography describes a similarly fascinating but entirely different trajectory to Picasso's, and for an entirely different set of reasons.

Perhaps the most remarkable thing to note about Guerrero is that Spain even produced an Abstract Expressionist—that group of wild-haired, Manhattan-centric, anti-European paint (and drink) throwers, who defined themselves by burning the bridges that linked them to, well, painters like Velázquez and Goya—in the first place.

Guerrero has a genuine underdog biography, unlike Picasso's comfy upbringing in that smart townhouse in Plaza de la Merced, even if Guerrero's adventure would take him from his birthplace in Granada, via Madrid and Paris, to New York—and then back, in the thick of the Franco era, to Cuenca, Granada and finally Nerja, along the coast from Málaga. When his father died in 1929, Guerrero, aged only fourteen, was forced to find work to support his family and began work as an apprentice carpenter. A few jobs on, his employer told him he should improve his skills by taking night classes in art at the Escuela de Artes y Oficios, where a friend secured him—in an almost impossibly cute biographical detail—access to Alonso Cano's old studio in the bell tower of Granada's cathedral, where he could paint to his heart's content in return for ringing the bells when told to. He wrote, in a piece reproduced in a *Seleccion de escritos de Guerrero* published by the Museo Reina Sofía in 1994: "From the tower one could see the whole of Granada; it smelled of vegetation, of chocolate, of spices, of fish. There were the sounds of the street sellers, of voices from the Albaicín, of the bells that I was ringing."

In 1935, aged 21, Guerrero was conscripted, an unfortunate date to walk into this particular set of circumstances, with the Guerra Civil about to erupt. He served in the forces as a soldier and sketch artist until 1939 and after the war studied briefly in Madrid before returning to Granada. He was already under the thrall of Picasso, Miró and Gris, and experimenting in landscape and representation somewhere between Fauvism and Cubism. With the help of grants he studied in Paris and then Rome, where he met his future wife, the North American journalist Roxane Whittier Pollock (no relation, it would seem, to the more famous Jackson), with whom he emigrated to the USA in 1950, settling in Greenwich Village, and even taking US citizenship in 1953.

Guerrero had already tested the waters of Abstract Expressionism while hanging out with the likes of the Gallego sculptor Eduardo Chillida in Paris a few years earlier. In New York he swiftly located the notorious Cedar Tavern, Jackson Pollock's favourite falling-over-drunk venue, and the clubhouse to Marc Rothko, Willem de Kooning, Franz Kline and others. While Roxane went to work at *Life* magazine, Guerrero found a studio and fell in with "The Irascibles", as *Life* dubbed them, among them Kline, de Kooning, Robert Motherwell, Barnett Newman, Ad Reinhardt, Rothko and Clyfford Still.

The two most important contacts Guerrero made in New York were Betty Parsons, a painter who had turned herself into a gallery owner and the "den mother" to the Ab Ex crowd, and James Sweeney, director of the Guggenheim Museum (then on the Upper East Side and some years off its move to Frank Lloyd Wright's shiny white spiral on Fifth Avenue). Parsons was the first person to give Pollock, Rothko and Still gallery space, some time before Peggy Guggenheim's chauffeur found the address, and her friendship with Guerrero drew Sweeney of the Guggenheim, who offered Guerrero space in a "Young Americans" show at the Guggenheim in 1954.

Spanish art historian, critic and curator Manuel Romero has written that "the Guerrero we know was born in 1950." This is the year when the formative Guerrero became the *immigré* Ab Exer in New York: big canvases, bold gestures, lots of paint. One of his best early pieces, "Signos" (1953), is an assertive family group of big slabs of black (an abiding trope throughout his career) against a Rothko-like red colour field. One of his late masterpieces, painted just two years before his death, "Azul añil" (1989), a big, brushy mat of royal blue with a red line splashed up the right edge of the canvas, resembles, maybe even waves hello to, the notorious colour fields of his friend Barnett Newman, with their famous "zips" both dividing and balancing the fields.

Along with Rothko, Newman was probably Guerrero's greatest friend in the Ab Ex gang. In his book *About Modern Art* (2001), Francis Bacon's friend, the critic David Sylvester, introduced Newman's philosophy by saying, "In the search for the absolute and commitment to the new, it was advantageous not to be a European, not to be steeped in a tired culture," which puts the Spanish *immigré* and newly-arrived Manhattanite José Guerrero in an interesting context. Sylvester went on to quote Newman from his own manifesto, "The Sublime is Now", a text Newman prepared for the first ever show of his vast, engulfing canvases: "I believe that here in America, some of us, free from the weight of European culture are finding the answer... are creating images whose reality is self-evident and which are devoid of the props and crutches that evoke associations with outmoded images, both sublime and beautiful. We are freeing ourselves of the impediments of memory, association, nostalgia, legend, myth, or what have you, that have been the devices of Western European painting. Instead of making 'cathedrals' out of Christ, man, or 'life', we are making it out of ourselves, out of our own feelings."

It could be that Manhattan and the USA offered Guerrero a *tabula rasa* on which to write himself anew. Equally, it could be that time would prove the motivations of these painters to be more complex than previously thought. Newman's philosophy of Abstract Expressionism has long been held to be the consensus among the Abstract Expressionists, although with the passage of time attitudes have softened and opinions changed. In the twenty-first century we are now beginning to consider, following the huge Tate Gallery (as was) retrospective in 1999, that Jackson Pollock's equally vast canvases might not be so abstract or expressionist after all, and that titles such as "Blue Poles", "Lavender Mist" and "Summertime" might actually have representational resonance, the last perhaps even alluding visually to Goya.

So, too, we might reconsider Guerrero's abstract expressionism. Marriage and ambition took Guerrero to Greenwich Village, and what turned out to be a lifelong marriage to Roxane Pollock underpinned his decision to take US citizenship. There was little to keep him in Spain, and having lived through both the Civil War and the subsequent *años de hambre* ("years of hunger") in the 1940s, he might (as others did) have looked for a more convivial life among other artists elsewhere. Yet in hindsight, this would appear to be mere paperwork; within a matter of years, and perhaps tellingly after Guerrero had experimented with psychoanalysis, the Guerrero family was heading back to Spain, to Madrid, then Cuenca, where he helped found the Museo de Arte Abstracto Español with his friend the painter Fernando Zóbel, the Manila-born businessman who trained at the Rhode Island School of Design (a few decades before David Byrne) and used his wealth to found what is today Spain's greatest collection of home-grown twentieth-century art.

The Guerrero family stayed bicoastal, or perhaps bioceanic, for a number of years, commuting between New York and Spain, finally to a home in Nerja. Back in Spain Guerrero's Ab Ex tendencies started applying themselves to his home soil. Starting around the time of his "Albaicin" (1962), named after the famous Granada barrio, Andalucía started to appear in his adventures with paint and canvas. In his brief exile in New York Guerrero had become friends with the Lorca family, and his interests took him to that *barranca*, ravine, outside Viznar where the poet had been assassinated. The visit produced a key mid-career work, "La brecha de Viznar" (1966), *brecha* being Spanish for breach, opening, gap or gash. This seemingly abstract work becomes explicitly, almost violently, representational when you consider that it represents either the mass grave where Lorca and three other men were murdered on 19 August 1936, or perhaps even a gash in one of the men's bodies, with its unambiguous splash of blood red spilling off the bottom of the canvas. Considering its era, this could be said to have been more political than even "Guernica", although luckily for Guerrero the *Franquistas* were looking the other way.

Guerrero would find his soil (not least that black earth) recurring in his later work, and with increasing, almost urgent, frequency in works that were acquiring representational and narrative titles. He said of his favourite (non-)colour, black: "for me, perhaps, it is the colour of colours," and once titled a New York exhibition "The Presence of Black":

> My black is living, vibrant, transparent, it is not a dead black. The Spanish black is alive; You see it in the countryside; there is always something black that moves, a gorse bush, a goat, a woman in mourning... Ever since I can remember, black was always there, as a part of life: in people, in the landscape, in solitude. It was always like something in movement, like cries representing life and not death.

He also wrote of other favourite colours: "Blue... has a lot of my childhood. It was the colour I used in order to paint the skirting boards of my house." Red was "the red ochre that we used in the villages of Andalusia... a red taken out of the earth." And white: "Andalusia, nothing more. The dazzle of a whitewashed wall." Another earth colour: "Ochre is the earth with which I played. Grey, the Andalusian mountains... at least those of Granada... there the mountains are grey."

His abstraction, then, while far removed from the drip and action paintings of Pollock and those big blue cathedral spaces of Newman, might be seen alongside that of a Terry Frost, responding quite directly to the landscape around him, but using the lexicon of abstraction. You can see it, for free, at the handsome, if hard to find, Fundació Guerrero museum, which maintains his archive and also stages shows by other contemporary artists, hidden in a small alley off the north-west corner of the Plaza Bib-Rambla, at Calle Oficios 8, and probably the best kept secret in the whole of Granada.

When Guerrero returned to Spain in the 1960s and accepted Zóbel's invitation to Cuenca, he found himself among a group of younger painters who in 1957 had formed the now legendary El Paso group, among them Rafael Canogar (Toledo, 1935), Martin Chirino (Gran Canaria, 1925), Luis Feito (Madrid, 1929), Manolo Millares (Gran Canaria, 1926), Manuel Rivera (Granada, 1927) and Antonio Saura (Huesca, 1930-98). If anything, Guerrero might have been one of their influences, as this group, formed to launch a "plastic revolution" against the sorry state of Spanish art under Franco, was fired in part by the inspiration of the Ab Ex crew. Their manifesto, however, issued in the summer of 1957, also criticized the "artificial solution of artistic emigration" as one of the causes of that same sorry state of Spanish art. The manifesto also stated, with a snarl, that "the action of El Paso will continue while the conditions against exhibition continue in our country." They called it a day in 1967, perhaps when the Franco regime was beginning to realize that some of its most successful overseas ambassadors were trouble-making men (and they were, almost exclusively, men) wielding paintbrushes.

That same year, others in the Spanish and Andaluz diaspora were busy elsewhere. Self-exiled to Paris, sculptor Jorge Oteiza, from Vizcaya, called a meeting of like-minded *exiliado* friends who would become the highly influential Equipo 57, numbering among their ranks Andaluces Juan Serrano (Córdoba, 1929) José Duarte (Córdoba, 1928) and Juan Cuenca (Puente Genil, Córdoba, 1934). Reacting against the "bourgeois" ideal of the artist as romantic individualist visionary, Equipo 57, as their name ("team") implies, worked as a collective, on paintings, sculpture, furniture and even films that explored the relationship between creativity and everyday life in a style that prefigures pop art. The group dissolved itself in 1961, when one of its members, the sculptor Agustín Ibarrola

(Vizcaya, 1930), was jailed in Burgos for his work as a communist activist. (Today, Ibarrola is one of the leading lights and a co-founder of ¡Ya Basta! [Enough Already!], the umbrella group that protests against ETA violence.)

There is perhaps one more loner we should recognize, Luis Gordillo (Seville, 1934), nowadays based in Madrid, a 2007 recipient of the prestigious Velázquez Prize for artistic achievement, and the perhaps unwitting head of a school known as *Gordillismo*, which seems to be defined by an almost biological (and, like Guerrero, psychoanalysis-based) preoccupation with organic forms, and processes, giving his paintings an at times disquietingly visceral appearance, and sheen. Unsurprisingly, he is often named alongside the likes of Joseph Beuys and Sigmar Polke among postwar European painters.

Dos Extranjeros: Bomberg and Richmond

Ultimately, artists, like writers, rarely recognize borders, unless they are put in their way, gravitating towards sympathetic locales where they might expect to encounter like-minded souls, in maturity sometimes choosing to return "home", or settle somewhere else entirely. Yet with few exceptions all the above artists, and a few left to appear below, have been at least partly defined by the accident of geographic origin, and where they chose to produce their work. For some, their link to Andalucía is utterly irrelevant; for others (as Guerrero found) it is utterly essential to their work and their being.

There is of course another type of artist we should consider, the *foraneo*, adjectivally foreign, who settle or spend a lot of time somewhere else, and apart from the small army of happy weekend daubers who get out and about with their easels and oils, some serious painters have also sojourned in Andalucía. Most famous, if perhaps from an Anglophone viewpoint, is the British painter David Bomberg (1890-1957), who spent long periods before and after the Civil War in Ronda, returning in 1954 to spend the last few years of his life there. An early fellow traveller of Wyndham Lewis and the Vorticists, he recanted his belief in this British arm of Futurism after his experiences in the trenches in the First World War and set out to find a humanist form for his uncompromisingly avant-garde philosophy of representational art straining at the limits of representation.

His semi-abstract landscapes of the area crackle with heat and light even on the pages of a catalogue—the most likely place to find Bomberg's work today. Although there are some now in the Tate collection, and a famous early work, the—quiza—Cubo-Vorticist "Ju-Jitsu" (1913), is displayed at Tate Modern, he spent much of his career suspiciously overlooked by the establishment. Bomberg's career seems to have been one of brief periods of happiness snatched from longer periods of disappointment, and there is a distinct subtext that on more than one occasion—being sidelined by the British war artists' programme in the 1940s, teaching in London and Spain—Bomberg may have been the victim of institutionalized British anti-Semitism.

The eminent British critic Richard Cork wrote in a catalogue for a 2004 show in Ronda, a town where Bomberg had been known mainly as an eccentric who could not speak Spanish, that "Ronda fired Bomberg to incorporate an apprehension of seismic violence in the work he produced there. His paintings are charged, now, with the landscape as a world riven by convulsive geological stress."

Bomberg passed on this interest in seismology to his former student, sometime assistant and lifelong friend, Miles Richmond, who followed Bomberg to Ronda and even today enjoys a similar late-career flourish, with shows touring Spain and Britain in the 2000s. Richmond invokes Cézanne, perhaps Bomberg's greatest influence, as the painter he admires most after Bomberg, and his own style both refers back earlier than Bomberg to Cézanne's landscapes and also later and beyond Bomberg, to representations of landscapes almost identical to those painted by Bomberg but in which Richmond dismantles the constituent parts of the landscape, in a work like "El Cerro Verde" (1973), atomizing an Andaluz hillside into shards of intense colour. Like Bomberg, he is on a difficult voyage in search of an authentic form in which to portray the essence, maybe even spirit, of landscape, not unlike perhaps Georgia O'Keeffe's insistence that she was painting *her* sunflower, and nobody else's. A retiring figure who is disinclined to sell his work, Richmond has an unusual fanbase led by none other than John Berger, author of the seminal *Ways of Seeing*, who contributed this to a 2008 catalogue on Richmond's work, commenting on his muscular blue and yellow mountainscape "The Pass over the Mures" (1981):

It didn't come from the mere act of observation, any more than it came from any manual act of gesturing. It came from quitting the self, and feeling, with all six senses, his wary way into the jurisprudence of the elemental, which holds together the known (and unknown) laws of geology, climate, anatomy and the longings of the soul.

In the 2000s, Seville's Centro Andaluz de Arte Contemporaneo was leading the recuperation of the history of the Andaluz avant-garde, not least when it organized a fiftieth birthday retrospective for the surviving members of the Equipo 57 group. More interesting, however, for anyone with an eye on the future, was a special project the CAAC commissioned from young Andaluz artist Jesús Zurita, born in Ceuta, Morocco, in 1974 but raised and educated in Granada. His "La Llanura Baja" ("The plain below") is a site-specific work for the chapel of Santa Ana at the Monasterio de la Cartuja, which houses the CAAC collection. The chapel dates back to the fifteenth century and is also known as the Capilla de Colón, Christopher Columbus. Zurita, who has created eerie floating paint and sculpture works for the Arco show in Madrid and shows elsewhere, conceived his "plain" as an intervention into the chapel's architecture and its symbolism, undermining both by transforming it into a woodland scene. His preparations made the national newspapers and the evening news. Four hundred years after the indoor gardeners of Seville, it seems that some Andaluz painters are still taking the landscape indoors...

CONTEMPORARY *ANDALUZ* INDOOR GARDENERS

Of all the arts in Andalucía, the visual arts, particularly contemporary visual arts, seem to attract the most support from government, private sponsors (banks are big art sponsors, probably for tax-break reasons, across Spain) and audiences. Perhaps even thirty years into a democracy, art still has a secondary journalistic function in the tradition of Goya, Picasso and Guerrero, while remaining ambiguous enough to survive the interrogations of suspicious authority. As well as the Fundacio Guerrero and CAAC, Andalucía boasts two feisty contemporary art spaces that rarely make it on to the itineraries of most visitors. The first, dead centre in the city where most tourists land, Málaga, is the unfortunately acronymed CAC, Centro de Arte Contemporaneo, a former market building off the Alameda Principal overlooking the Rio Guadalmedina flood channel. This brilliant white box has a small permanent collection of largely North American works—Nan Goldin, Jenny Holzer, Julian Opies, Ed Ruscha, Andres Serrano (but not *that* notorious Serrano work) and Cindy Sherman, as well as Europeans such as Louise Bourgeois and Damien Hirst, and an army of Spanish artists led by the late Juan Muñoz, whose unintentional farewell prior to his sudden death aged forty-eight in 2001 featured those enigmatic lifts going up and down in the Tate Modern Turbine Hall in his huge "Double Bind" installation.

The second is the spookily unvisited NMAC culture foundation, in the countryside outside the pueblo blanco of Vejer de la Frontera, almost perfectly preserved behind its castle walls on a mount with views in the direction of Baelo Claudia and the Atlantic. Almost equally spooky is the fact that NMAC, the Fundación NMAC Montenmedio Arte Contemporaneo, shares its vast sculpture park with a golf course, perhaps more baffling to the golfers than the art lovers, particularly when they come face to face across a water bunker dominated by Fernando Sánchez Castillo's sculpture, "Fuente" ("Fountain", 2003). This comprises a police anti-personnel wagon that appears to have been hurled backwards into the small lake, presumably by angry rioters. If you press a button on a pole by the edge of the water obstacle, the riot wagon's water cannon, originally designed to dispel unruly crowds, becomes a pretty fountain in the middle of all this lush and manicured grass, and even produces rainbows on sunny days.

Elsewhere in the park, which can take the best part of a day to explore, there are mysterious obelisks, sunken neo-prehistoric observatories, sound and wind sculptures, surreal garden furniture, a perverse version of one of the tiled bridges from Seville's Parque Maria Luisa lobbed into some bushes, a large monument by Sol LeWitt, and shortly the park will acquire a mediated daylight sculpture, "Stupa" (2008), by James Turrell.

Perhaps the most interesting—and unquestionably the most entertaining—exhibit is one of the few indoor pieces in the small group of what were once army barracks in the woods. "Tú también puedes caminar" ("You too can walk") by the video artist Cristina Lucas (Úbeda, 1973) is a video short that needs careful consideration, particularly in its end credits. It takes its inspiration from Virginia Woolf's essay "A Room of One's Own", her celebration of earlier women authors in which she quotes Johnson's disparaging comment: "Sir, a woman's preaching is like a dog's walking on his hind legs. It is not done well; but you are surprised to find it done at all."

Like Woolf, Cristina Lucas, who has exhibited around the world, disagreed with Johnson, enough to round up a group of dogs and take them for a walk on their hind legs through nearby Vejer de la Frontera to prove him hilariously wrong. Armed with only her camera and doggy pals, Lucas shoots them and the townsfolk of Vejer as the dogs, led by one particularly agile standard poodle, dyed a fetching orange-pink, walk through the town and out into the countryside, applauded by baffled and cheering citizenry. Some of the poodles appear to breakdance, while others just mince rather queenily. It is one of the funniest films this sometime film critic has ever seen.

Keep an eye out for the credits, however, and Lucas' film takes on a greater resonance than its post-feminist riposte to Johnson. As well as crediting a local dog trainer and his canine stars, it acknowledges that the film was made with the assistance of an organization of widows, divorcees and single women in Vejer, one of the multitude of assertive community groups that have sprouted across modern Spain, and which gives "Tú también puedes caminar" an even deeper, local, significance in a country where domestic violence affects one in ten households (the statistic even applies to "gay" households) and inspires an annual national day of protest at violence against women.

ANDALUCÍA ON SCREEN
Film was and remains the Cinderella of Andaluz, and Spanish, arts, partly due to the lack of commercial and state funding, partly because it is a far more centralized industry—you have to be on the doorstep of producers, distributors, the studios and technical resources needed in this intensely collaborative field—but also by a quirk of geographical distribution; beyond Madrid and Barcelona, northern and eastern Spain seem to have more filmmakers per square yard than elsewhere. It costs astronomically more to make a film than it does a painting or book, and when a country's sole star onscreen export is Banderas, its sole star off-screen export Almodóvar, with Victor Erice able to make just one film a decade, this does not bode well for a home-grown film culture, particularly when the multiplexes are jammed with dubbed Hollywood blockbusters. (This does underline an amusing quirk in Spain's cinema industry, though: it is said that

a small but powerful mafia of voiceover artists in Madrid controls the trade so completely that in theory a Spanish person could live and die and never hear what Jack Nicholson or Susan Sarandon actually sound like in person.)

Andalucía is not without its cinema greats, however, in history and today. The first ever Spanish talkie, *El misterio de la Puerta del Sol* (1928) was directed by Francisco Elías Riquelme (Huelva, 1890-1977), and is available today on DVD. His near contemporary José Val del Omar (Granada, 1904-82), a film editor and sound technician, a friend of Lorca and Cernuda, destroyed his one full-length film, *Un Rincon de Andalucía* (1925), because he considered it an artistic failure. He did, however, develop an early form of stereo cine sound and construct experimental electro-acoustic music soundtracks for others, and also developed a now-lost early version of Sensurround, which he dubbed TactilVision, and which sounds like a real-life version of Huxley's "feelies", or perhaps the gimmicks deployed by John Goodman in the affectionate B-movie spoof, *Matinee* ("Mant! Half-human! Half-ant!").

Another, José López Rubio (Motril, Granada, 1903-96), a writer, director, poet, theatre historian, humourist and a member of the Generación del 27 literary movement (more of whom anon), worked as a screenwriter and translator in Hollywood during the early 1930s, where he was friends with Chaplin and worked alongside Buster Keaton and Laurel and Hardy. His politics took him to Mexico and Cuba during the Civil War, although he returned to Spain in 1940, to direct the film version of the Nobel prize-winning writer Jacinto Benavente's novel *La malquerida* (The unloved).

More recent achievements have included those of Benito Zambrano (Lebrija, 1965) who studied film in Cuba and won no fewer than five Goyas (the Spanish Oscars) for his 1999 film, *Solas*, including best director. He won the best director Goya again in 2005 for his *Habana Blues*. One of his contemporaries, Antonio Cuadri (Trigueros, Huelva, 1960), won rave reviews, the collaboration of British actor Bernard Hill and a hefty twelve million-euro budget for his 2007 film of Juan Cobos Wilkins' book, *El corazón de la tierra*, a novel set during a real-life industrial dispute at the Rio Tinto mines in the late nineteenth century. Hill, naturally, plays the English nasty who sends the troops in to crush the workers' revolt.

While many bemoan the state of Andaluz and Spanish cinema, younger filmmakers are making some headway, thanks to affordable lo-tech equipment, DIY aesthetics and sensibilities developed from too many nights spent watching Tarantino. Alberto Rodriguez (Sevilla, 1971) and his young star, Juan José Ballesta, won a Concha de Plata award at the 2005 San Sebastian Film Festival and a best new actor Goya for actor Jesús Carroza for 7 *Virgenes*, a *Last Detail*-meets-*Trainspotting* escapade that follows a teenager on a weekend of excess through a mocked-up version of Seville's notorious Tres Mil gitano ghetto (real-life setting for Dominique Abel's scripted documentary, *Poligono Sur*).

His contemporary Pedro Temboury (Málaga, 1971) has so far produced two full-length features, *Karate a muerte en Torremolinos* (roughly, "Death by Karate in Torremolinos", 2001) and *Ellos robaron la picha de Hitler* (again, roughly, "They Stole Hitler's Dick", 2006), both Z-movies in the style of his mentor Jesús Franco, the god of Spanish trash aesthetic cinema (some fifty-odd released to date). The latter film, in particular, places him firmly in the realm of Roger Corman and Russ Meyer, being the tale of a band of young neo-Nazis who steal Hitler's penis (don't ask) in the hope of having their master cloned back to life by Nazi scientists living in hiding in Marbella. (This last bit, at least, is in fact probable, as we will shortly find out...)

While Temboury's films may revel in the sordid antics of Jesús Franco, Corman and Meyer, they also refer back to a certain post-punk schlock-art aesthetic that produced films such as Slava Tsukerman's *Liquid Sky* (1982) and Rosa von Praunheim's *City of Lost Souls* (1983), as well as earlier works such as Curt McDowell's *Thundercrack!* (1975, but rehabilitated in the wake of punk). They also refer back to another, specifically Andaluz, cultural phenomenon, and one that is only just being excavated by younger writers, critics, historians and urban archaeologists: what the writer, poet and novelist Juan Bonilla (Jerez, 1966) calls, in his book of the same name, *La Costa del Sol en la hora pop* (The Costa del Sol in the era of pop, 2007), an extraordinary, brief and to some entirely illusory miniature golden age, the Costa's very own version of Swinging London, or, as the artist Richard Hamilton famously had it, "Swingeing London".

Before we explore that, however, we have to consider how Andalucía has been treated by foreign writers over the past two centuries, and how its own writers write their version of Andalucía.

Chapter Sixteen
ENGLISHMEN ABROAD:
THE CURIOUS HISTORY OF
ANGLOPHONE WRITERS IN ANDALUCÍA

"Nothing gives more pain to Spaniards than seeing volume after volume written on themselves and their country by foreigners."

It all begins with Richard Ford (1796-1858), who made this observation in his *Gatherings from Spain* in 1846. The book was a selection of "tit-bits" from researches for his three-volume *Hand-book for Travellers in Spain*, published the previous year. The gatherings were "hors d'oeuvres" intended for the home reader who was unlikely to travel, or for the amusement of ladies who might find the prospect of the full three-volume *Hand-book* daunting. The observation reflects the fact that the *Hand-book* was just one of many English gentlemen's books on Spain being published then, not all of them with the wit, erudition and good cheer of Richard Ford. He may, however, have lived to rue his own words: by the time of his death his *Hand-book* and its companion had become the definitive guide to Spain in English, and set the template for future generations of foreign writers causing yet more pain to the much-written-about Spanish.

Read today, Ford seems like science fiction, although science fiction garbed in the dress and mores of early nineteenth-century England. His books were written by an English gentleman for other English gentlemen, and one can imagine his dismay at the idea that later editions of his books may have fallen into the hands of the lower orders. Ford was born into the British aristocracy, educated at Winchester and Trinity College, Oxford, and was called to the Bar at Lincoln's Inn but never practised. Instead, he used his wealth to fund his travels around Europe and in particular to Andalucía, where he and his family spent three summers in Seville and three winters in quarters in the Alhambra complex at Granada.

They had, at my count, at least four servants, and were wealthy enough to have acquired works by both Zurburán and Murillo.

Even though Cervantes had made Castile and La Mancha famous, Andalucía was and remains the honeypot destination among all Spanish destinations for writers, travellers and we mere tourists. It seems fair to say that Ford and his successors are the reason we went there.

The year 1846 is a long time ago. It took six days to sail from Southampton to Cádiz, and most travellers travelled armed. Ford is unambiguous in his opinions, as perhaps only a writer from his background can be: "Every Spaniard has the same right in law and equity to kick and beat his own ass to his own liking, as a philanthropical Yankee has to wallop his own nigger." Given that the Abolition of the Slave Trade Act had been passed in 1807, and the decisive Slavery Abolition Act in 1833, we might allow Ford a certain irony here, if not necessarily a get out of jail free card. Ford is a very stylish and entertaining guide, a polymath and polyglot, and is usually a gregarious and sympathetic stranger in a strange land. Yet he sets the tone for the Englishman writing about elsewhere that would inform almost all later writers about Spain, and about anywhere else. Going places and being rude about the people who live there is nothing new, from Homer to Paul Theroux, and Paul Fussell in his essay "Travel, Tourism, and 'International Understanding'" (in his collection *Killing, In Verse and Prose*) detected a phenomenon he calls "post-tourism", in which, citing the writer Hilary Mantel, the modern writer abroad "must sometimes pay it the compliment of hating it."

Ford's writing, while often generous to his subjects, betrays a mindset that most travel writers packed along with their cleft sticks and malaria tablets. He compares "the gay and voluptuous Andalucian" to the "sly vindictive Valencian." While noting that Spain is "the most romantic, racy and peculiar country of Europe", he cannot help noticing that "pride and laziness are here as everywhere the keys to poverty." "The lower classes of Spaniards, like the Orientals, are generally avaricious," he explains, adding, "As a mass, they are apt to indulge in habits of procrastination, waste, improvidence and untidiness."

Park yourself in an expatriate bar in Fuengirola or Estepona and you will hear these sentiments expressed, less elegantly, by Britons (or indeed by Germans, Lowlanders or Scandinavians) today, the Britons probably carrying a copy of *The Daily Mail* or *The Sun*. Then as now, the more cautious visitor might question the authority behind this carefree amateur psychoanalysis of an entire people. They might also wonder how, beyond the exigencies of journalism (Ford qualified that opening quote by damning those writers "who have only rapidly glanced at one-half of the subject"), they assume to make sweeping generalizations about people they do not even know.

This feeds into another aspect of this mindset. Most travel writers, and a good many of their readers, assume, often quite comically, that they are superior to the people whose country they are visiting (at least Ford could claim to be the progeny of both a Lord and a Lady). Ford's work was written for the English gentleman who could count on gentlemanly treatment from Spanish people of his own caste on presentation of his gentlemanly credentials. But woe betide the English gentleman who fell into the hands of lesser mortals, who were more often than not duplicitous, lazy, venal, and not a few of them homicidal maniacs. Ford's gatherings cover an encyclopaedic array of everyday information for the traveller, from the choice of a horse to the selection and treatment of servants, but to anyone born out of his caste or later than his lifetime, the planet he describes is as bizarre as Borges' "Tlön, Uqbar, Orbis Tertius".

Ford's writing also displays another aspect of that mindset, the Englishman's curious fondness for dressing up in drag, literal and metaphorical, which can still be observed today. The cover of the latest edition of his gatherings features a portrait of him by José Becquer, "Richard Ford as a Majo", the Spanish slang for, as Ford describes it, a "dandy". This crossdressing, what is known in the culture of transvestism as "passing", would recur through English writing on Andalucía in particular. George Borrow took this to the extreme of almost trying to become a gitano (just as twenty-first-century writer Jason Webster would do, in a different setting). And unless he was on his way to a fancy dress party, the famous photograph of painter David Bomberg on the back of a burro and togged up like a bandit just looks sad.

The cautious visitor should, of course, avoid falling into the temptation of amateur psychoanalysis, but it seems safe to draw two conclusions from this flirtation with cultural drag. While it would be cruelty in the extreme to belabour an old man in fancy dress on the back of a donkey with even the paperback edition of Edward Said's *Orientalism*, this approach to Andalucía as a mysterious Other suggests two interesting but dangerous misreadings by certain writers and visitors. Firstly, it elevates, or perhaps recasts, Andalucía and its people into the role of an exotic culture to be both admired and feared. Readers of anyone from Claude Lévi-Strauss to Umberto Eco will have passed by here before, but it is as though the Andaluz, place or person, is somehow more traditional, rooted, *authentic*, in possession of certain philosophical secrets that have so far evaded the pale and weedy Englishman (witness Chris Stewart: "The Andaluces seem to be in touch with things the rest of us can scarcely understand."), and therefore a splendid exemplar worthy of emulation. Sometimes this wisdom can be acquired simply by dressing up like them; at other times it can be discovered at the bottom of a freshly-dug cesspit in the high Alpujarras. Secondly, the flipside, the reason they are to be feared, is, crudely put, that the Andaluz, place or person, is "a piece of rough", tough men and perhaps even tougher women living tough lives in a tough place. And a piece of rough is, of course, something—person, object, place—to be "cruised", for pleasure, cheap or dangerous thrills or simply cultural slumming.

This idea—and, really, we're only a few blocks away from the idea of the Noble Savage here—makes the Andaluz, person or thing, something like a mythical beast, to be engaged, negotiated, confronted, set out against like some medieval quest epic, battled with, *taken by the horns*. Going there, on holiday, to write a book, or even moving there is an adventure, a crusade (Ford compared it to a military campaign), a Homeric odyssey with whirlpools and monsters lying in wait. (For the people who live there, of course, it's just, well, home.) Like a tribal initiation ceremony, the test will either impart wisdom, or destroy you.

And all the while, of course, the subjects of these fevered imaginings are just living there, doing the stuff they do, leading perfectly ordinary lives, utterly unaware that they have been cast as extras in some mind-boggling land-based version of *Pirates of the Caribbean*, helmed jointly by Fellini and Buñuel, say, with intertextual nods in the direction of *The Sheltering Sky* and *that* scene from *Suddenly Last Summer*.

Of the several writers considered here, only three—Laurie Lee, Alastair Boyd and Paul Richardson—avoid falling into this trap. Interestingly, they also represent, roughly, three different, consecutive generations of writers, which suggests two things. One is that suspicion of the myth of the Spanish Other is nothing new; the second is that some among at least three generations of writers have had either the wit or the savvy to see through this myth. There is, of course, a third and maybe even a fourth aspect to this: some writers find it to their advantage to talk up the myth of the Spanish Other; the fourth is that maybe some Spanish people find it amusing, perhaps at times even lucrative, to go along with the Englishman's fancy for cultural drag.

This myth permeates every level of writing about Andalucía, from the loftiest to the lowliest. Ernest Hemingway is considered at greater length later in this book, but it seems fair to say that he fell hook, line and sinker for the myth. It also affects much journalism on the region. The myth reaches its true nadir in foreign-language journalism—especially English-language journalism aimed at expatriates—particularly along Andalucía's littoral. It plumbed its utmost depth so far a few years back in the form of a banner advertisement strapped across the top of the front page of *Sur in English*, the weekly journalism lite version of the beefier, but unfortunately Spanish, daily newspaper, *Sur*. It may "only" be an advertisement, but they are carefully tailored to a newspaper's readership profile, and *Sur in English* obviously had no qualms about running it. The advertisement was for the Gibraltar branch of the British supermarket chain, Sainsbury's, and read, resonantly, "Labels you can read, food you can eat." To their credit, many readers wrote to *Sur in English* complaining that the advert was racist, but the advertisement repeated on the front page for a good few more issues before either disappearing or being withdrawn. There is neither space here nor, really, the will to dismantle all the implications of that one line, but suffice to say, it appears to libel the reader as a monoglot idiot, while simultaneously implying that the Spanish food processing industry is one vast conspiracy hell bent on poisoning foreigners.

WASHINGTON IRVING'S *PARQUE TEMATICO*

The worst offender of all in mythifying Andalucía and the Andaluces, people and things, is Washington Irving (1783-1859). This estadounidense author (in lieu of an English adjectival phrase that describes North Americans without lumping in Canadians) actually lived in the Alhambra the year before Richard Ford and his family took up residence. Irving was, of course, norteamericano, born into a wealthy New York family, but he was a near contemporary of Ford, just thirteen years his elder, and died a year after him. While an ocean and a war of independence separated the two, their worldview when visiting other people's countries to write about them was almost identical, although this too needs careful negotiation.

A career journalist and writer, Irving was outspoken in his criticism of the USA's treatment of native American Indians, although this radicalism did not make it into his luggage when he set sail for Europe, where he lived and travelled for seventeen years. In the later part of his four years in Spain he served as US Ambassador to Spain, in Madrid. He spent time in both Seville and Granada, and in the latter had the remarkable good luck to be offered accommodation in what was then the near-abandoned ruin of the Alhambra complex (further proof that, before the advent of mass tourism and modern archaeology, the past was just stuff you used to build the future with).

In literary terms, he was a contemporary of James Fenimore Cooper, and is credited with encouraging younger writers such as Hawthorne, Longfellow and Poe. He was a friend of Dickens, won early fame as the author of both "Rip van Winkle" and "The Legend of Sleepy Hollow", and, we should bear in mind, first won acclaim as the author of social satires that earned him comparisons to Jonathan Swift.

If this puts us on our guard when approaching his *Tales from the Alhambra* (1832), the text itself is puzzling in its perhaps intentional naïveté. Irving spoke fluent Spanish and spent at least three months studying older Spanish and translations of Arabic histories at the Jesuit Library of Granada University. Put politely, the *norteamericano* set his sense of irony aside when writing about the Alhambra and Andalucía. Put crudely, he became the first Spanish correspondent that *Condé Nast Traveler* magazine never had, the man almost single-handedly responsible for the high romantic notion of Andalucía as a place of poets and adventurers, *gitanos* and *bandoleros*. The first man, in fact, to construct the notion of Andalucía as a theme park.

Compared to Irving, Ford was a fully paid-up member of the Dirty Realist school. Although writing in the early-mid-nineteenth century, Irving slips into—perhaps we should admit, he affects—a curious cod-Elizabethan English: his sentences are peppered with "nays", "damsels", "demesnes" and "fains", not to mention the highly popular "yon". Clearly, Irving had supped, as he himself might well have quoth, alongside Shakespeare, possibly Sir Thomas Malory and Edmund Spenser too. His tales—

and again we ought to keep a strong hold on that precise word, for ballast—from Boabdil's Granada are pitched at the level of Arthurian legend (if there is a buzzword in here, it is "chivalry") but told in the manner of children's fairytales. The reader will lose count of the number of times he begins a tale with "There once lived a…"

Even overlooking his frequent lapses into brochurese ("I see you raise your eyes to the snowy summit of yon pile of mountains, shining like a white summer cloud in the blue sky"), he has a curiously simplistic grasp of the geopolitics of the region, in both his own era and the one, some five hundred years earlier, addressed in his book. This might almost be explained by his era and cultural background, but it is strange for a man of his education and extensive researches to write the following:

> The Moslem empire in Spain was but a brilliant exotic, that took no permanent root in the soil it embellished… Their whole existence was a prolonged, though gallant and chivalric struggle, for a foothold in a usurped land… The exiled remnant of their once powerful empire disappeared among the barbarians of Africa, and ceased to be a nation… Such is the Alhambra. A Moslem pile in the midst of a Christian land; an Oriental palace amidst the Gothic edifices of the West; an elegant memento of a brave, intelligent, and graceful people, who conquered, ruled, flourished, and passed away.

And then there is this historical oddity: "[T]he fiery courage of the Arab was at length subdued by the obstinate and persevering valor of the Goth." Which at least asks the modern reader the interesting question, who indeed was supplanted by Tariq ibn-Ziyad in 711, and who was still around 781 years later to "reconquer" al-Andalus? Are we, and were Irving's contemporary readers, expected to reconsider the Reyes Católicos as Visigoths?

A Marxist brawler might argue that Irving was the brainwashed dupe of Occidental colonialists and supremacists, configuring Andalucía as one great bucolic pastorale staged as an entertainment for wealthy gentlefolk as they passed through in their heavily-armed caravanserais (many actually paid agents to pre-arrange a "hold-up" by bandoleros, the *pièce de la résistance* of their holiday), but even this one wonders if that would not be breaking a butterfly on a wheel. It is likely, however, that the next time you trip over a cliché about Andalucía, it will have Washington Irving's fingerprints all over it.

It's possible that the author of the pseudonymous Swiftian satires of Diedrich Knickerbocker and George Crayon was simply caught up in the giddy romance of his time living in the Alhambra, although given the state he found it in the romance was more shabby than giddy. Certainly, it is impossible to imagine the Alhambra then when visiting it today as one of the "limited" number of 8,800 visitors allowed in each day, each allotted a thirty-minute window to make the mad dash for the entrance to the Nasrid palaces. Perhaps Irving's sweet and slightly dotty tales do not deserve such rough manhandling, and ought to be left in peace in their flower'd bower in Andaluz mythology as just that, fairytales of knights, kings, fair damsels, "squires" and "varlets". Although, as one twenty-first-century Andaluz novelist told this writer, "I'd sooner read the '1001 Nights' any day…"

GEORGE BORROW AND THE GYPSIES OF SPAIN

The story of George Borrow (1803-81) is perhaps the strangest of all these stories of Englishmen abroad in Andalucía. Unlike almost every other author mentioned here, he had no university education, although he did attend Norwich Grammar School, near his birthplace of East Dereham, Norfolk. He displayed a precocious gift for languages at an early age, and at his death was said to be either fluent in or conversant with one hundred languages. He first studied law, but turned to literature and languages. He began the first of many voyages at the age of twenty-two, walking through France and Germany, and later visited Russia, Portugal, Spain and Portugal. Working as an agent for the proselytizing Protestant British and Foreign Bible Society, he oversaw the production of a Russian edition of the *New Testament*, and was such a successful salesman for the Bible Society that he was sent to Catholic Spain in 1835. He spent five years in Spain overseeing Spanish editions of the scriptures and distributing them by hand, an experience that would produce his best-selling book, *The Bible in Spain* (1843). It was preceded, however, in 1841 by his *The Zincali; or, An Account of the Gypsies of Spain*. Even Borrow aficionados admit that his work is an uneasy mix of reportage and fabulation—he himself declares at the opening of *The Bible in Spain* that he is no author or travel writer. He describes his years in Spain as the happiest times in his life, but calls its working class "heartless thieves and drunkards". This may be due to his religious background, for Borrow was gripped by an unwavering belief in his mission to take the Protestant testaments to the Spanish and just about anybody else he met. His descriptions of the Spanish he encounters are often withering, and in *Zincali* his descriptions of gitano life—he calls them Roms or Cales; we, conversely, are Gorgios or Busnes—can be eye-wateringly rude. (One modern-day Roma website observes: "This book does not appear to be sympathetic to the Gypsies.") Worse, his syntax and tendency to upper-case passages he wants to stress at times give *Zincali* the appearance of an unhinged pamphleteer's rant.

Yet Borrow clearly considered himself the gitanos' friend and brother, spoke the language(s) fluently enough to trade the richest insults with them, and defended them against what today would be called racist stereotyping, even if he considered, sometimes from personal experience, that not a few were cutpurses, poisoners and even, perhaps, cannibals. His passages on gitano ethnography and social rituals are fascinating, but much of *Zincali* reads like a period curio—and, unfortunately, one that underpins much later writerly comment on the gypsies of Spain. The modern reader seeking live contemporary gitano culture might be better served by films such as Tony Gatlif's *Gadjo Dilo* or Dominique Abel's *Poligono Sur*, and the music of Taraf de Haïdouks or Shukar Collective (only Abel's documentary emerges from Spain, specifically the Tres Mil ghetto of Seville, but this is after all a culture in diaspora).

Dyspepsia was a common ailment among Englishmen writing on Spain until well into the twentieth century, and we might date the turning point at the arrival of Gerald Brenan. Other aspects of the Englishman's relationship with his subject were also shifting, not least his position in his home country's class system. Like Borrow, Brenan was not a toff down from Oxbridge, although he was born into a comfortable middle-class family and educated at Radley College public school. He thwarted his father's ambitions for his son to study at Sandhurst by running away to China with a friend, turning back when they ran out of money in Bosnia. Brenan entertained ambitions of joining the Indian Police Service, but that was set aside at the outbreak of the First World War, in which he served for two years, being awarded both a Military Cross and a Croix de Guerre. His time in the trenches, even as an officer, affected him profoundly, and on being demobbed he decided to quit England in disgust at a society "petrified by class feeling and by rigid conventions". The decision was no doubt influenced by a fellow officer and later a lifelong friend, Ralph Partridge, who introduced him to the Bloomsbury Group, among them Lytton Strachey, Virginia Woolf and Dora Carrington, later Brenan's lover.

By his own admission, Spain was not his first choice of destination, but on his meagre officer's stipend he could not afford to travel to Italy or Greece. He did not even know much about the country he arrived in at La Coruña in 1919: "Almost all I knew about that country was that it had been neutral in the war and would therefore, I imagined, be cheap to live in." His first experiences of Spain were dispiriting—the dreary landscape of the central Meseta, rain in Madrid, accommodation run by "harpies" and "crones", foul food, bug-infected beds, a bout of dysentery—and on his arrival Brenan seemed to be shaping up as that classic literary archetype, the English whiner. Even George Orwell succumbed to this, not least when describing his frightful digs above the tripe shop in *The Road to Wigan Pier*, and the one thing English whiners seem to have in common is the solipsistic conviction that other people's misery has been put there solely to put a crimp in the English whiner's own day. But as soon as he was installed in a small house in Yegen, in the Alpujarras, south-west of Granada and halfway to Almería, Brenan was transformed, as his rhapsodic descriptions of his new surroundings attest.

What distinguishes Brenan from his predecessors is his decision to live among the peasants of this tiny mountain village, where the only concession to modernity was a rough road connecting it to the outside world. Water was taken from a village well fed by mountain streams, and Yegen had yet to join the larger surrounding villages in the network supplying that innovation, electricity. He would remain an outsider, but was grateful for their acceptance and soon became a part of village life. He romanced the girls, and later scandalized the village with certain aspects of his private life but, as anyone who has read Julian A. Pitt-Rivers' *People of the Sierra* will know, mountain peasants are no strangers to scandal themselves.

The book he wrote about the "six or seven" years he lived in Yegen between 1920 and 1934, *South from Granada*, was only published in 1957 and was written, as he admitted, with the benefit of twenty years of hindsight. Yet half a century on, it remains the most balanced account by an

English writer about life in an Andaluz village. It has aged, inevitably, and there is a hint of both misanthropy and perhaps even a subtext of miscegenation—his later life would be attended by posthumous biographical scandals of the sort that attended both Robert Graves and Lawrence Durrell—but as a record of Andaluz life it would have no match until a good two decades later.

Brenan's books have a curious chronology. He published his first Spanish book, *The Spanish Labyrinth*, in 1943, four years after the end of the Civil War and while living in England. Similarly, *The Face of Spain* (1951) was written on a visit to the country and he only returned in 1953, four years before publishing *South from Granada*. He died in 1983 in his adopted home of Alhaurin el Grande, between Málaga and Coin, where a main road and a cultural Foundation are named after him. Similarly, the house he rented in Yegen now bears a plaque, and perhaps uniquely among Englishman abroad in Andalucía, Brenan has been lionized by his Spanish hosts.

In 2003 Spanish film director Fernando Colomo made a film "of" *South from Granada, Al Sur de Granada*, jointly written by Colomo and Brenan's official biographer, Jonathan Gathorne-Hardy. In fact, it is a conflation of Gathorne-Hardy's biography, *Gerald Brenan: The Interior Castle* (the title itself another reference, to the key text by medieval ecstatic mystic Teresa of Avila, subject of an unfinished book by Brenan and famously iconized by Bernini) and parts of Brenan's book. As a film, it has the right to establish its own narrative, although the appropriation of the title from Brenan's best-selling autobiography for this semi-fictional confection might be a liberty too far for some. It is a bucolic period idyll, aimed squarely at the same market as *Il Postino, Cinema Paradiso, Mediterraneo* and any number of other European art movies that promise the viewer a cultural suntan. Yet it flies in the face of everything Brenan wrote about Andalucía and its people. In the movie version of Gerald Brenan's Andalucía it is sunny all year round, no one starves and everyone seems to have a bath every morning and puts on fresh clothes. Nowhere are there the middle classes reduced to begging, women unable to attend mass because their clothes are so ragged, people whose faces are ingrained with dirt because they can't afford the water to wash it off. Brenan himself, as some reviewers pointed out, does not come out of it terribly well either, effectively abandoning the village girl he impregnated, returning years later almost as though nothing has happened.

LAURIE LEE'S MOMENT OF WAR

It could be that his experiences in the Great War impelled Brenan and his wife Gamel Woolsey to leave Spain at the outbreak of the Civil War, but it is notable that a great many others were heading in the opposite direction, among them Laurie Lee and George Orwell. Orwell, of course, was heading for Barcelona, where his experiences would produce *Homage to Catalonia*. Lee's exploits, recorded in his two later volumes of autobiography, *As I Walked out One Midsummer Morning* and *A Moment of War*, also need careful consideration.

His three major works appeared over a space of forty years, interspersed among collections of poetry, essays and memoirs. *As I Walked Out...* was published in 1969, ten years after *Cider with Rosie* and some thirty-five years after the events it describes. *A Moment of War* was published, with surprising anachronicity, in 1991, nearly half a century after the events it describes and when Lee was seventy-one (he died in 1997). The latter book sparked a minor (if, while he was still alive, private) controversy on its publication, not least when surviving veterans from the British battalion of the XVth International Brigade disputed Lee's presence at the battle of Teruel during the winter of 1938-9. (Lee's Civil War experiences were all in the north, some way from Andalucía.) It has been said that Lee never joined the International Brigades, failing the medical when it was discovered he suffered from epilepsy, but eyewitness reports and papers later found at the Comintern archive in Moscow, cited by Lee's biographer Valerie Grove, prove that he did (the epilepsy was a fact; he was given light duties and later invalided out of the war). Careful checking of the chronology of *A Moment of War* also seemed to place Lee in the wrong places at the wrong dates, something that may have to be considered in the chronology of *As I Walked Out...*, leading the baffled reader to conclude that these too were also works of the imagination.

No one doubts that Lee was indeed in Spain, and Andalucía, during these periods and visited the places he describes, although owners of a map of Andalucía will be left scratching their heads by his wayward itinerary between Toledo and Cádiz in *As I Walked Out...* It also seems that the coastal town of "Castillo" mentioned towards the end of the book was a carefully disguised portrait of what is now the busy resort of Almuñecar, which is indeed his specified "sixty miles east of Málaga", and where a monument to Lee, resembling a tall country chimney, was erected above the beach in 1988.

Lee's reasons for fictionalizing his experiences in Andalucía went to the grave with him, although his sympathetic but unflinching biographer Valerie Grove, in *Laurie Lee: The Well-Loved Stranger*, considers this all of a piece with an intensely secretive man who few got to know well. He himself described his work as neither autobiography nor fiction, but a new genre somewhere in-between. *As I Walked Out...* and *A Moment of War* end and begin with the same anecdote and the same exchange ("'I've come to join you,' I said. '*Pase usted*,' he said."); both also feature the mysterious Frenchman who guides Lee on his way across the Pyrenees. But the two books were written by entirely different men. The first was written by a middle-aged man remembering his youth (he was twenty-three when he arrived in Spain), and his description of "Castillo" at the outbreak of the Civil War has a young man's passion for the Republican cause (he may not have been a card-carrying communist, but he was definitely a fellow traveller). His dedication of the latter book to "The Defeated" suggests it was written by an old man still angry at the several betrayals of a people and a generation in that time. Certainly, enough histories—not least those by Anthony Beevor, Paul Preston and Hugh Thomas—existed, along with numerous actual autobiographies from the era, to make it obvious that there were enough people still alive and able to expose the inaccuracies and inconsistencies of the later book, which, indeed, is what promptly happened (the controversy only went public after Lee's death).

The tone of *A Moment of War* is self-deprecating, but not in the cutely disingenuous way of most self-deprecating literature. He and his colleagues were there (or not) because of a "shared historic daftness". They "had yet to learn that sheer idealism never stopped a tank." He portrays himself as neither hero nor buffoon, but as a believer caught up in a confusing war in which strings were being pulled from as far afield as Moscow, Washington, London and Berlin. Those who did fight at Teruel and at the Ebro and elsewhere were right to pick him up on his inconsistencies and the fabulation of their experiences. But considering that he could not have expected *A Moment of War* to go unchallenged, it might be considered a populist poet's attempt to capture and salute the spirit of place, and time. He might even have believed that in the 1990s it needed saying again—in the urbanizaciones of "Castillo" and elsewhere the Civil War is nowadays as remote as the Battle of Hastings, less understood even than the "Reconquest". Read as historicizing fiction, it has the taut and spare poetry of another historical fabulizer, Michael Ondaatje.

As I Walked Out... was perhaps unique, though, in its narrator's attitude to his surroundings, and the people living there. As might be expected of a working-class youth from a Cotswold village, Lee arrived in Spain with even less metaphorical baggage than his actual baggage of a violin and his knapsack. As their social equal, he recorded the lives of the people he encountered without condescension, although perhaps not without flourishes of embellishment. Their conditions were neither appalling nor pitiable, just the way things were for people like them living there and then (hence his enthusiasm for the—lest we forget, democratically elected—Republican government). While it was written from comfortable hindsight, the young Lee had come from an English village not unlike their own villages. His description of Estepona, San Pedro, Marbella and Fuengirola as " salt-fish villages, thin-ribbed, sea-hating, cursing their place in the sun" had more than a touch of Dylan Thomas about it and might be said to touch on the reasons why those places were so willing to transform themselves into hives of tourism three decades later. Certainly, he unwittingly prefigures the expatriate culture that was to blossom there in the 1960s, describing 1930s Málaga with its English debutantes "sipping at glasses of pallid tea." (Nowadays, of course, it would be Pimm's.) We may suspect the poet of embellishment, but Andalucía had finally been visited by a foreign observer who did not write like an amateur anthropologist, snob, racist or a visitor from Mars.

ALASTAIR BOYD'S IDYLL, J. G. BALLARD'S HEART OF DARKNESS

Curiously, it was a writer from the other extreme of the British class system, and a Lord, no less, who would match Lee's affection and enthusiasm for his subject. Alastair Boyd, who prefers not to use his hereditary title of Lord Kilmarnock, has lived in and around Ronda on and off for the best part of half a century. If he had followed the path proposed by his father, he would have pursued a career of banking, City and ermine. Instead, he moved to Andalucía, founding first a language school, then opening a bar and later moving his young family to a *huerta*, small farm, in the outlying

An offshore realm: Puerto Banús, likely inspiration for J. G. Ballard's Costa del Sol dystopia in *Cocaine Nights*

hamlet of La Indiana, where he began to write and where he and his wife live quietly today.

In 1958 he published a young man's picaresque novel, *Sabbatical Year* (nowadays only found in antiquarian book stores). Life, adventures, two marriages and a son intervened before he published another book, *The Road from Ronda* (1969), followed by the *Companion Guide to Madrid and Central Spain* (1986) and *The Essence of Catalonia* (1988). He published his second Andalucían book, *The Sierras of the South*, in 1992. *Road from Ronda* and *Sierras of the South* were republished by the small *andaluz* press Santana Books in 2004, and a Spanish translation of *The Road from Ronda*, *De Ronda a las Alpujarras*, was published in 2007 by the cultural foundation La Serranía.

The earlier book describes a journey on horseback from Ronda to the Alpujarras, the latter a motorized version of same around the mountains of his adopted home. What marks Alastair Boyd out from earlier and contemporary writers on the region is his interest in his subject's past, present and future. He too has read Ford and Brenan, and was a friend of the latter, but he is also interested in the opinions of young Spanish feminists and ecologists about what is happening in their society and landscape, and is not fazed by engaging with a high-falutin' cultural critic such as Marina Warner, among others. The later book, especially, is the most catholic and rounded single volume on the region this writer has read.

He also shares the sanguinity of some younger writers such as Paul Richardson, discussed later, about the complexities and seeming contradictions of life in modern Andalucía, and even uses a quote from Brenan on the problematic relationship between foreign writers on Spain and their subject as an epigraph to *The Road from Ronda*. This was thrown into sharp, and for many scandalous, relief in 2006 when he and two other extranjeros were cited in a court case in which the developers of a proposed golf course and luxury housing development on land outside Ronda were seeking damages for comments Boyd and the others had made to the press about the project's unsuitability inside a "protected" UNESCO Special Biospheric Reserve in the Sierra de las Nieves mountains. Simply for telling a journalist that such a development might be "unsuitable" in such a setting, Boyd was being asked to pay a cool twenty million euros for the damage his comments had done to the future of the project. The case was eventually thrown out by a judge, but not before things became a lot nastier, with local Spanish ecologists receiving anonymous threatening phone calls late at night, and *El Pais* printing a letter from one brave Rondeña woman claiming that the climate of fear in Ronda was akin to Al Capone's Chicago.

There is no way to compare Alistair Boyd's factual Andalucía and the fictional landscape of J. G. Ballard's novel *Cocaine Nights*, published in 1996 and followed promptly by its Spanish translation, *Noches de Cocaina*. As with other novels by Ballard, it is a morality tale set somewhere exotic where a seeming paradise is revealed as an inferno.

The *Independent* newspaper called *Cocaine Nights* "dazzlingly original", although to anyone familiar with Ballard's ironically dystopian fiction it was a familiar Ballard theme played out on the playas and in the gated urbanizaciones of a fictionalized Costa del Sol resort, Estrella de Mar, "star of the sea", just down the road from the real-life Calahonda. If not dazzlingly original, it is probably the book where Ballard confesses his unlikely debt to T. S. Eliot and one of the key inspirational texts in "The Waste Land", Frazer's *The Golden Bough* and the myth of the Fisher King, the figurehead who has to die so that his lands can be reborn. In brief summary, a man arrives on the Costa to investigate his brother's mysterious admission of guilt in a series of murders and in essence finds that his brother has surrendered his freedom in order to maintain a horrible dream.

Anyone who read Ballard's *Observer* article in the early 1990s about a new breed of super-Europeans tanning and exercising themselves on the beaches of the Costa del Sol could have seen *Cocaine Nights* coming—just as anyone who read his 1973 story collection, *Vermilion Sands*, might have suspected that it was only a matter of time before Ballard was spotted leaving Málaga airport in a rental car with a notepad on the seat next to him. (His protagonist, Charles, in fact arrives via Gibraltar, allowing Ballard to skewer that British enclave en route as well.) Put simply, letting Ballard anywhere near the Costa del Sol is akin to giving a pyromaniac a lighter for Christmas.

Noches de Cocaina was well received by the Spanish press and public. Its warm reception at first seems odd—with typical glee, Ballard portrays the Costa as a moral sewer where bored wife-swappers watch staged gang rapes to relieve their ennui—until you realize a key fact about *Noches de Cocaina*: there are no Spanish characters in this novel. Jesús Gil y Gil, the now deceased jailbird gangster mayor of nearby Marbella, might have been appalled by Ballard's portrayal of extranjero culture, but cleverly and possibly unintentionally Ballard did not commit the offence of besmirching Spanish culture, only his own. And, if it still needs saying this late in his career, Ballard is in fact a deeply moral writer and ironist, whose patron saint is probably Jonathan Swift.

Ballard's fictive Costa del Sol is an offshore realm (we could have some fun with the idea of his Costa as an English taifa), completely detached from the landmass it occupies. He starts from the assumption that while Estrella de Mar is nominally in Spain, it is actually in another space, another place, perhaps even on another planet entirely. As with other Ballard novels, set in parts of Britain where society has reverted to savagery, or exotic locales overcome by climate or strange transformations of landscape, the setting simply provides the players who will be put through their paces by the author.

The most striking factor, for this reader at least, is how even J. G. Ballard's moral fable is frequently outstripped by the reality of the Costa del Sol. Anyone keeping an eye on the Andaluz press during the year 1999-2000 would have noticed an unusual spike in Ballardian events on that coastline. Chief among these was the brutal murder of Rocio Wanninkhof, a young woman killed in a gruesome assault on her way home from a local feria. Suspicion first fell on her mother's lesbian lover, Dolores Vázquez, and Vázquez spent a year and a half in jail for the crime. Only later did DNA tests identify the true killer as British criminal Tony King, who probably killed her with the aid of an accomplice in a sex attack after a binge of porn videos, drugs and booze. The media, Spanish, foreign-language and overseas, lapped up every sordid detail.

Other grisly murders popped up along the Costa that year. Bodies left in fields. Bodies left in suitcases. Bodies left on beaches. Bodies chopped up and democratically distributed in plastic bags left in waste bins along the coast. With the constant background hum of its reputation as the Costa del Crime, given a fillip by the film *Sexy Beast*, and the underbelly of low-level crime, from timeshare scams to drug running, it seemed as though Ballard had in fact underestimated the hell that sometimes flickers into view in the wrong parts of what is also known as the Costa del Golf.

Homeowners, and they are almost all, in an interesting socio-economic quirk, homeowners in that last Andaluz dream zone, would no doubt be outraged at the representation of their landscape as either a Ballardian dystopia or as a body-strewn killing ground. It is only a small part of Costa culture, but their lives are constructed around the denial or avoidance of the fact that it is there, which is why Ballard went snooping through their garbage. This is not what they came for, or indeed what they see beyond their faux-Arabic housing developments, the lush and manicured fairways of their golf courses, the lifestyles marked out by Conservatives Abroad social occasions, Little England charity events, the lunches along the Paseo Marítimo in Marbella, the gala evenings at Puerto Banús. It would not need a Mike Davis, however, to point out that the architecture of their gated urbanizaciones, with their armed patrols and CCTV surveillance, like those in Britain and elsewhere, is the architecture of urban siege, food riots, civil unrest, and worse. Read the English-language "ex-pat" media here—if you can bear to—and you get a chilling idea of the minds living behind those walls.

Ballard declined to be interviewed for this book due to ill health, although he did tell this writer in an earlier interview that he considered his *Vermilion Sands* to be a theme park of the imagination, like the Costa, that he liked to visit from time to time. He made some more interesting revelations—not least that he would not mind moving to Estrella de Mar—to the writer Damien Love, for an interview in the Scottish arts magazine, *The List*, in 1996, around the publication of *Cocaine Nights*. In the interview he told Love that the genesis of the book came from "watching the growth of the Costa del Sol and similar places along the Mediterranean over the last 40 years that I've been going there, and seeing a microcosm of a future that's waiting for us all."

> You know, these security obsessed enclaves with tele-surveillance and armed guards and smart cards and all, the whole paraphernalia, like a kind of maximum security state, reduced to the size of a village… As you drive along that coast, from Marbella to Málaga, or from Gibraltar to Málaga, you pass all these condominiums and pueblo-style housing estates, and you think "Well, they're a bit odd, I wouldn't want to live in one myself." But you don't realise how odd they are until you go into one, and then you realise that tens of thousands of Brits, along with Dutch and French and Germans and so on—many of them retired there permanently, are all living these very strange lives.

Again, to anyone with a passing knowledge of Ballard's oeuvre, this is pretty much par for the course. In fact, it is almost a Ballard party-piece, an *épater-le-bourgeois* act that sometimes looks just a little too slick. But Ballard knows how to push buttons with his readers: "I can imagine, 50 to 100 years from now, social-historians looking back at the closing years of the 20th century and saying, 'My God, it opened with the flight of the Wright Brothers; halfway through they went to the moon; they discovered scientific miracle upon miracle. And then they ended with people sitting in their little fortified bungalows while the tele-surveillance cameras sweep the streets outside, and they watch reruns of *The Rockford Files*.' It's a nightmare vision."

Chris Stewart's Lemon Crop

New times bring new writers to the curious business of writing about Andalucía. Two immediately stand out; Chris Stewart, author of the million-plus bestseller *Driving Over Lemons* and its two sequels so far, and, less famously, Jason Webster, author of (so far) three Andaluz-themed books, the first, *Duende*, being a confessional autobiography of romantic obsession, impossible gitano divas and cocaine-fuelled adventures in the carjacking trade that deserves slow and careful reading. Although they both hail from public school backgrounds, the two men have nothing whatsoever in common apart from the fact that both are inveterate fibbers.

Chris Stewart, it should immediately be said, is on the side of the angels here. Published in 1999, *Driving Over Lemons* was every author's and publisher's dream; the unexpected, out-of-nowhere runaway success. His jocular tale of a linguistically challenged Brit throwing himself into the foolhardy adventure of buying and renovating a rundown *cortijo* halfway up a mountain in the remote Alpujarras had "you'll love this book" written all over it. It also had some outside help.

The first has to be his cover designer, who deserves an award for the simple but brilliant juxtaposition of that impossibly blue Andaluz sky and the blinding yellow of the titular fruit in a book cover image that simply demanded to be placed on top of the pile of books everyone was taking on holiday that summer. As a semiotic sign, the cover itself could be considered a triumph in cynical subliminal marketing.

The second has to be his publisher, Sort Of Books, launched by Mark Ellingham and Natania Jansz, the former Stewart's friend and sometime employer at the Rough Guides series, which Ellingham and his partner Jansz founded and for which Stewart is an author. Due credit must go to their publicity machine, which, again perhaps a little cynically, lifted one minor detail from Stewart's author biography, gave it a gentle nudge and watched a little white lie go haring off around the world, spawning untold numbers of newspaper and magazine headlines.

That little mistruth is still doing the rounds and in June 2007 appeared on the cover of *EPS*, the Sunday glossy supplement to *El Pais*: "De bateria de Genesis a la soledad literaria en las Alpujarras" ("From drummer for Genesis to literary solitude in the Alpujarras").

Unfortunately for Stewart and his publishers, some of the people who bought his book knew a thing or two about the history of Genesis. Some of them, indeed, might have been former rock journalists who may even have been on the road with Genesis. An even larger number might have gone through their record collections to check if they had overlooked his name on any of the album credits. Some might have signed on pseudonymously to the Genesis fan club website and gone looking for evidence of Stewart's headline-catching connection to said band.

To be fair to Stewart, according to reports of at least one of his public appearances in Andalucía promoting the book, he has been discreetly backpedalling on what might simply be a partial myth that got out of hand. He did in fact drum on the very first two singles recorded by Genesis, while they were still schoolboys at Charterhouse, the sort of minor detail usually noted only by anoraks and band historians. He left shortly, and swiftly, afterwards, as much by his own design as by any of Messrs Gabriel, Rutherford and Banks. (He told *EPS* that he was sacked, or thrown out.) He described himself to *EPS* as possibly the worst drummer in the world (intriguingly, Peter Gabriel was originally meant to be the drummer). But it cannot be denied that the white lie, aided undoubtedly by the short attention-span and desperate cynicism of subeditors the world over, helped his career far more than it might have been helped by headlines referring to his later, longer-lasting, avocation, that of peripatetic sheep shearer.

A decade later, Stewart seems to be suffering from a mixture of sequel-backlash, Peter Mayle Syndrome and, alas, the law of diminishing returns. While *Driving Over Lemons* made him financially comfortable, he sports none of the appurtenances of the rich bestseller author, and still lives in his ecologically sustainable *cortijo*, farm house, up in the Alpujarras, where winters remain as grim as ever. His books have, unsurprisingly, inspired others to follow in his footsteps, including one poor soul seen on the British television series, *A Place in the Sun*, carting a portable computer to a wrecked Alpujarran *cortijo* in the hope of emulating his achievement in what might well be a post-modern form of cargo cult. He has also been accused, quite preposterously, of "ruining" the Alpujarras (Peter Mayle Syndrome), a familiar cry to anyone who has ever fallen foul of People Who Moved Here Before You Did. His loudest critic was, bizarrely, the Labour MP for Luton South Margaret Moran, who also owns a cortijo outside their nearest town, Orgiva. Moran sparked small riots when she began blocking communal paths that cross her property, and in the well-publicized hubbub that ensued she accused Stewart of single-handedly triggering an influx of ghastly Brits into the Alpujarras. (Her property remains a "holiday home".) One unimpressed neighbour was moved to comment that the "Socialist" politician was "behaving like an English imperialist from the last days of the Raj."

Anyone who has visited the Alpujarras will know that the region does not need Chris Stewart's help to change or ruin it. Progress manages that quite nicely, and in 2007 Stewart himself was saying that he gave Andalucía only four years before it was ruined by development, corruption and greed. No change there then.

For all the media hullabaloo, *Driving Over Lemons* was a charming tale of a plucky public school dropout getting his hands dirty and mixing up his Spanish tenses in a landscape where no one with an affection for running hot water would dream of living. His ellipses of narrative (he starts out needing a translator but is soon an eloquent Hispanophone; we hardly ever hear from his wife; the narrative ends in mid-air and almost mid-sentence) are the ellipses of most books like his. (As for the business about his connection to Genesis, at least he got out before they started making white disco muzak and threatening to leave Britain if a Labour government got in.)

No such good humour accrues to the work of Jason Webster, although we have to tease out the dynamic at work in his first book, *Duende*, quite carefully, not least because this text, like any published text, has a contractual libel clause looking over its shoulder.

Something—well, quite a few things—does not sit quite right with this book. It is subtitled "A Journey in Search of Flamenco", although curiously, Webster begins his search in Alicante, moving to Madrid, and arriving in the home of flamenco, Andalucía, only in the last third of the book. It is pitched as autobiography, and most reviewers took it as such, although some cheerfully assumed it was a work of the imagination and reviewed it as same (Robert Carver in *The Times*: "The traditions of the Bildungsroman and the rites-of-passage novel have migrated into the travel genre").

The first problem with *Duende* as autobiography, for this reader at least, is the dialogue. There is so much of it one can only assume that either Webster has perfect total recall or was carrying a digital recording device throughout his adventures, some of which take place underwater. The second, perhaps more serious, is the milieu in which he sets his adventure. Webster paints a convincing unvarnished portrait of his life among gitano musicians and the urban *demi-monde*, although anyone with a passing knowledge of a) the Spanish underworld b) gitano culture and c) the cocaine trade (it was a long time ago, officer, honest) will surely wonder how a willowy blonde "English" (his term) academic medievalist whose air-brushed author photo resembles the young Stephen Spender gained entry to any of these deeply secretive societies in the first place. If one were to be deeply cynical, *Duende* could be seen as a truly brilliant literary hoax: a caper set in such an extreme social sub-set that it is almost certainly impossible to disprove (should we want to). Before we delve further into Webster's book, we should record, however, that his unsparing yet sympathetic view of modern Spain is a far cry from the overheated froth that is served up in many books about Spain, even if his sympathy does not extend to either cats or homosexuals.

His musical chops—and there are a lot of musical chops in this book—seem sound, although not without some minor oddities that again do not sit well in a book about flamenco. When he finally arrives in Granada, Webster notes with awe that it is the home of modern flamenco legend Enrique Morente. It is his birthplace, but Morente moved to Madrid aged fourteen to begin his career and pursued it elsewhere from then on. He notes also that Morente, famed and damned in equal part for expanding the flamenco repertoire, recorded the legendary *Omega*, a setting of Lorca poems and some Leonard Cohen covers (more on which later), with "a heavy metal band". This was in fact Lagartija Nick, probably the greatest post-punk group Spain has ever produced, and calling Lagartija Nick a "heavy metal band" is a bit like calling The Sex Pistols a skiffle combo. They do come from and still live in Granada, and might be called the most important modern group Andalucía, and Spain, have yet produced. Again, minor points, but something that someone immersed in Andalucía's musical culture might have got right.

When "Blondy", as Webster is nicknamed by his Brechtian band of homeys, is finally accepted as a flamenco guitarist and goes on the road, we learn very little about what life on the road is like, although they do a lot of coke and drink heavily. But even his description of his cocaine use is eerily detached, so much so it might almost have been copied out of someone else's homework, and he kicks the habit in a blink of an eye, despite confessing to losing a stone after two months of coke-fuelled mayhem.

Granada itself features little in the final section, apart from some lofty travel journalism on the Alhambra and Generalife gardens. Here the book shifts into the realm of magic realism; some baffling adventures with a delightfully eccentric seventy-year-old Englishwoman who takes him to a gypsy wedding (where they are the only *payos*, outsiders, in sight), an encounter with a knife-wielding angel of death, who spares the narrator, and an encounter with Paco de Lucia ("Paco" throughout) when they share the same bush while having a pee backstage at a de Lucia gig in the Generalife.

Earlier, there is an amusing, if unlikely, account of Webster's stint on an English language "ex-pat" newspaper and an exciting, if also unlikely, high speed car chase in which he and his soul brother Jesús are pursued by two police cars through the centre of Madrid in the early hours of the morning. But considered in its parts it does not add up to very much about music, people or place. His one moment of *satori* is when a friend tells him that he will only find his *duende* (Spanish for imp or goblin, but taken to mean soul) within him. This is what is known in the trade as false Zen.

There are two possible explanations for *Duende*, both of which would invite a minibus-load of French literary critics to defend the theory, if not the text itself. One is that it could be part of the Richard Rayner School. In his first book, *Los Angeles without a Map*, Rayner fabricated a similar adventure of a hapless Brit pursuing love and adventure in a hyper-real LA. Twenty years on, it is still marketed as "non-fiction". Another, which struck this reader late on in *Duende*, is that perhaps Webster has taken an obscure first-person literary narrative from an earlier era and dressed it up as modern-day low-life Spain. That minibus of French intellectuals, with perhaps Roland Barthes at the wheel, would applaud the conceit, although they might feel short-changed by the result.

At this point, we might also acknowledge two of the more mature commentators on contemporary Andalucía. The work of Ian Gibson, nowadays the owner of a Spanish passport, is considered in greater length in the following chapter, but it is worth recording that his historical work on the lives of Lorca, Dalí, Antonio Machado and others has won him a unique position in Spain's cultural life. Similarly, art historian and writer Michael Jacobs, author of the definitive English historical study, *Andalucía* (1990), and the warmly received *Factory of Light* (2003), just one of a number of books Jacobs has published about his adventures in Spain and elsewhere, succeeded without recourse to car chases or Class A drugs. Some have even described Jacobs' adventures in his adopted Spanish pueblo, Frailes, as a modern-day equivalent to Cervantes.

PAUL RICHARDSON'S VANISHING SPAIN

It is a genuine pleasure, then, to head into the hills and further with the latest arrival in this increasingly cramped literary genre, Paul Richardson. From one brief and really little more than mischievous reference in his *Our Lady of the Sewers* (1998), it is clear that Richardson too is no stranger to Colombian marching powder; he compares a shot of Sanlúcar sherry, rather disingenuously, to a hit of cocaine, but this is perhaps a hangover from the research for his earlier book, *Not Part of the Package: A Year in Ibiza* (1994). While young enough to know both rave culture and fast drugs, but born perhaps two generations after the older writer, Richardson is more akin to Alastair Boyd in the generosity of spirit and sheer affection he brings to his book, subtitled "And Other Adventures in Deep Spain".

Only part of his book covers Andalucía. It travels to Murcia, Catalonia, Madrid, the island of Gomera and elsewhere, but enough of it is about Andalucía to deserve inclusion here. The reason for setting out on his adventures is to record vanishing Spanish culture, from witchcraft to *la transhumancia* (transhumance, the seasonal droving of pastoral flocks), via small fiestas, bizarre sports competitions and much more. Like Alastair Boyd, he is an erudite and witty commentator, and fluent enough in

Spanish to walk into any outlandish scenario, from feigning an ailment on a visit to a witchdoctor to taking part in Friday prayers in a Granada mosque, without embarrassment. Unlike Alastair Boyd, however, he is queer, and sometimes takes his boyfriend Juan on his adventures.

Very much like Alastair Boyd, though, he sees Spain as a (perhaps nearly) modern country in constant dialogue with its past. He quotes Ford and James Morris, but disparages the snobbery of earlier literary visitors. He has neither agenda nor baggage, and takes Spain as he finds it, treating it with respect, but not reverence. He has travelled sufficiently far into "deep Spain" to have left the clichés far behind, except when he feels the urge to debunk them, which he does with a modest, if bawdy, humour. He sees no contradiction in the way that "classical" Spain can live side by side with modern Spain, plastic and cardboard alongside *marmol y yeso*. He accepts, and even celebrates, the flux and ambiguity, ironies and sometimes hilarious contradictions, that collide to make modern Spain and modern Andalucía a somehow workable chaos, while acknowledging that post-Franco Spain has embraced modernity and the future with some force. This, at last, is the Andalucía that some of us *guiris* outside the gated urbanizaciones believe ourselves to be living in.

He is also, perhaps uniquely, the only travel writer with the *cojones* to ask a shepherd, during several days and nights of la transhumancia, if it is really true that they fuck their sheep.

But you'll have to read his book to find out the answer to that one.

At the end of barely two hundred years of English writing on Andalucía, we might find ourselves contemplating the truism than most of these writers were writing not so much about Andalucía as about themselves. This is not in itself a sin; some of the best and some of the worst travel writing foregrounds the author. It may serve to underline the fact that almost every visitor constructs their own Andalucía, many of them cheerfully unaware of death-of-the-author theory.

It will also serve to illustrate, by comparison, how Andaluces write Andalucía, which is why the guiris and foraneos come before the indigenous authors here. We can assume that their Andalucía is written from insouciant authority, and without the preconceptions, cultural misreadings and personal baggage of foreign authors. They are not running away from anything, less still attempting to build John Winthrop's "Citty upon a Hill". They are, as it were, already *home*.

The last word here, though, has to go to Richard Ford:

> Let no author imagine that the fairest observations that he can take and make of Spain as she is, setting down naught in malice, can ever please a Spaniard.

We have been warned.

CASARES 8-7-1885
SEVILLA 11-8-1936

A Sta ANA
LLA) Cueto

Land and freedom: one of the many shrines to the father of *Andaluz* independence,
Blas Infante, here at Ronda

Chapter Seventeen
FEDERICO GARCIA LORCA'S LAST NIGHT ON EARTH:
ANDALUZ WRITERS WRITING ANDALUCÍA

Prior to exploring writer Ian Gibson's ever-expanding corpus of works on the poet Federico Garcia Lorca (Fuente Vaqueros, Granada, 1898-1936) and his era, I mistakenly believed that I had slept in the same house in Granada—perhaps even in a neighbouring bedroom—where Lorca spent his last night on earth.

This is no feat of investigative journalism, less still a favour curried through privileged contacts. Simply, the owners of what is now the Reina Cristina Hotel in Granada are happy to explain that their hotel, much renovated since 1936, was originally the house where Lorca was staying the night in June of that year when the fascists came looking for him (probably today's room 310, if you are interested).

In fact, I was around forty-eight hours too early for the actual site of Lorca's last night on earth: according to Ian Gibson's decades-long investigations into the events around Lorca's death, the poet was assassinated two days after being taken from what was then the house of his friends the Rosales family. He was first held in a nearby government building along with dozens of other detainees, and then taken to a killing ground outside the town of Viznar where he was shot, along with three other men, lined up against an olive tree that stands there today. Their bodies were then dumped in an unmarked grave that remains the subject of a controversy over whether or not the bodies should be exhumed for definitive identification and conventional burial. It has to be said, of course, that Lorca and the three other men killed that night outside Viznar were only four among hundreds of thousands of Republicans killed by fascist opponents of the democratic government during the Civil War.

This is only the first in a lengthy list of complications we have to negotiate when approaching the life, work and cultural significance of Federico Garcia Lorca. Modern Spain has embraced him as perhaps *the*
cultural icon of the twentieth-century nation, and certainly Andalucía
has been dining out on his artistic reputation ever since the death of
Franco allowed Lorca's work to be rehabilitated and reinstated in the libraries and bookshops where it had been banned since his death. (Ian
Gibson even says that at some points mere ownership of Lorca's writings
could be read, or perhaps played, as a crime, in a country where the po-
liceman's gun was still law.) Simultaneously, Lorca is the locus of the *sub
rosa* discussion about how modern Spain refurbishes its recent history,
particularly during the years 1936-9. The twenty-first-century EU state
that iconizes Lorca also loathes his memory, is mortally embarrassed and
enraged by the memory of him and what it did to him, and wishes he
would somehow simply go away.

And that includes some members of his surviving family, who still
resist grimly any attempts to exhume either his or the three other bodies
believed to be under that olive tree outside Viznar. The families of the
junior school teacher Dióscoro Galindo González and the anarchists
Joaquín Arcollas Cabezas and Francisco Galadí Melgar who were also shot
alongside Lorca do not seem to have been given much of a say in what
happens to the remains of their dead forebears, largely, it seems, because
the Lorca clan, while happily prepared to celebrate (and collect royalties
from) the career of Lorca the writer, do not want the more controversial
side of Lorca's life—leftist, homosexual, communitarian, friend to the dis-
enfranchised and dispossessed of the world—dredged back up out of that
Viznarino mud. And, truly tragically, most Spanish people seem to agree
with them.

The Lorca celebrated in theatre festivals and heritage trails has become
a free-floating sign, cut adrift from the reality of his life and work, and
rendered harmless, antiqued or varnished, *embalmed* for presentation to
the tourists who fetch up in Granada and elsewhere. When we consider all
that has gone on around, in and under the sign of Lorca, we might wonder
if the Spanish as a people ought to have the cultural object Federico Garcia
Lorca taken away from them.

We would also seem to have the support in this of another great
Andaluz poet, Antonio Machado, whose poem "El crimen fue en

Granada" ("The Crime Was in Granada") about the poet's assassination points an unwavering finger at the population of Granada, and the country at large.

Ian Gibson's latest book, *Cuatro poetas en guerra* (Four poets in war), revisits the era of his earlier famous work, *The Assassination of Federico Garcia Lorca* (1979) and the later *Life* (1990), to explore the lives and works of four poets—Lorca, Machado, Juan Ramón Jiménez and Miguel Hernández (all Andaluces barring Hernández)—who were profoundly, some fatally, embroiled in the Civil War.

In his introduction Gibson evokes the marvellous euphoria that these poets felt at the installation of a democratically elected Republic on 16 February 1936. Some seventy per cent of voters awarded the left-wing Frente Popular 257 seats of a total of 453 in the Cortes, handing them what the newspaper *La Voz* trumpeted as an absolute majority. None of these poets was a member of any particular party—argument still rages over Lorca's reluctance to commit himself to a party line, and the future Nobel Prize winner Jiménez, a lifelong hypochondriac and depressive, was already despairing of the Spanish left that February—but each saw a left-leaning democracy as the best way to win a better life for a populace done very few favours by 444 years of well-dressed aristocratic gangsterism.

Unfortunately for Lorca and his fellow poets, their Republic was already in trouble before it was even elected. While the history of the Civil War has been exhaustively mapped by historians such as Anthony Beevor, Paul Preston and Hugh Thomas, it is still worth recalling—as Gibson does—some of the events that were already happening on the periphery prior to the 1936 election.

In public the monarchist right were cocksure about their imminent victory and their plans for the future—leader Gil Robles appeared on a huge illuminated sign on Madrid's central Puerta del Sol plaza declaring "Give me an absolute majority and we will give you a greater Spain!"—although in private they were not so sure that they should not take the precaution of having a few words with their friends in the armed forces, Church, media, big business and the newly arrived fascist powers in Germany and Italy in case the *rojos* (reds) somehow won the election. Before the vote was even in, aristocrats and industrialists were seen quietly leaving the country—to the extent that some worried the Spanish economy might collapse as the rodents left the proverbial craft in distress—

and their thugs were already active on the sidelines. Two days before the elections, Lorca, the communist poet Rafael Alberti (Cádiz, 1902-99) and others held a "civic funeral" at a Madrid theatre for the revered Gallego poet Ramón del Valle-Inclán (1866-1936), which included tributes from figures such as Pablo Neruda and Luis Cernuda, only for the event to be almost cancelled amid rumours that fascists were planning to attack the theatre and wreck the event.

As events in Gernika and elsewhere would also show, the Spanish right also had some well-equipped friends outside Spain only too ready to step in and help. (Ubrique, the Gaditano hill town west of Grazalema, centre of the Andaluz leather industry and a radical stronghold, was buzzed by planes that dropped leaflets warning the townsfolk that unless they put white sheets on their roofs to signal their surrender, they too would be bombed. Ubrique left its sheets on its beds and walked en masse into the hills instead, a mute invitation to the bombers to do their worst. The planes did not come back.)

Even as far afield as the west coast of the United States, a powerful figure such as William Randolph Hearst, shortly to be skewered by that adopted Andaluz Orson Welles in *Citizen Kane*, lent his media empire to the propaganda war against the reds. The British, in the form of Neville Chamberlain, and to the intense and repeated scorn of Machado, feared "burning their fingers on the Spanish question."

The Republic lasted just four calendar months and a day. On 17 July Franco led his well-planned uprising in Morocco and the first city to fall was the Andaluz capital, Seville, to General Gonzalo Quiepo de Llano. With the far subtler analyses of writers such as Beevor, Preston and Thomas easily to hand, there is little point in rehearsing the events of the Civil War here, except to note how they affected Ian Gibson's four poets in war. Lorca, the applause of New York and Buenos Aires still ringing in his ears, and with *La casa de Bernarda Alba* set for its premiere that autumn, was revelling in his success and the acclaim that led to him being mobbed by admirers whenever he appeared in public—a celebrity that in hindsight undoubtedly contributed to his demise.

The elation of those early days of the Republic that Gibson describes soon turned to a rising sense of dread, as the victors in this latter-day re-conquest began to flex their muscles and their frontera, with cities and towns falling one by one to the right. The Franquistas soon went looking for revenge on the left-wingers who had brought two years of right-wing misrule to a decisive close in that election. Lorca knew that he more than anyone had reason to fear the right—for his outspoken left-wing politics, his no less unabashed homosexuality, but perhaps worst of all his betrayal of the Granada petit bourgeoisie he dismissed as "cursi", the argot for "cursileria", an obscure concept of middle-class snobbery and tastelessness (see under "hortera"), discussed in Noël Valis's book, *The Culture of Cursileria: Bad Taste, Kitsch, and Class in Modern Spain* (2002)—but mere days before his own arrest he was still brave or brash enough to march into a police station to demand to see a friend who had been arrested.

As Ian Gibson writes, Lorca was one of the early victims of the Civil War. It would be nice to be able to say that his last night on earth involved some heroic sacrifice, or that he went out with all guns blazing. Alas, Federico Garcia Lorca is said, from the few reliable sources recorded, to have been led to his death sobbing, shaking and terrified, after newspapers tipped off the police that he had returned to Granada, and one particularly vindictive thug decided that Lorca's scalp would be his. The bitterest irony is that he was arrested at the house of a prominent Falangist, his close friend Luis Rosales, who would later make strenuous attempts to secure the poet's safety and, he hoped, release. By that time, however, Lorca had, along with hundreds of others, been disappeared into the Falange's murder machinery—what Gibson, no bug-eyed leftie he, feels capable of describing as "el holocausto Granadino"—led away late at night by members of the notorious Escuadra Negra death squad, bundled into a car and taken to a holding site at Viznar, where around 2,000 men and women are believed to have been executed on the site of what is now a pretty if eerie public park dedicated to Lorca's memory.

Despite recent changes in law and attitude, in 2008 Federico Garcia Lorca still moulders in his unmarked grave outside Viznar, while his family prays against all hope that this *ovieja negra* or black sheep will somehow go away. Like the image of an object falling into a black hole, which is theorized to remain on what is known as the "event horizon", Lorca's image remains on the event horizon of recent Spanish history, while the man, his work and everything he stood for have vanished into the maw of the black hole and been blasted either out of existence or into a nearby parallel universe. You could bet very good money that the vast majority of Spanish people probably have not read the poetry or drama of their country's greatest poet of the twentieth century. Even if they did, you could probably also bet on the likelihood that while they might have understood the point of his "Romance de la Guardia Civil de España"—his assassins almost certainly did—they would have been baffled by the "night benighted by night", or elsewhere by the "small pain of an ignorant leopard", just why those boys were "mauling small squirrels" in those piles of saffron, and any of the hundreds of other crazily beautiful surrealistic metaphors inspired by Baudelaire, Rimbaud and the Whitman to whom he dedicated his famous "Ode to Walt Whitman", imagining the poet's "beard full of butterflies".

They may have even seen, or been dragged to, Lorca's plays such as *Yerma*, *Bodas de sangre*, or even the posthumously-staged *La casa de Bernarda Alba*, but it is unlikely they would have caught the poet's point in any, least of all the nearly autobiographical criticism of Andaluz class structure and misogyny in *Bernarda Alba*. The Federico Garcia Lorca whose casa natal in Fuente Vaqueros you can now visit on a guided tour of the newly invented Lorca Trail (thirty euros and lunch included, although it remains cheaper doing it by bus on your own) is not the author of the *Romancero Gitano* or *Poeta en Nueva York*, but a hologram, and nothing whatsoever like the body still rotting under that olive tree outside Viznar.

LORCA'S QUESTION TO THE FUTURE

Lorca's hologram is also mouthing a question at us: what does it mean to call a writer an Andaluz or even, more generally, Spanish? More so even than painters such as José Guerrero, writers are ambulatory creatures, foragers or adventurers, who cannot be tied down to one place, even though they may declare a link or anchorage to a specific point. They are, to quote the famous pun, citizens of the word.

We can read Lorca's own words, in his poetry and the dramas he toured with his La Barraca theatre group, taking socially engaged art to the working people (and probably inspired by the movie trains and other mass cultural innovations of Soviet Russia) that won him the adulation of those crowds who mobbed him in Madrid, Granada and elsewhere. Lorca wrote with the tradition of Andaluz poetry and folklore at his side, but as a sworn modernist and internationalist who saw no contradiction in being who and what he was in his *pueblo*, and in every sense of that word. He wrote, "I think that being from Granada I tend towards a sympathetic understanding of all those who suffer persecution. That of the gypsy, the negro, the Jew... the Muslims, [the persecution] that we all carry inside us." He also wrote that "a good Chinese person is closer to me than a bad Spanish person... I am a citizen of the world and a brother to all." He repudiated the notion of "art for art's sake", insisting that art must have a social function and purpose.

Identity is a theme that runs like a seismic fault through these writers, and others besides across the centuries, carrying with it all the cinematic special effects that the simile implies. María Rosa Berocal, approaching Cervantes from the interesting angle of a medievalist who could be said to be reading Cervantes as futurology, sees the *Quijote*, that ur-text of Spanish literature (you have never argued with a Spanish intellectual until you have argued with a Spanish intellectual about the *Quijote*) as a book written in the smoke of the book-burning that followed the "Reconquest" and the destruction of the great Muslim libraries. A poet who looms large in the work of modern writers, not least the Generación de 27, Luis de Góngora (Córdoba, 1561-1627), famed mainly for giving the dictionaries the words *Gongorismo* and in English Gongorism, the term for florid, archly stylized and recondite poetry and prose (it is also known as Culteranismo), has been claimed by a whole raft of twentieth-century Spanish poets as the inspiration for much of their poetry. He is also credited by a recent editor of his *Soledades*, John Beverley (citing Michel Foucault) with subverting the writer's role in society, particularly the way in which the writer addresses the social order and, specifically, the Spanish class system.

In the twentieth century the concern over national and regional identity would lead to another assassination, on the road from Seville to Carmona, on 11 August 1936, of the writer and philosopher Blas Infante Pérez de Vargas (Casares, 1885-1936), also by fascist gunmen. Getting shot at by unappreciative right-wing reviewers seems to be almost part and parcel of the avocation of writer in Andalucía, possibly even *de rigueur*, and might even be seen as a rather drastic form of literary criticism.

Blas Infante was the founder and author of the mission statement of the Andalucismo autonomy movement. He also oversaw the design of the green and white Andaluz flag and wrote the words to the "Himno Andaluz" anthem, set to a traditional farm workers' song, "Santo Dios" (you can hear it at the website of the Fundación Blas Infante at www. fundacionblasinfante.org). It is a rather twee ditty but it is also a historic as well as heroic text, containing the famous cry for "tierra y libertad", "land and freedom", which names the splendid if forgivably sentimental Ken Loach movie of that title. No two versions of the hymn agree on the exact spelling, but this is the official spelling:

"Himno de Andalucía" (1933)

> La bandera Blanca y Verde,
> Vuelve tras siglos de guerra
> A decir paz y esperanza
> Bajo el sol de nuestra Tierra.
>
> ¡Andaluces, levantaos!
> ¡Pedid tierra y libertad!
> Sean por Andalucía Libre
> España y la Humanidad.
>
> Los andaluces queremos,
> Volver a ser lo que fuimos
> Hombres de luz que a los hombres
> Alma de hombres les dimos.
>
> ¡Andaluces, levantaos!
> ¡Pedid tierra y libertad!
> Sean por Andalucía libre,
> España y la Humanidad.
>
> (The white and green flag,
> returns after centuries of war
> to call for peace and hope
> under the sun of our land.
>
> Andaluces, rise up!
> Call for land and freedom!
> It will be for a free Andalucía,
> For Spain and Humanity.

We Andaluces want
To return to who we were
People of the light
That gives us our souls.

Andaluces, rise up!
Call for land and freedom!
It will be for a free Andalucía,
For Spain and Humanity.)

Infante also wrote half a dozen published works, out of a total of perhaps three thousand manuscripts, including *Motamid, ultimo rey de Sevilla* (1920), a poetic reverie of Muslim Seville, and *Cuentos de Animales* (1921), a collection of didactic children's stories, but his key work was the earlier *Ideal Andaluz* (1915), which laid the foundation for the next two decades of his brief life's work. In it, he posits a harmonious balance between regional and national identity, hazarding, for example, that "there is perhaps more spiritual distance between the gravity of the Castellanos and the happy Andaluces than between them and the expansively frank Valencianos." Above all, he writes, "life is beautiful", *hermosa*, in Andalucía, where, despite its unambiguous problems, the people are defined by the simple "joy of living". But, he insisted, all could be united in a modern or modernized Spain.

This is an over-simplification of Infante's thesis, which delves deeper into Andaluz identity and its origins in African, Greek, Roman, German, Muslim and other cultures (Infante is rumoured to have flirted with Islam) than can be sketched here. But he sees these as complementary, rather than oppositional, identities, and moreover as the building materials for a truly great modern, egalitarian society. In 1918 he staged the first conference on Andalucismo, in Ronda, and a year later was a signatory of the *Manifiesto Andalucista de Córdoba 1919*, which called for the establishment of a modern, liberated Andalucía, free from corrupt central government as much as from local *caciquismo*—the rule of the *caciques*, local bosses, installed by the rich absentee landowners. It also called for a free Andalucía to become part of a federal Spain, something it almost but not quite resembles in the newly constituted autonomous regions of modern-day Spain.

Like Gibson's poets, Infante was a utopian, and one who saw a possibility of building a better society in Andalucía. Which is why he and three other men were arrested en route to Carmona by Franco's troops that night in August 1936, on the pretext that they lacked the correct papers, and shot on the side of the road, at kilometre four outside Seville, where a shrine to Infante now stands, one of many that now dot Andalucía.

His birthplace, Casares, is one of the most dramatic of the pueblos blancos, a tangle of white houses and alleyways wrapped around a steep peak inland from the grim fag end of Estepona (the grim fag end, that is, and not Estepona itself, which retains some charm). His casa natal is nowadays a tiny museum to his life and work, in what is a surprisingly well-preserved hill town given its proximity to the Costa del Sol. It overlooks a large wind farm, whose shiny new turbines and sails look like a gigantic white Alexander Calder mobile strung out across the mountains. The turbines, visible from as far away as postcard-pretty Gaucín up in the Serranía de Ronda, also have a delightful, if unintentional, extra cultural aspect. Standing between Gaucín and its expensive views of the Mediterranean, Gibraltar and Africa, the wind turbines really annoy the Brechtian carnival of characters—which includes at least one Guggenheim, retired philanderer Cecil Parkinson and a regatta's-worth of disagreeable rich Brits, a deposed gangster mayor, sundry Costa crime figures looking to gentrify their alibis and any number of Andalucía's richest cocaine dealers, for Gaucín these days is Charlie Central in this cocaine-hungry part of a country with the biggest recreational cocaine habit in the world—who ru[i]n Gaucín, and who may have unintentionally twinned this picturesque motorway lay-by in Theme Park Andalucía with the doomed city of Mahagonny …

While the murders of Lorca and Infante were shocking enough, the most tragic story is that of the poet Antonio Machado (Seville, 1875-1939), who rallied passionately to the Republican cause, somehow managed to evade the unwanted attentions of the Franquista gunmen, but died having fled across the border into France after the fall of Barcelona in circumstances that might be described as a death foretold in one of the poet's own works.

Machado is the oldest of Gibson's four, and a member of the Generación de 98, that group of writers—although the grouping is hotly contested by some critics and historians, including Ortega y Gasset—formed by their reaction to the disastrous events in the Spanish-American war in that year. Its stars included Miguel de Unamuno, Valle-Inclán, the Nobel Prize winner Jacinto Benavente, the Álvarez Quintero brothers of Utrera, and the brothers Antonio and Manuel Machado (1874-1947).

The Machado brothers collaborated on many joint works in their youth, but at the outbreak of the Civil War found themselves both physically and philosophically on either side of the front. Antonio virtually disowned Manuel—during the conflict the latter was alleged to have broadcast his own panegyrics to Franco on Franquista-run radio—and mention of the poet's fascist brother's name is said to have caused the republican of the two great distress.

Machado won fame in his twenties with the publication of his first major collection, *Soledades* (perhaps an allusion to Góngora), in 1903. This and later works marked out his singular melancholic lyricism, particularly his haunting evocation of landscape. This is counterbalanced by his work in prose, often under the most famous of his pseudonyms, Juan de Mairena, a figure in the manner of Flann O'Brien's numerous pseudonyms, who allowed Machado free(ish) rein to say the often unsayable to the consternation or amusement of those in the know. (There is a Juan de Mairena active in the blogosphere today, where he or she shares space with an equally amusing collaborator, the opera-loving Otis B. Driftwood.)

When the Republic was declared, Machado, by now a nationally renowned figure, committed himself to the cause with gusto, writing almost daily in a variety of newspapers and magazines, making public appearances, leading conferences, but always declining to join any party. (It is said that he may have been briefly tricked into identifying with the communists, although authorities doubt this.) Indeed, his *denuncias* against the fascists were so fiery that, given the atmosphere of the time, it is remarkable that he survived the Civil War more or less unscathed. In 1937 he was joined by the likes of W. H. Auden, Malcolm Cowley, André Malraux, Pablo Neruda, Tristan Tzara and others at the Segundo Congreso para la Defensa de la Cultura in Valencia. This was probably a time when the Spanish left and their allies still believed they had victory in their sights.

Machado threw himself into the effort to defend the Republic, even moving from city to city, although this was often largely for his safety and that of his family. At the beginning of 1938 he was living in Valencia but eyeing routes to the Republican stronghold of Barcelona should Valencia fall to the Franquistas. That spring he began work on a "Historia poética de la Guerra", now assumed lost, uncompleted. Despite failing health, Machado was still writing and speaking on behalf of the Republic and even finding time to indulge the opinions of Juan de Mairena in print.

As events began to cascade towards the fall of the Republic, Machado and his family were evacuated from Barcelona on 26 January, the day the city fell. They joined the exodus heading north towards France, their progress hampered by his frail and elderly mother's condition. Finally across the border, having had to abandon most of the cases they were carrying—including a case of Machado's texts—they found shelter at a hotel in the French town of Colliure. Penniless and virtually possessing only the clothes they stood, or lay, in, they were taken in by French sympathizers. The already sick Machado began to worsen and died on 22 February 1939, his mother three days later. He was buried in Colliure, where his grave is now a shrine.

It is quite common for commentators to quote the final verse of his poem "Retrato" ("Portrait") when writing of Machado's death, as indeed Ian Gibson does (it in fact supplies the title for Gibson's biography of Machado, *Ligero de equipaje*, 2006), although I must thank Miguel Ruiz Trigueros for pointing me towards it.

> Y cuando llegue el día del último viaje,
> y esté al partir la nave que nunca ha de tornar,
> me encontraréis a bordo ligero de equipaje,
> casi desnudo, como los hijos de la mar.

It loses its rhyme in my clodhopping translation:

> And when the day of the last voyage arrives,
> and the ship from which no one returns is ready to leave,
> you will find me aboard with very little luggage,
> almost naked, like the children of the sea.

Sentimentality aside, Machado also leaves us a furious poetry with an unintended resonance for twenty-first-century Andalucía. In March 1937 he wrote an impassioned broadside, "Meditación del día" ("Thought for the day"), in which he described the Civil War as a *huracan* sweeping across the whole of Spain:

Pienso en España vendida toda
de río a rio, de monte a monte, de mar a mar.

In a Spain I think has been completely sold,
from river to river, from mountain to mountain, from sea to sea.

He continues, in a prose continuation of the same text, that Spain has been sold—perhaps sold out—from sky to land to subsoil.

He returned to this trope a year later, in another poem, "Alerta (Himno para las juventudes deportivas y militares)" (Alert, hymn for the young athletes and soldiers) in which he describes a Spain where everything—from the coastlines and beaches, to the winds in the mountains, the landscape, the playing fields, the mines, everywhere except the earth where the people will be buried—has been sold to foreign exploiters. Machado was a liberal Christian socialist, who probably did not believe in life after death, but we might indulge a brief fantasy of his ghost stalking the golf courses and urbanizaciones of modern Andalucía, reciting those terrible stanzas. He closes the poem, in the manner of Coleridge's Mariner hectoring the unfortunate wedding guest, "Alerta, alerta, alerta!"

JIMENÉZ, THE TRANSCENDENTALIST OF MOGUER

The story of Juan Ramón Jiménez (Moguer, 1881-1958) is complicated by a number of factors, not least his lifelong ill health and tendency towards profound depression, as well as other psychological problems, including a persecution complex. This last inspired his decision to leave Spain, for good, during the Civil War, exiling himself and his wife Zenobia first in the United States, then Puerto Rico, where he lived until his death. His paranoia probably inspired the fear that he was on "Gil Robles' 'black lists'", which Ian Gibson says drove him into exile unnecessarily, but it seems likely that the poet's fragile health would not have survived the conflict to allow him to produce the body of work that he did.

Like his friend Machado, Jiménez was also strongly influenced by the Symbolists and German Romantics, although filtered through his first major influence, the great Nicaraguan poet, Rubén Dario. Dario, teaching in Madrid, helped Jiménez publish his first collection of poems, *Almas de violeta* (Souls of violet) in 1900—a book he later attempted to erase from his life in embarrassment at its sentimentality. It was a later work, however, that established his name—and in certain circles his notoriety—the prose work *Platero y Yo* (Platero and Me), his lyrical evocation of life and landscape around his birthplace of Moguer, one of the ports from which Columbus sailed, and the littoral of the Huelva province. The titular Platero is a *burro* (donkey), the narrative Yo his philosophically-minded owner, and they have become much loved folk figures across Spain and beyond, figures in children's literature who can also be enjoyed by adults. (Jiménez's fame during his sojourn in the USA was due in part to a translation of *Platero y Yo* into English.) Its folksy tone also earned him hate mail from avant-gardists such as Buñuel and Dalí, who penned a joint letter to him saying that his book was, in their opinion, a piece of shit, but signed off "Yours sincerely" nevertheless.

It was later, richer works such as *Voces de mi copla* (Voices of my song, 1945) and *Animal de fondo* (The deep animal, 1947), where Jiménez was merging modernism with spirituality and sensuality—work compared to the Transcendalists Emerson and Thoreau—that brought him to a wider international audience. In particular, it caught the attention of a group of people who meet in Stockholm every year to talk literature, and who in 1956 awarded Jiménez that year's Nobel Prize for Literature. He is, so far, only one of four Spanish Nobel literature laureates, along with Camilo José Cela, Jacinto Benavente and José Echegaray. Jiménez remains, again so far, the only Andaluz, and his nomination had nothing whatsoever to do with any of the Spanish judges and nominators (if, indeed, there were any that year). The Nobel prizes are discussed in secret, judges and proposers selected by invitation only, but in the autumn of 2007 journalist Lola Galán revealed in *El Pais* that, having had sight of fifty-year-old secret Nobel files, she found that the only person to have nominated and championed Jiménez was the eminent English scholar and wit Maurice Bowra, then warden of Wadham College, Oxford. Presumably the Spanish Nobel officials were rooting for others among the thirty candidates nominated that year (among them, Borges, Camus, Green and Pound).

Nobel committee member Ragnar Granit, a Finnish neurophysiologist who himself won a Nobel a decade later, gave the award speech and spoke of "the sheer visual beauty of his landscape, lovely Andalusia, its birds, its flowers, pomegranates, and oranges. Once inside his world, by leisurely reading and rereading, one gradually awakens to a new *living insight* into it, refreshed by the depth and richness of a rare poetical imagination." (Sensibilities that would appear to have bypassed those perennial shit-stirrers Buñuel and Dalí.)

Jiménez was unable to travel to accept the award, "besieged by sorrow and sickness" in Puerto Rico and probably aware that his gravely ill wife Zenobia was close to death; she would die just three days after the award was made. He followed her two years later, and both are buried in Moguer, where their home and his casa natal are both museums to their lives and work. If in his later years Jiménez seemed to take on a faintly saint-like aura, his aura was dimmed somewhat shortly before Lola Galán's revelations by the discovery of a previously suppressed collection of distinctly unholy erotica, some of it dedicated to individual nuns in convents where the younger Jiménez was sent to convalesce. The poems have yet to appear in public, and are still the subject of debate as to whether they are works of the imagination, or autobiographical porn.

MIGUEL HERNÁNDEZ, POET OF THE TRENCHES

The saddest and grimmest of all these stories of poets harmed by the Civil War is that of Miguel Hernández (1910-42), the youngest of the four and, while not an Andaluz, a neighbour from Orihuela, outside Alicante in Valencia. His neighbours called him the "poet-shepherd" and were astounded when this uneducated twenty-something from a poor country background started appearing on national radio reciting his own poems. He began writing at the encouragement of a village priest—Hernández remained an unorthodox Catholic, despite his communist politics, throughout his brief life—and fell under the spell of Góngora, Dario, Jiménez and particularly Neruda, whom he revered as a "poet of blood and not reason" and who later championed and befriended the younger poet.

A chance meeting with Lorca in Murcia while Hernández was preparing his first book of poems, *Perito en lunas* (Expert in moons, 1933), won him an *entrada* into the literary world, an encounter probably not unconnected to the fact that Hernández was a wide-eyed but heterosexual young beauty. (The remarkable lemur-like eyes were in fact a side effect of hyperthyroidism.) Lorca encouraged him in his writing and politics, but did not effect the career gear-change Hernández might have hoped for from his famous fellow poet. Ian Gibson, in his analysis, believes Hernández was just another of Lorca's "victims", people caught up in Lorca's gravitational field but mistaken in thinking he was their new best friend. Regardless, Hernández revered Lorca throughout his own career, the older poet's murder becoming a familiar, anguished theme in his own work.

After an unfortunate run-in with the Guardia Civil left Hernández battered and bruised, the newspaper *El Socialista* published a manifesto in his defence, led by Lorca and signed by the likes of Neruda, Rafael Alberti, Luis Cernuda and many others. As well as Neruda, he also found a surprising champion in the usually retiring Juan Ramón Jiménez. Unlike many others on the intellectual left—whom he criticized in his poetry— Hernández was rare in seeing action at the front, joining the Quinto Regimiento (fifth regiment) and serving for two years, in which he fought on various fronts around Madrid, at the famous battle of Teruel and elsewhere. He also became friends with Octavio Paz and Alejo Carpentier in Madrid, and worked on several projects alongside Neruda. The "poet-shepherd" was now being lionized as "the poet of the trenches".

More so even than Lorca, Hernández's scabrous attacks in poetry and prose on the Franquistas—including El Caudillo himself, the "mono" (monkey) of Hitler and Mussolini in Spain—were stacking up karma for the young poet, and when it came, it came in spades. At the collapse of the Republic, with many scrambling for the exits, Hernández was treated rather shabbily by his former compañeros, effectively being left to fend for himself (he now had a young family) while others were flown out to safer climes. Inevitably, he was caught trying to cross the Portuguese border, identified and interrogated brutally, during one ten-hour session being beaten so badly he urinated blood. He was charged twice, on different charges, and even briefly bailed, but arrested again on a more serious charge, which should have carried the death sentence. Ian Gibson cites other sources from the time quoting Franco and others as being wary of "another Lorca", so Hernández's sentence was commuted to thirty years and a day. In fact, he might have chosen a firing squad rather than what followed. Others who encountered him when he was let out of solitary confinement and into the general prison population described the thirty-year-old as looking thirty years older. He was bronchitic and, worse, was chain smoking, as if from nerves. The bronchitis turned to tuberculosis and Hernández died in a prison hospital on 28 March 1942, having famously, if apocryphally, scrawled his last poem, "Adiós, hermanos, camaradas y amigos, despedidme del sol y de los trigos" ("Goodbye, brothers, comrades and friends, say goodbye from me to the sun and the wheat fields") on the wall of the prison hospital where he lay.

LUIS CERNUDA'S SONGS OF THE LAND

There is one other poet—among many, not least the aforementioned Rafael Alberti—whom Gibson does not focus on but who, for at least two reasons, deserves our attention: the Seville-born Luis Cernuda (1902-63), who can be spotted in the background at various points throughout Gibson's book, not least in the throng with Auden, Cowley, Malraux, Neruda and Tzara at the Segundo Congreso para la Defensa de la Cultura in Valencia in 1937. It might be that Gibson left him out of his four poets because Cernuda had not so much a love-hate as a hate-hate relationship with his birthplace, which he fled as soon as he could, and that he also fled Spain, for good, shortly after the start of the Civil War (not long after, in fact, the Congreso in Valencia). Certainly, his politics were as stalwart as any of his fellow poets, even after leaving Spain, a decision that Cernuda, also uncomplicatedly homosexual in person and in print, may have thought sensible after the murder of Lorca.

His position in the pantheon of twentieth-century Spanish poetry is assured, even if some of it was written from his office at Mount Holyoke College in Massachusetts, where he taught between 1947 and 1952. Like many of his compatriots in the Generación de 27, he was born, metaphorically at least, under the sign of Góngora, but was also heavily influenced by the Symbolists and Surrealists, notably Baudelaire, Mallarmé, Valéry and Verlaine, and also later, perhaps unusually, Eliot. Like that of his counterparts, his work brims with the symbols of his *país*: sea, mountains, sky, landscape and that highly charged Spanish word *tierra*, which never simply means earth or land. Given that Cernuda moved from the USA to Mexico in 1952, we might also imagine that his experience as an exile took on a poignancy of almost Lowryesque proportions.

He also wrote and taught critical theory, but he will be remembered for marking the high tide of his generation's experiments with symbolism and surrealism, and using these to develop what Barthes would have termed a *langue d'amour* of homosexual love. Perhaps the sweetest example is his 1956 poem "Contigo" (With you, or, perhaps simply, Us):

¿Mi tierra? Mi tierra eres tú.
¿Mi gente? Mi gente eres tú.
¿El destierro y la muerte para mi están adonde no estés tú.
¿Y mi vida? Dime, mi vida, ¿que es, si no eres tú?

(My land? My land is you.
My people? My people is you.
Exile and death, for me, are where you aren't.
And my life? Tell me, my love, what is it, if it isn't you?)

It is possibly interesting to note that people were getting thrown into paddywagons for writing that sort of stuff north of the Mexican border at this time. More interesting, however, is that uniquely for his generation, however much exile may have pained him, Cernuda appears to have lived a happy, fulfilling and, from that poem alone, loved life. He never returned to Spain and died of a heart attack in Mexico City in 1963.

ENTER GOYTISOLO, BRISTLING

It is little surprise, then, given the way it treats them, that Spain should have bred several generations of writers who felt that the most apposite riposte to, if not their country, then to the government that ran it, was to spit in its face. It is true, in the spirit of balanced reporting, that the forces of darkness and chaos also had their poetic voices—not least the respected modernist Manuel Machado—but it seems blatantly obvious that most writers, like most decent people, voted with their feet during these dark years, and later.

If the authorities thought that the post-war clampdown might have finally silenced their literary critics, they were probably taken by surprise by the appearance of Juan Goytisolo. While born a Catalan (in Barcelona in 1931) and for many years now self-exiled in Morocco, Goytisolo has addressed himself to Andalucía and notions of cultural and national identity throughout his career as a novelist and particularly as a journalist. It was he, if we recall, who denounced the squalor of the Guadix caves in the 1960s. More recently, in 1998 he was declared *persona non grata* by the mayor of El Ejido, the town west of Almería that houses the biggest concentration of North African guest workers in Andalucía, estimated between 12,000-30,000, depending on who you listen to. Goytisolo's crime was to criticize the treatment of that guest worker community, perhaps a fifth of the entire population, most of them working in slave conditions in the *mar del plastico,* sea of plastic, that covers the region's vast forced fruit and vegetable industry. (Are North African guest workers part of Andalucía's cultural history? They indeed are. This is something else that modern Spain has to grow up about.) Two years after Goytisolo's criticisms, El Ejido went up in flames as race riots against the guest workers broke out and the (same) mayor refused to intervene. This was Andalucía's own small and shameful *Kristallnacht,* although luckily the comparison ended after a few days of arson, vandalism, beatings and racial terror while the cops stood idly by. (In a curious coincidence, the incident was said to be one of the events that triggered the resignation of someone we are about to meet again in more detail, novelist Manuel Pimentel Siles, then the minister of labour in José María Aznar's centre-right Partido Popular government.) More recently still, in his role as a peripatetic correspondent for *El Pais*, Goytisolo has been indulged the luxury of centrespreads in the paper's weekend editions to denounce white mischief in the Muslim world, in particular Turkey, the Middle East and North Africa.

Goytisolo might best be explained as a cultural phenomenon in relationship to his late friend and mentor, Jean Genet. Like Genet, he is a maverick, renegade and champion of the oppressed. Whenever he opens his mouth on the subject of Spain, the novel, cultural identity or racism, Goytisolo starts breathing fire.

Interviewed by the writer Julio Ortega in 1975, around the time of his major trilogy of novels—*Señas de identidad, Reivindicación del conde don Julian*, and *Juan sin Tierra*—Goytisolo had this to say about what he called, unintentionally or perhaps intertextually echoing Kyd, "the Spanish tragedy":

> The Spanish tragedy—the consciousness of a national tragedy which has been felt so acutely by our best intellectuals since the middle of the eighteenth century—reached its paroxysm during the Civil War of 1936-39, in terms which moved and mobilized the entire liberal and progressive intelligentsia of the world. When I read or meditate on what happened in those years, it is difficult for me to hold back my emotions and not think of what Spain meant to so many writers and intellectuals and to thousands of people of different means and ideologies, races, re-

ligions, and languages, who left their countries, their work, their families, and their friends in order to fight and die for our country. It is evident that the Spanish cause appealed to a universal conscience in the clear-cut dilemma which was then being faced politically, and that explains the passion and the generous sacrifice of so many lives.

But the Spain which emerged around 1960, beginning with its economic miracle, created by the invasion of tourists, can no longer result in impassioned dedication on the part of its intellectuals, and even less on the part of foreign intellectuals. This does not mean that Spanish intellectuals do not continue to have a reasonable and pragmatic interest in the destiny of their country. What I am saying is that their passion, when it exists, will be channeled in other directions.

What that direction might be is perhaps something like Goytisolo's own work, which could be described as the Post-Modern (and Post-Colonial) Expedition to discover ways of melding narrative, poetry, prose, fiction, autobiography and reportage into a radical and dangerous new form of writing. (As you might imagine, Goytisolo's opinion of 99 per cent of contemporary writing would probably best be expressed using a large outdoor space, sizeable quantities of dynamite and earplugs.) Yet no consideration of present-day Spanish literature can be conducted without including this eloquent, angry *nomada*.

The aforementioned Manuel Pimentel (Seville, 1961), whom we first met when exploring Andalucía's obsession with the Atlantis-qua-Tartessos myth, and the also aforementioned Miguel Ruiz Trigueros (Málaga, 1961), might be considered fellow travellers in that expedition.

The real cause of Pimentel's quite abrupt and noisy departure from the Partido Popular in March 2003 was the Aznar government's involvement in the Iraq war, which Pimentel saw as a *'guerra illicita'*, an illegal war. (Aznar is rumoured to have kicked furniture in utter rage at such a respected figure quitting his cabinet.) Pimentel is possibly unique, or at least unusual, in having a great many admirers on the Spanish political centre and left, who respect his principled stand on issues such as Iraq and El Ejido. For the Anglo-Saxon reader and writer, it probably also speaks to subtle differences and ambiguities in political alliances in Spain that perhaps elude the guiri used to the left/right binarism of Britain.

Pimentel had launched his literary career three years before he walked out on Aznar's government, with his first novel, *Peña Laja* (2000), a contemporary mystery involving the human genome project, a mysterious hominid discovery in Andalucía and media and police skullduggery. He followed that with *Monteluz* (2001), a literary conundrum set in a booming coastal town where the mayor and governor are up to no good (it is, of course, in no way, shape or form based on Jesús Gil y Gil's Marbella…). His other novels have also looked at contemporary Spain through the prism of its history. *La Puerta de las Indias* (2003) has a young archeologist discovering a mystery among the *conquistadores'* archives at the Archivo de las Indias in Seville, and pursuing the mystery to the jungles of the Yucatan Peninsula in Mexico. *La Ruta de las Caravanas* (2005) conflates a vanished library, the lost cities of the Sahara and the highly topical subject of the calls for a new caliphate stretching from Baghdad to the beaches of Bolonia.

His most recent novel, *El Librero de la Atlántida* (The librarian of Atlantis, 2006), as well as pushing numerous buttons wired to the Tartessos/Atlantis myth, is also his most outrageous book to date, mixing not only Andaluz history with contemporary Spain—its several narrative strands span the destruction of Atlantis and twenty-first-century Andalucía—but also the threat of both global warming and a new ice age that will cover northern Europe in forgetful snow. It is set in Cádiz, Sanlúcar and elsewhere at a time when archeologists believe they may have found Atlantis in Andalucía (ring any bells?). The novel even comes with an apocryphal press file at the back, as if to give credence to the narrative, but this is perhaps about as trustworthy as Eliot's notes to "The Waste Land". It also includes perhaps the most outlandish and funny narrative conceit in his career: to wit, that the recent orgy of land speculation and uncontrolled property development in Andalucía has been masterminded by rapacious developers who see the rest of Europe flocking to Andalucía to flee the glaciation elsewhere and, of course, buying homes in their uncontrolled property developments.

Curiously, the second novel by Miguel Ruiz Trigueros, *La Noche de Arcilla* (Night of clay, 2006), also turns on a archaeological excavation—this one in London's Docklands, where a Spanish archeologist is unearthing mysterious prehistoric relics down among the tube tunnels—and also spans prehistory, from pre-Christian Iberia to the British occupation of Gibraltar in the eighteenth century and the modern day. Where Pimentel packs the special effects of an upmarket Michael Crichton, Ruiz (keen-eyed readers will recall he features prominently in the acknowledgements to this book, but is Señor Ruiz here, for professional reasons) is a more pensive writer—Spanish reviewers have praised his felicity of language, perhaps not surprising for a writer who tends to cite Marquez and Proust as heroes when he appears in public to discuss his work. In particular, Proust's treatment of time is something that preoccupies Ruiz, along with the notion of *azar*, chance, as an agency affecting the lives of his characters and how they interact, across both space and time. He is capable of scintillating, lyrical passages—again, the tropes of sea, landscape and *tierra* recur—but he is also capable of laconic and even, in his first novel, *Los bailarines de Kronvalda* (2003), almost cruelly comic set pieces. That first novel, a border-hopping picaresque tale of a sly naïf abroad in the world of financial impropriety on the Costa, in the USA, Eastern Europe and elsewhere, featured certain passages—a pyramid selling scam at a casino in Las Vegas, the narrator encountering a disappeared Beat Generation legend panhandling on the streets of San Francisco—that had this reader laughing aloud on public transport. Ruiz is currently threatening a possible future literary caper following another of his heroes, Orson Welles, into a staged disappearance from public life, for reasons as mysterious as the real-life disappearances of the quixotic auteur.

Both Pimentel and Ruiz are writers who seem aware that their historical responsibility stretches back some distance before the Civil War, the Republics, the Carlist Wars, the Reconquest, even Tartessos-qua-Atlantis, to what we might call deep Spanish history, measured in time spans as long as those of the Long Now Foundation. As writers such as Verdaguer found—not to mention the Generación de 27, and their obsession with Góngora—the sedimentary layers of the past provide rich pickings for writers negotiating a problematic present. Younger writers are finding different ways of negotiating both past and future.

Juan Bonilla, Literary Gunslinger

The future undoubtedly belongs to writers such as Joaquin Pérez Azaústre (Córdoba, 1976), who won the 2007 Unicaja de Novela Fernando Quiñones Award (worth €30,000) for his fourth novel, *La suite de Manolete*, a book mixing biography and fiction and based on the short, spectacular life of the Córdobese bullfighting legend of the title (more of whom also anon) and written under the confessed influence of Hemingway. Right now, however, the fastest gun in town, and likely to remain so for some time, is Juan Bonilla, poet, novelist and columnist for *El Mundo*. Bonilla (Jerez, 1966) seems to enjoy his reputation as a literary bad boy, and might at first, in novels such as *Los principes nubios* (translated into the singular English as The Nubian Prince, 2003), seem to be the Spanish Michel Houellebecq, but in fact Bonilla is too much a moralist in the vein of a Ballard or Burroughs to follow Houellebecq down the path of nihilism *à la* Céline. In fact, as you will find if you Google for his website, Bonilla's hero is the late linguistic mischief maker, Georges Perec.

The Nubian Prince, published in translation in the USA in 2007 (Bonilla has yet to be snapped up by a British publisher), is in fact his fourth novel and follows on from eight volumes of short stories, four collections of poetry and five collections of his journalism from *El Mundo* and elsewhere. Its Ballardian narrative pitches its rather wimpy narrator, the perhaps pointedly named Moisés Froissard, a comically disillusioned puppeteer for homeless children in the hellholes of the world's worst slums, into a decadent new career: that of a talent scout for a shadowy international escort agency that fields a small army of the world's most beautiful bodies for hire to rich sybarites around the globe. The titular prince is an impossibly handsome Nubian street fighter, the dream catch of Moisés' career, if he can catch him, and as the pursuit becomes even more desperate Moisés finds himself sinking deeper and deeper into moral degradation.

Bonilla clearly likes pushing the envelope, as one of his short stories, translated into English, further proves. His "Monica's Letters" is the unsettling tale of an adult who finds himself "grooming" an underage girl through a pen pal relationship, even imagining them consuming their relationship physically, until Bonilla delivers the expected, if still surprising, narrative twist at the end. In reality, however—at least from his writing—Bonilla is too much of a nice guy to play a convincing monster, although that does not mean he is not sometimes dangerous to be around.

His latest non-fiction work, the aforementioned *La Costa del Sol en la hora pop* (2007), is deceptive. At first it appears to be a coffee-table book about the Spanish seaside—all pastel colours, pop art graphics, overexposed Kodachrome images of Beat Girls and Hippie Chicks gyrating alongside leathery middle-aged women and hemorrhoidal middle-aged men in Sixties Costa nightclubs—until you naively start reading Bonilla's text. You then find yourself negotiating what might be the Spanish equivalent to Tom Wolfe's *The Electric Kool-Aid Acid Test*, maybe even his *Radical Chic & Mau-Mauing the Flak-Catchers*. We might consider it alongside *Fear and Loathing in Las Vegas*, or Barthes' *Mythologies*, Debord's *Society of the Spectacle* or Baudrillard's *Cool Memories*. We might equally compare it to Burchill and Parsons' *The Boy Looked at Johnny.* (their full-stop there by the way) or Jon Savage's *England's Dreaming*. It might even be compared to what Greil Marcus failed to pull off in his *Lipstick Traces*. It is, in short, nothing less than a hellfire tract of guerrilla cultural criticism that blasts Spain's swinging Sixties to smithereens—but not before it has fingered the guilty parties, among them the fugitive Nazi war criminals contentedly pottering about the Costa's golf links in their electric golf buggies…

The beauty of Bonilla's deeply subversive book is that it uses what seems to be a terminally uncool period of recent Spanish history as a focus to highlight what writers such as Machado and Goytisolo had also been writing about; the *España vendida* of Machado's poem and Goytisolo's "Spanish tragedy". Bonilla names the guilty men, and not just the elderly Nazis who turn their urbanización homes into mini indoor Nurembergs, nor the jailbird criminals like Jesús Gil y Gil, but the great promoters of swingeing Marbella such as the wastrel rich kids Ricardo Soriano and Alfredo Hohenlohe who, as Bonilla witheringly points out, may have created a playground for their jet-set pals, but rather thoughtlessly left *the Spanish* out of their architectural plans.

Bonilla also identifies a lively underground—not least in the back-street queer bars of the Sixties, which may have seen their own miniature versions of the Stonewall riots—erected in resistance to this wholesale takeover by the filthy rich. Nor does the innocent passerby get off lightly, either: in a book where the word *joder*, 'fuck' (as in, "How did things get so fucked up?"), begins to appear with increasing frequency as the pages pass, Bonilla repeatedly points out that many of the people responsible for "fucking up" the Costa were corrupt politicians voted in by democratic majorities.

In passing, he also throws light on a whole subculture of younger writers, critics, historians, musicians, tribal anthropologists and urban archaeologists—not unlike Borges' secret society of conceptual geographers in "Tlön"—who are, in Mike Davis' phrase, "excavating the future", and not in downtown LA but on the playas and in the nightclubs of Torremolinos and Marbella. One of the best places to view this urban archaeology is at the website of torremolinoschic.com, which has been lovingly constructed as a cyber-shrine to everything that came in dayglo, pop art shapes or swirly psychedelic typography from a Costa del Sol that might have been fashioned as the backdrop to a B-52's song.

Bonilla writes like a dream—well, in fact he writes like a hipster semiotician with his pants on fire—and offers us the pleasure of concluding this chapter by observing that, as long as Andalucía, and Spain, has writers such as Bonilla—and Pimentel, and Ruiz—at large, then the dreams of Lorca, Jiménez, Machado, Cernuda, Goytisolo and others still live on.

Dangerous summer: the parade of the enganches, horse-drawn carriages, during Ronda's annual September Goyesca bullfighting festival

Chapter Eighteen

DEATH IN THE AFTERNOON: HEMINGWAY, ORDOÑEZ AND THE CORRIDA

"Bullfighting is the only art in which the artist is in danger of death and in which the degree of brilliance in the performance is left to the fighter's honour."

Ernest Hemingway, *Death in the Afternoon* (1932)

Whatever you may think of either the man or the art, Ernest Miller Hemingway (1899-1961) offers probably the best summation of the spirit of the *corrida* in that one, typically crisp, sentence. Hemingway's sentences are commonly praised by his admirers for containing far more than what appears on the page, and this is true of that sentence. He touches on the fact that bullfighting is considered an art and not a mere sport, which is why it is written about on the arts pages of Spanish newspapers and not in the back pages along with the *futbolistas*. The subtext, or maybe the supratext, to the corrida is death, both the bull's and possibly the bullfighter's too. It is about performance, and brilliance in performance, which can be as ritualized as kabuki or Eastern dance forms such as kathak and gamelan. "Honour" is Hemingway's reading of the complex cultural codes that attend the psychology of the corrida, both for the matador and his assistants and for the spectators in the crowd. While *Death in the Afternoon* is Hemingway's most famous book about bullfighting, the key text is in fact another book entirely, his less known *The Dangerous Summer* (1960), which we will get to in a while. The corrida deserves some hopefully dispassionate history first.

The corrida provokes intense emotions among both its aficionados and its detractors. The former will fly the length and breadth of Spain to follow their heroes from fight to fight, just as in earlier times they would have taken less convenient transport across country to follow those heroes.

In many ways, the culture that surrounds the bullfight—history, litera-ture, legend, its secondary representations in art and music, the panoply of capes and swords and the *traje de luz*, suit of lights—resembles a small, self-contained universe. While less than thirty per cent of the population is said to support bullfighting, it looms large in the national psyche, to the extent that most Spanish people of a certain age will probably remember where they were the night Manolete (Córdoba, 1917-47) died after being gored at Linares, much as many North Americans will remember where they were when JFK was shot.

Others, particularly foreigners, find the spectacle simply revolting. The British in particular (and even more particularly, Britons living in Spain) become quite heated in their opposition to the corrida. It could be argued that, with two million cows dead from the last BSE alert in Britain, and the continued abuse of farm animals to feed a daily diet of cheap meat (a diet even the carnivorous Spanish find baffling), often forcing herbi-vores to eat the infected remains of other species, Britons do not have much of a case when it comes to arguing animal rights. But like the expa-triate campaigns to improve the conditions of cats, dogs and donkeys in Spain—a decent-hearted concern, but hard to measure against the cam-paigners' lack of interest in, say, child poverty—the dispassionate observer is asking for trouble interposing themselves between the British and their anthropomorphism, particularly when the anthropomorphized object is furry and has big sad eyes.

BULL SYMBOLISM, FROM PERSIA TO PAMPLONA

The bullfight has its origins in Spain's prehistory, and as we saw at Acinipo and Itálica, probably begins in the human-animal contests of Rome, pos-sibly before. Spain's *tauromachia*, bullfighting culture, has its counterparts in Portugal and France, and the Spanish themselves transported the "art" to the Americas in the fifteenth century. The symbolism of the bull first appears with the legend of the sun god Mithras, who slaughtered the bull whose blood would bring forth fecundity on the earth and protect hu-manity from harm, a mythology that has been tracked back to Persia and India two thousand years BCE. It also overlaps with Judaic and Christian beliefs in the sacred bull and the golden calf. This symbolism recurs in the ox frequently present in Christian nativity scenes and cribs, and in the elaborate Spanish *belén* (crib) displays at Christmas. A confusion of religious legends has conflated St. Saturninus, martyred in the third century BCE by being tied to a bull and dragged to his death, and St. Fermin or Cernin of Amiens, born the son of a Roman general in the Spanish city where he is now patron saint, Pamplona. His festival, the San Fermín, probably originated in a cattle market in the city in the fourteenth century, linked to the summer celebrations around the feast of St. John the Baptist in June, and the symbolic running of the bulls became an annual festival in early July during the sixteenth century. The bulls were, and still are, run through the streets of the casco antiguo of Pamplona to the city's plaza de toros, where they are corralled for the contests of the afternoon's corrida, an event that put Pamplona on the world map with the 1926 publication of Hemingway's *Fiesta* (the English title), better known as *The Sun Also Rises*. Here, however, even the disinterested observer has to step back and confess misgivings about the odds stacked against half a ton of angry herbivore facing as many as a dozen men armed with sharp prods, lances, swords and, if the kill is messy, a bolt gun powerful enough to turn its brain to mush.

Despite what its supporters say—and they include the Scots novelist A. L. Kennedy, whose curious *On Bullfighting* (1999), starts with her accepting the book commission as a way of writing herself out of the depression that, as it opens, has her on her Glasgow window ledge, urging herself to jump to her death—the corrida's days are numbered. As its predominantly older aficionados die out, fewer younger people are attending the spectacle. It is being slowly but surely nudged off television, particularly during primetime when children might be watching, and some cities (Barcelona among them, at least in theory) and towns have banned bullfighting altogether. But reports of its demise are premature, particularly if you consider the annual September Goyesca bullfight in Ronda, probably the most flamboyant in the whole of Spain, where royalty, politicians and Hollywood A-list names are helicoptered in for an afternoon's overdressed carnage where tickets can change hands for over two thousand euros a piece on the black market. (In 2007 both Robert de Niro and George Clooney were rumoured to be schmoozing with the matadors in the VIP zone of Ronda's plaza de toros. Sensible folk tend to flee the town until after the feria.)

The Goyesca, so called because participants and some attendees affect the dress of Goya's sketches and watercolours of Rondeño tauromachia scenes from days of yore, might invite the three word description that Hunter S. Thompson applied to the Kentucky Derby: "corrupt and depraved". It is, in short, a carefully stage-directed entertainment of the sort that might have been scripted by the Walt Disney Corporation. With so much tourism industry money riding on it, the Goyesca could never be allowed to proceed otherwise.

While much blood is spilt on to the sand, it is a curiously bloodless event. The stages of the corrida, signalled by the president and his hanky from his box in the *sombra* (shade) section of the bullring, proceed by a series of pre-ordained steps, each announced by a fanfare from an out-of-tune amateur brass band. The *picaderos* or lance-holders and *bandilleros*, the guys with those pretty beribboned spikes, will, if things have gone well, have lanced the bull's neck muscles so that it cannot support the weight of its own head, leaving it vulnerable to the matador's sword in the *estocada*, the final blow (the ultimate being the *estocada recibido*, "received blow", in which the matador stands still as the charging bull impales itself on his sword, severing its spinal cord, although normally the end is far messier). The "brilliance" of the artist's performance—the feints and flourishes with the *muleta*, the red or pink cape (the bull is in fact colour blind; the angry herbivore is after anything in its blood-soaked vision that moves, which usually means the padded, blindfolded and terrified horses), the jokey conversations with the stunned animal, the fighters leaning an elbow on its head, the others who clown around miming telephoning it to explain what is happening—is all that stands between it, us and either the estocada recibido or the bolt gun. It is, in essence, showbusiness, and even eighty years ago Hemingway himself was already accusing the corrida of being corrupt and depraved and in the service of the entertainment industry, in the pages of *The Dangerous Summer*. Among his criticisms were the controversial shaving of bulls' horns, which weakens the animal and gives advantage to the matador, crude nobbling of the animal by dropping heavy objects on to its spine, and doping (the animal, for a change) with tranquilizers. Hemingway's criticisms of the shadier practices in and out of the plaza de toros earned him death threats when they were mistaken as criticism of the aforementioned Manolete, who had and in some circles still has a powerful iconic aura to rival even Hemingway's.

In 1953, when, as he opens, none of his friends was in jail anymore and he felt it safe to return to Spain, Hemingway took his wife Mary to

Pamplona (which he had "written once and for keeps" in *The Sun Also Rises*) and then on down south to Andalucía, where he connected with the great twentieth-century Rondeño matador, Antonio Ordóñez, whose father Cayetano, also a matador, Hemingway portrayed in *The Sun Also Rises*. Ordóñez and his brother-in-law, Luis Miguel Dominguín, were about to set off on a tour around Spain, France and Portugal where each night the two fought *mano a mano*, not literally hand-to-hand, but in the same ring, each man with a different set of bulls in a season that would become famous in bullfighting history. Hemingway and Ordóñez became fast friends, the bullfighter calling the writer "Papa Ernesto". Photographs of them together in Ronda, like the photographs of the bullfighter with his other pal, Orson Welles, have become so iconic they are the Spanish equivalent of Alberto Korda's famous photograph of Che Guevara.

Hemingway tagged along for the ride with Ordóñez and Dominguín, afterwards writing what is very probably the best book ever written about bullfighting. To aficionados it is the most authentic record of the life of a bullfighter as lived outside the bullring, an insider's view of the private world the aficionado never sees. Detractors might find that it confirms their worst suspicions about these petulant little *princesas* with their fawning retinues, who behave like spoilt rock stars and their flunkies on the road.

Hemingway, like bullfighting, also tends to divide observers, sometimes quite violently. Even his great champion in the dog days around the publication of *Across the River and into the Trees* (1950), James Michener, who hailed him as "the man who had set free the English sentence," admitted that he could be nasty, spiteful, childish and a boor. His health, dependency and emotional problems have been discussed at such length elsewhere as to render any further discussion here redundant. We might, however, find space and reason to reconsider Hemingway the writer, in the light of his writing in Spain and Europe.

Hemingway was, by his own many acts of *bricolage* as much as the acclaim of the critics, the first rock star of twentieth-century North American literature. As a journalist, Hemingway arrived at his assignments (wars, revolutions, bullfights, fishing trips) wrapped in and indeed preceded by his own aura, an aura which we might consider bearing in mind a phrase minted by the cultural critic Richard Dyer, "hysterical masculinity". Dyer invented the term (in his book, *Only Entertainment*, 1992) when decoding a publicity shot of a pipe-smokin' Humphrey Bogart surrounded by the accoutrements of huntin', fishin', shootin' and other manly pursuits. The studio had obviously ransacked the sports department of a nearby department store to dress this PR shot, clearly unaware that the pipe was connected to the smoking-related lung cancer that would eventually kill Bogart. Just why the studio wanted to beef up the macho persona of the star of *The Big Sleep* and *The African Queen* remains a mystery. Hemingway, however, seemed to be fighting off his own demons with the hard-drinkin', huntin', fishin', shootin' blowhard persona, and his hysterical masculinity—a persona fatally betrayed by that ultimate macho wimp-out, his suicide in 1961—has rubbed off on latter-day wannabe Mini-Hemingways such as Sebastian Junger and the likes of Jason Webster.

Some find his slapped-thigh, lantern-jawed straight talk invigorating, while others just find it wearying. Hemingway was no match for his Paris sparring partner Gertrude Stein in the "and and and" stream of consciousness stakes, and his contemporary John Dos Passos' techniques in *Manhattan Transfer* and *USA* outdo anything Hemingway attempted with stylistics. There is no doubting his courage while covering the Spanish Civil War and other assignments, although his work lacks the holy moral rage of Upton Sinclair's *The Jungle* (1906), or even the (perhaps comfortable) compassion of a John Steinbeck. It might also be time to consider the possibility that his sometime wife—although she spent the rest of her life metaphorically snipping "Papa" out of her wedding photos—Martha Gellhorn (1908-98) was the better journalist of the two. Her essay "Justice at Night" bests even Orwell's "A Hanging", all the more so because a woman correspondent got to the story before any men did. Moreover, Gellhorn's outstanding record in her sixty years as a troublemaking journalist was achieved without the posturing and bluster of the ex-husband whom she briskly disappeared in her book *Travels with Myself and Another* (1978).

We might also take a look Hemingway's bosom buddy Antonio Ordóñez (Ronda, 1932-98) through the prism of Richard Dyer's notion of "hysterical masculinity", although in truth it applies to virtually every matador, up to and including the iconic Manolete, recently portrayed with uncanny likeness by Adrien Brody in Menno Meyjes' biopic, *Manolete*. Matadores, their cronies and their aficionados live in a little world of their own—much in the way superstar footballers do—where the visitor has to sign on to their cockeyed version of reality or risk expulsion from their magic kingdom.

It would not take Roland Barthes to point out that the subject in question, the *punctum* of any photograph of a matador, is male sexuality, specifically male sexuality under threat. If the corrida were a sport and not an art form, the matadors would wear protective clothing—not least a cricketer's box, codpiece, or padding—rather than impossibly tight clothing that is the sartorial equivalent of painting a bullseye, no pun intended, around the matador's groin. It begins with the faintly religious ritual of dressing the matador; the penis is strapped to the preferred leg, "for protection", the histories tell us—and as Hemingway reported, almost naively given the way it would be re-read later, even the matador's underwear has to be perfectly clean, as any dirty cloth entering a wound if the matador is gored might infect the wound. If they have not already, those North American academics from the Queer Theory faculty would make excellent mileage out of the valences between goring and penetration here, and more besides.

Miguel Ruiz Trigueros has written, rather gingerly, in an article for the Andaluz cultural and political magazine *El candil de Diogenes* ("Diogenes' lamp", from the legend that the philosopher carried a lighted lamp through ancient Athens in daytime to help him in his search for "one honest man"), that the corrida is based on binary gender oppositions, and oppositions that are only revealed and perhaps even reversed at the moment of the engagement between man and bull. He writes that, "Images of bullfighting always carry an aura that is essentially sexual. The black, macho bull with its horns is naturally masculine; the matador counterposes a world that is not entirely masculine." Thus, it would seem, the matador is in effect feminized by the act of confronting the far more powerful bull.

It is perhaps impossible for an outsider to comprehend the particular part of the Spanish psyche that can engage in this psychosexual gameplay, just as it is possible that most Spanish aficionados of the corrida go to the bullfight to watch a group of men execute clever balletic manoeuvres against a dumb herbivore that is almost certainly doomed before it finds itself released and baffled into the bullring.

The masculine culture of the corrida also needs addressing, as women make up a sizable part of the audience, which counterbalances the macho sheen of the bullfight, although rarely the personnel. The most notable exception is Cristina Sánchez (Madrid, 1972), who won fights, awards and more ears than you could shake a stick at (if you don't know what the ears are about, you are better off not knowing) in plazas de toros in Spain, Mexico and Ecuador. Her career was studied in detail, along with the culture around the bullfight, in Sarah Pink's book, *Women and Bullfighting: Gender, Sex and the Consumption of Tradition* (1997), which also looked at the roles of women elsewhere around the plaza de toros: the mothers, sisters and girlfriends (and in that particular hierarchy) in the barerra de sombra, the front-row VIP seats, and in the audience and outside. Despite her international successes, and all those problematic ears, Sánchez retired after less than six years in the limelight, angry at the hostility of some men in the culture who could not and would not tolerate a woman in their space, and some who simply refused to fight in the same plaza de toros as a woman.

We can content ourselves with the observation that the corrida has become so far removed from its origins, and so bound up with the world of showbiz, that it is indeed an impossibly over-stylized production number in the manner of kabuki or gamelan dance. If the statistics that only thirty per cent of the Spanish population supports the corrida are true, this adds weight to the anti-bullfighting lobby's claim that the other seventy per cent are actually tourists and foreigners observing (Erwin Schrödinger and his cat again) and in so doing keeping alive something that is in fact in the process of vanishing.

As for Hemingway himself, some observers believe that his experience on the road with Ordóñez and Dominguín was one of the main contributory factors in his suicide in 1961. Psychiatrist Christopher D. Martin, in an article for the journal *Psychiatry: Interpersonal and Biological Processes*, wrote a "Psychological Autopsy of a Suicide" about Hemingway in 2006 that listed, among other ailments:

> bipolar disorder, alcohol dependence, traumatic brain injury, and probable borderline and narcissistic personality traits. Late in life, Hemingway also developed symptoms of psychosis likely related to his underlying affective illness and superimposed alcoholism and traumatic brain injury. Hemingway utilized a variety of defense mechanisms, including self–medication with alcohol, a lifestyle of aggressive, risk–

taking sportsmanship, and writing, in order to cope with the suffering caused by the complex comorbidity of his interrelated psychiatric disorders. Ultimately, Hemingway's defense mechanisms failed, overwhelmed by the burden of his complex comorbid illness, resulting in his suicide.

Which is what the guys in the white coats think of the author of *The Sun Also Rises*.

José Luis Castillo-Puche, in his 1974 book *Hemingway in Spain: A Personal Reminiscence of Hemingway's Years in Spain by his Friend*, believed that Hemingway had been "betrayed" by both the promoters and even the bullfighters, particularly Ordóñez, in the events described in *The Dangerous Summer*, and that this was a, if not the, contributing factor in his suicide a year later.

Los Ingléses en la Plaza de Toros

Perhaps the most curious sidebar to the corrida in Andalucía is the number of foreigners who attempt to enter this almost exclusively Spanish, male, enclave. The first recorded was probably Ernest C. Boss, a former British soldier who studied *el toreo* in Madrid and made a name for himself fighting in Mexico. Ernest's one grazing pass with history was a note in the *City of Mexico Herald* that he had arrived there in 1901.

No fewer than three Englishmen made a name for themselves in Andalucía's bullfighting culture in the past century. Frank Evans, "El Inglés", only retired in 2005, having started fighting in 1966 when he was just 17. Evans was guided by an even earlier English bullfighter, Vincent Hancock, whose 1959 autobiography, *Torero*, originally inspired Evans to track down Hancock and seek his advice. A North American matador, John Fulton, based in Seville until his death in 1998, fought his last corrida as recently as 1994.

Most noteworthy, however, is the career of Enrique Cañadas, also known as "El Inglés", but plain Henry Higgins on his birth certificate. Higgins (1944-78) originally came to Spain to study art and flamenco dance, quickly developed a passion for the corrida and was even briefly managed by Beatles manager Brian Epstein, until Epstein's death in 1967. He also won the blessing of the spiky intellectual Kenneth Tynan, who in 1955 had published a respected book on the subject, *Bull Fever*, and contributed a laudatory preface to Higgins' own co-written life story, *To Be a Matador* (1972). Higgins seems to have been an intellectual matador and one with a social conscience—the autobiographical sections of his book display a sharp awareness of social difference in Andalucía, and at one point his co-writer James Myers proposes the corrida as a symbol of social tension between the haves (the expensive sombra seats) and have-nots (the cheaper sol seats), with the latter dreaming of revolutionary vengeance against the former.

Possibly the most interesting revelation in a book dedicated to perhaps too much of the workaday concerns of the bullring is the quite candid culture of corruption that Higgins had to tolerate simply to be considered for fights, not least of all the envelopes of cash handed to bullfighting journalists after the corrida to ensure these notorious crooks would say something nice in print. The most profound, and for Higgins himself profoundly depressing, revelation in the book is this: "[A]n English novillero, no matter how well he fought, was one of the lowest forms on bullfighting's tree of life."

THE ANTI-CORRIDA MOVEMENT

The aficionado lobby and the dispassionate tendency have had a fairly easy ride here this far, so we should consider the growing din from the opposition. The Barcelona-based Asociación Defensa Derechos Animales has been working to defend the rights of all animals, from squirrels to big cats, since 1975. In 1975 it revealed a study made by the *ajuntament* of Barcelona that estimated as many as 76 per cent of the population are against bullfighting. Pollsters Gallup estimate that as many as 81 per cent of Catalans oppose it, and 72 per cent of the general population across Spain. Google for the League Against Cruel Sports and the information on their website may well put a crimp in your day if you just shelled out two thousand euros on a seat at the Goyesca. The World Society for the Protection of Animals also supports the Asociación in Barcelona, and reports that in 2007 the city of Baños de Agua Santa in Ecuador declared itself a corrida-free zone. In the USA, where the corrida is popular in Sun Belt regions, it is against the law to harm, let alone kill, the bull, which must be defeated symbolically by the matador swiping a rose fixed on its neck.

The Animal Liberation Front, as you might imagine, has its own trenchant opinions, although not without either style or humour. It claims that at least thirty-two Spanish cities have now banned the corrida. In 2000 the Ronda tourism office was actually refusing to give the date of that year's Goyesca over the telephone to overseas callers, fearing interventions by the likes of the ALF. The Front has an amusing section on its website which salutes famous personalities who have, perhaps more in spirit than in declaration, supported its actions, and which airily embraces Plato, Socrates, Milton, Shelley, Tolstoy, Voltaire, Mark Twain, Franz Kafka, H. G. Wells and George Bernard Shaw. It has also corralled musicians ranging from Paul McCartney to Prince, via the Smiths and Robert Wyatt. Among the Hollywood crowd, it has co-opted, or perhaps kidnapped, Tobey McGuire, Charlize Theron, Alicia Silverstone, Darryl Hannah, Jamie Lee Curtis, Kim Basinger and even Mickey Rooney for its campaigns. It is early days yet, but the anti-corrida movement seems to be on a roll.

Flamenco nuevo: José Merce, one of the greatest contemporary flamenco stars, channelling his *duende*

Chapter Nineteen

THE SHRIMP FROM THE ISLAND: BY CAB FROM ZIRYAB'S GARDEN TO THE MOSH PITS OF GRANADA

If we are to identify the key musical figure in the history of Andaluz music, beyond our fabric queen friend Ziryab, that is, it can only be El Camarón de la Isla, "the shrimp from the island". He was born José Monje Cruz in 1950, but an uncle nicknamed him the "shrimp" because of his unusual blonde hair, and the rest of the nickname came from his birthplace, San Fernando, the satellite-cum-suburb that was once one of the islands that formed the archipelago around Cádiz.

Alas, we identify Camarón as an icon for a series of largely unfortunate reasons, quite apart from his voice, and reasons that elevate him to that pantheon of sad musical casualties alongside Charlie Parker, Billie Holiday, Chet Baker, Janis Joplin, Jim Morrison, Jimi Hendrix, and many more besides. His death, aged 41, in 1992 from lung cancer was probably hastened by a history of serious alcohol, cocaine and heroin use, which at one point rendered him so out of control that he caused the deaths of two other drivers in a car crash while driving under the influence. Some aficionados argue that the lifestyle was part of the art, and certainly part of the myth, but from performances near the end of his life, the voice, which sounded as pure as water when he was younger, was showing signs of damage. None of this has harmed sales of his records, nor really dented the myth, and his standing as the legendary voice of gypsy flamenco remains inviolate.

The greatest living flamenco artist today is the Granadino singer and composer Enrique Morente (Albayzin, 1942), whom we came across briefly when exploring Jason Webster's *Duende* a few chapters back. His work is sniffed at by the purists who guard the myth of Camarón (there was no such enmity between the two men themselves; in fact, they worked together), and he is probably outsold by the works of a newer flamenco star, José Merce, but more than anyone else Morente has kept flamenco alive and engaged, connected both to its tradition and its future, not least in his *Misa Flamenca* mass (1991), which used texts from medieval writers such as Lope de Vega and Fray Luis de Léon, and more contemporary works such as the aforementioned *Omega* (1996). This recording is a landmark in Spanish music of the past quarter century, recorded with fellow Granadinos Lagartija Nick, and more conventional collaborators such as the guitarists Tomatito, José Manuel Cañizares, Vicente Amigo and Paquete, joined by singers El Negri and Morente's own daughter Estrella, herself, no pun intended, a star in her own right.

Omega was remarkable for its daring but clever mix of fluid, passionate contemporary flamenco and lo-fi post-punk guitar noise from Lagartija Nick, who do indeed take their name from the 1983 single by the British new wave band, Bauhaus. Their style might be triangulated somewhere between vintage Sonic Youth, the New York maximalist composer Glenn Branca, and classic Can (when they play *Omega* behind Morente live, Lagartija Nick almost *are* early Can). It was also Morente's canny choice to mix texts by Lorca and the Canadian folk legend, Leonard Cohen, including famous Cohen tracks such as "First We Take Manhattan" and "Hallelujah". Cohen, as Morente must have known, was smitten as a poet himself by Lorca when quite young, and even named one of his daughters Lorca. When he discovered Morente's recording, Cohen told a Los Angeles radio interviewer: "What I like about Morente's work is that he takes my songs right into his own terrain. He doesn't feel obliged to make any references to my version or they are very subtle. The fact that he saw there was a flamenco reality to the work is what touches me most deeply. So he brings it right into the centre his own tradition and manifests it as an artifact of his own culture. That's what I love about it, that it is his."

And Cohen's first reaction to hearing *Omega* is also worth recording: "I sent him two dozen roses."

Omega is not the only recording of Lorca's work among Morente's twenty or so recordings since his 1967 debut, *Cante Flamenco*. In 1999 he recorded one of his finest works to date, *Lorca-Morente*, also with the help of Cañizares, Paquete, the admired jazz bassist Carles Benavent and Morente's childhood friend Pepe Habichuela, responsible for the outrageous *Yerbagüena*, which the guitarist, one of the famed Habichuela flamenco dynasty, recorded in Bangalore and elsewhere with the Bollywood Strings orchestra. *Lorca-Morente* is Morente at his most mature, straddling flamenco, jazz and other strands, showcasing his voice in a way that impels this critic to compare him to the sublime Brazilian singer, Milton Nascimento.

It seems as though Morente has worked with everyone worth working with in Andalucía, from the jazz guitarist Gerardo Nuñez (Jerez, 1961) to Málagueño chill/trip-hop darlings Chambao (more on both later), and via the young dancer Israel Galván, for whom he composed a soundtrack to accompany Galván's contemporary dance interpretation of Kafka's *Metamorphosis*. He also appeared in Carlos Saura's film about the Barcelona-born composer Isaac Albéniz, and is the subject of a recent Saura documentary about his own work. Morente has played sold out concerts from Madrid to Paris to New York and beyond, and if it is a cliché to say that he is an ambassador for Andalucía and flamenco, it is also important to say that if this music is to have a future beyond nostalgia and cliché, its future is in the hands of musicians such as Enrique Morente.

Morente is also aware of the cultural pressures on flamenco musicians to toe the traditionalist, or purist, line, which he dismisses, telling one interviewer: "Art must not have frontiers… flamenco is a kind of music that is alive, very up to date and it can perfectly mingle with other instruments from all over the world."

He also dispenses with some of the worst clichés about flamenco and its origins: "They often think that you need to have pudgy fingers from harvesting potatoes in order to play the guitar with feeling. And I say 'Look, both jobs are honest, but I can assure you that a person with fine and fussy fingers won't be able to pick potatoes properly; but I also assure you that a person with pudgy fingers from picking potatoes won't be able to play the guitar properly…'"

Having acknowledged these two titanic figures of Andaluz musical culture, we might usefully join the aforementioned Pepe Habichuela on a journey back in time to its origins. Habichuela (Granada, 1944) conceived his *Yerbagüena* as an only partly tongue-in-cheek exploration of the theory that flamenco might be traced back to prehistoric India. There are two levels to this joke, the first being that Bollywood soundtracks, a soupier, orchestral version of the far livelier, and funkier, bhangra, are an invention of recent decades, and no earlier. The second is that both Bollywood soundtracks and bhangra have about as much to do with ancient Asian or Iberian folk music as The Monkees had to do with Mozart. But, brilliantly, Habichuela's camp mutation actually works, due probably to the quite serious musicological similarities between Indian and flamenco rhythmic metres, not least the fact that both involve a lot of complicated mathematics, and both are "counted" rhythms that come in algebraic packets. He even suggests analogues between flamenco and Indian musical forms—notably, the Gaditano tanguillo, "little tango", and the Indian counted rhythms of karnataka music (check Nitin Sawney's CD, *Beyond Skin*, for an Anglo-Asian take on these ravishing rhythmic structures)—as well as Indian forms that either mirror or fit in with flamenco forms such as the buleria (a faster version of the already lively alegria ["happy"] form), soleá (a tricky 3/8 rhythm) and seguiriya (a sixteenth-century form in triple time that is probably best heard in the "Près des ramparts de Seville" in Bizet's *Carmen*). The abiding impression from this immensely enjoyable recording, however, is that, history lesson aside, Habichuela saw the opportunity to have a great deal of fun leaping between genres, took it and ran with it.

It is, as we saw on that unlikely cab ride from Ziryab's garden in Córdoba to University Studios in Chicago, a long way from the prehistoric East to modern Andalucía, but the music began its journey there from Mesopotamia in at least the fifth century BCE, which is where archaeologists have found representations of early precursors to the oud/lute that would one day beget the guitar. Its history is only now being slowly pieced together by musicians and scholars such as classical guitarist Julia Banzi, her partner, the oud-player and multi-instrumentalist Tarik Banzi, and their multinational ensemble, al-Andalus.

Julia and Tarik Banzi nowadays shuttle between homes in Morocco and Oregon. In the former she has studied the history of women's Andalucían music ensembles, from the ninth century to the modern day, particularly the thriving tradition of these all-women ensembles in Tetuan in Morocco, and elsewhere. She has also studied shifting changes in the forms of flamenco music in Andalucía. As the core of their flexible ensemble, al-Andalus, they have toured the US, Europe and elsewhere with their repertoire, as well as collaborating with figures such as Paco de Lucia, the guitarist credited with inventing *flamenco nuevo,* new flamenco, in the 1960s, Yehudi Menuhin, Mike Shrieve of Santana,

Enrique Morente, jazz musicians such as Carles Benavent and saxophonist Jorge Pardo, and even helped to found local legends, the now disbanded Radio Tarifa, whose spirit lives on in the newly-formed Son de la Frontera.

Their music—they have released five CDs to date, and you can hear samples at their website www.andalus.com—spans medieval *cantigas*, which were devotional monophonic songs celebrating the Marian cult, *ladino* (Jewish-Spanish) forms, *nouba* suites in the manner of Ziryab and other forms of court music from the Muslim era and later styles, including what they have dubbed "Contemporary Andalusian" music, embracing flamenco and jazz, and the living folk music of North Africa (in that, the more modern al-Andalus sounds not unlike the North American pastoral jazz group, Oregon). It is probably the closest the modern listener can expect to get to hearing the music as it might have been played by Ziryab and his contemporaries.

One form of music that does not quite overlap with the Banzis' pan-continental researches and recordings, however, is Moroccan *gnaou* or *gnaoua* music, which, with its distinctive hand-percussion instruments, might have been the precursor of the Spanish castanet and thus a part of the flamenco armoury. If so, and this is likely, it is part of the hidden history of flamenco, too long held hostage by the theory that it was invented in the *tertulias* (poetry circles) of nineteenth-century Seville, when in fact this vibrant music is part of the pulse of musical expressions that have been reverberating around the Mediterranean basin for millennia.

While the Christian cantiga tradition carried traces of Muslim music, most indigenous music was torched in the wake of the "Reconquest". Devotional music came under the licence of Rome, and the Spanish court often looked abroad for its music, which is where some Spanish and Andaluz composers, such as Francisco Guerrero (Seville, 1528-99), migrated to develop their careers in more sympathetic climes. Spain's curious and enduring lack of home-grown classical talent, in tandem with its centuries-long resistance to its one great indigenous innovation, flamenco, continued into the seventeenth and eighteenth centuries, when guiris such as Scarlatti and Boccherini were appointed composers to the Spanish court. This trend was only really halted with the birth and ascendance of Manuel de Falla y Matheu (Cádiz, 1876-1946), who won Andalucía and Spain international note with his *Noches en los jardines de España* and the opera *El sombrero de tres picos*, better known as *The Three-Cornered Hat*, produced by Diaghilev and designed by Picasso.

De Falla was part of a generation that, along with Joaquín Rodrigo (Valencia, 1901-99), gave Spain a global identity in modern classical music. Rodrigo, perhaps one of Richard Ford's "sly vindictive" Valencianos, has a droll anecdote attached to his most famous work, the *Concierto de Aranjuez*. This gorgeous piece of flamenco-inspired orchestral music was famously adapted in 1959 by Miles Davis and Gil Evans for their landmark album, *Sketches of Spain*. Rodrigo hit the roof on hearing that a mere jazz musician had dared to adapt his work, and promptly told his lawyers to sue Davis and Evans. While lawyers' letters flew back and forth across the Atlantic, it is said that Rodrigo received his first royalty cheque from sales of *Sketches of Spain*, and quietly told his lawyers to drop their action against the trumpeter...

This was not the only time that Davis and Evans swung by Andalucía looking for inspiration. On the earlier 1958 big band album, *Miles Ahead*, the trumpeter adapted Delibes' "The Maids of Cadiz", delicately arranged by Evans, on an album that also included the track "Blues for Pablo" (Davis had met the Malagueño in Paris, and their genius was so similar—not least their overweening egos—that Davis is commonly called "the Picasso of jazz").

Spain did have its Pop Moment in the 1960s, as Juan Bonilla explains with mischievous glee, but the musical soundtrack was largely dire, an insipid form of beat pop called Ye-Yé (the Spanish equivalent of the Beatles' "Yeah yeah yeah"). Hipsters were more likely to be found listening to flamenco or jazz. It could be argued that Spain never quite "got" rock music, just as it could be argued that, conversely, its youth culture is unique in Europe in having maintained a link with its country's traditional music, namely, flamenco, which every child learns in school, a situation that finds no comparison in any other European country. A loosening of mores in the 1960s and Franco's pragmatic adoption of both tourism and North American trade brought a loosening of culture as well. Camarón and his collaborator, guitarist Paco de Lucia (Algeciras, 1947) established flamenco nuevo, mixing a raw, earthier version of the music, with an emphasis on the gitano origins that had been furtively airbrushed out of it since the days of Washington Irving, and strands from jazz, African music and elsewhere. De Lucia had and retains an extraordinary technique, which is why, after ten albums with Camarón, he started to stretch out stylistically and geographically, in 1979 joining another incredibly fleet-fingered guitarist, John McLaughlin, fresh from both the electric groups of Miles Davis and his own supergroup, Mahavishnu Orchestra, and Larry Coryell, of the US jazz-rock group Eleventh House, in what was simply called The Guitar Trio. Perhaps the most stunning fact about this self-taught genius is that until he was asked to record Rodrigo's *Concierto de Aranjuez* in 1991, he had not addressed himself to the skill of reading music, preferring in the mentoring tradition of flamenco to concentrate on spirit rather than academic technique. De Lucia told *Guitar* magazine: "I went to a house in the Caribbean where I was completely alone. I would spend the whole day working on the *Concierto*. I learned that piece with a book on hand, so I could look up what the value of the note was. I would look at the score, and if I saw any signs, I would look in the book to see what it meant. I translated like I had a letter or a book in Russian. You read what one word means in Russian and you go to the dictionary and translate it. After I spent half an hour reading, I'd get one note."

His time spent on one-note-at-a-time translation paid off; unlike Miles Davis, he produced a version of the *Concierto* that Rodrigo claimed was the best version he had ever heard.

LIKE PUNK NEVER HAPPENED... IN ANDALUCÍA

Franco's death in 1975 might have sparked the *movida* in cities such as Madrid and Barcelona, giving the world such disparate talents as Almodóvar and La Fura dels Baus, but there was no equivalent revolution in music. In Andalucía, 1976—the year the Sex Pistols swore on British television—saw the formation of the much-loved Malagueño band Tabletom, although thirty years on they remain a doper's goodtime boogie band, perhaps tellingly catalogued on YouTube alongside Lynyrd Skynyrd playing "Sweet Home Alabama". Nor was there any notable explosion in punk or new wave groups, as there was elsewhere in mainland Europe—Germany's *neue Deutsche welle* of the 1980s being an excellent case in point. Barcelona's La Fura dels Baus (politely, "the maniacs from the sewer") may have made a career out of scaring their audiences, but they have never approached the terror quotient of Berlin's road-drill-wielding Einstürzende Neubauten.

If the soundtrack in Andaluz youth bars and cars is a reliable barometer, then most Spanish youth have spent the past few decades contentedly nodding along to an uninspired choice of mainstream reggae, and particularly bad techno or *bakalao* (the linguistic curio being that with a C it is cod, with a K, it is bad techno). The former overlaps with Spain's ambiguous attitude to *hachís* culture, once legal and now re-criminalized, although the DIY marijuana crop in the countryside of Andalucía probably represents a sizeable percentage of its agricultural produce, and also involves a fair number of the otherwise law-abiding population, including at least one young mayor of a pueblo blanco known to this writer. The taste for dumbed-down electro—in a country where groups such as Kraftwerk, Yello and Orbital are virtually unknown—is baffling, particularly when rave culture would appear to have been more or less limited to foreign clubbers in the mega venues of Ibiza. It has, however, produced a sizeable market for ethnic and ambient chill music, dominated by the aforementioned Chambao, perhaps best described as a Mediterranean version of Everything but the Girl, whose lilting mix of African and flamenco rhythms and gentle trip-hop made their 2002 debut, *Flamenco Chill*, the summer soundtrack of Tarifa's kite-surfer bars and the hippie nudist beaches of Caños de Meca.

Camarón, de Lucía and their compatriots in the flamenco nuevo movement did inspire one abiding trend in Andaluz music, perhaps best typified by the aforementioned Radio Tarifa, who split in 2006 but whose constituent parts have regrouped as Son de la Frontera, a name that plays on the ambiguity that *son* can mean either "they are" or "sound", "of the frontier".

Radio Tarifa were neither a radio station nor from Tarifa. They came from Granada, Madrid and Sussex (their last bassist was Englishman David Purdye). They chose the name as it reflected their mix of Andaluz, Moroccan and other world music strands, naming it after the town where you can not only see Africa, as mentioned at the beginning of this book, but you can also tune in to TV and radio from across el Estrecho. Founder Fain Dueñas told *The Scotsman* newspaper, "That's us and our music, a meeting point between all the cultures that have come through and continue to come through that part of Spain." Dueñas also told *The Times*, "Our music unites Arabic and Western forms... We don't make fusion music. We mix cultures that live side by side and it's that interrelationship we are exploring."

Radio Tarifa were outsold by Ketama, who took their name from a Moroccan valley noted for the quality of its dope crop, and who numbered members of the Habichuela dynasty and other Andaluz musicians in their various line-ups, although Ketama achieved their popularity at the expense of the music, which at times verged on schmaltz (they disbanded in 2004).

Although punk never really took hold in Andalucía (even though both anarchism and dreadlocks did…), it can claim a number of slightly curious links to the genre. And in Andalucía, or Granada more precisely, all roads seem to lead to Joe Strummer, or at least his ghost. If you spend any time investigating the Spanish contemporary rock scene, you will find two things. The first is that a goodly number of British punks, among them the magnificent Vi Subversa of the equally magnificent Poison Girls, and Richard Nother, sometime 101'er with Strummer and drummer on PiL's legendary *Metal Box*, have been resident or in hiding in Andalucía for some years. (On the subject of PiL, their bassist Jah Wobble has been a regular visitor for decades.) The other thing you will find is that Strummer has left his mark all over eastern Andalucía, and especially in Almería, which he visited for the last twenty years of his life and until his death in 2002.

Even though it is perhaps only a quarter of the size of Seville, Granada is the centre of Andalucía's musical culture, with Almería threatening to overtake Seville in second place. If you search for information on the other main Granadino band, Los Planetas, you will find that their management company is not only called Spanish Bombs, but its website also plays you the Clash tune of that name, from *London Calling*, on its homepage. ("Spanish Bombs" the song was their homage to the Civil War left.) When you go looking for information on Lagartija Nick, you discover that in 2003, a year after Strummer died, the Nicks joined other Spanish post-punk groups alongside Mick Jones, Tymon Dogg and former Pogue Jem Finer (now the brains behind the Long Now's sound installation at Trinity Buoy Wharf in London) and other friends of Strummer in a *homenaje a Joe* in Granada. The affable and heroic Clash frontman, certainly the only believable rock star revolutionary this writer ever met, has left his fingerprints elsewhere in Andalucía's musical culture. While only nominally Andaluz, the fiercely political punk group Mano Negra (now also defunct, but survived by the irrepressible Manu Chao), who took their name from the mythical Andaluz anarchist group of that name—now believed to have been an invention of the authorities, looking for an excuse to beat up striking agricultural workers in the Guadalquivir plain in the nineteenth century—once coaxed Strummer, their musical idol, onstage to perform "I Fought the Law (and the Law Won)", the 1959 Sonny Curtis and the Crickets song that the Clash made their anthem in 1978. Mano Negra would later also coax Jello Biafra, of Dead Kennedys notoriety, onstage to duet with them, to perform the Dead Kennedys' reading of the same song.

Despite some shockingly intimate graffiti about them still to be found on walls around the centre of Granada, Los Planetas are, along with the Nicks, one of the key groups in the Spanish post-punk culture. Earlier releases such as their 2002 *Encuentros con entidades* (literally, "encounters with entities", but probably better read as "Close encounters of the third kind") could have tagged them, perhaps a little cruelly, as Spain's answer to Radiohead. In fact, as their version of Joy Division's "Disorder", from *Unknown Pleasures*, on the 1998 Spanish Joy Division tribute compilation, *Warsaw: un homenaje a Joy Division* suggested, there is something altogether darker about them. Their jangly, almost psychedelic buzz-saw guitar epics might invite comparison to trippier noise bands such as Spaceman 3, Harmony Rockets or even the impeccably cultish Bark Psychosis. Los Planetas themselves happily declare the influence of My Bloody Valentine and the Jesus and Mary Chain, although it has to be said that, particularly on their ecstatically noisy 2007 album, *La Leyenda del espacio*, when compositions vanish into a blizzard of feedback and echo, this music follows a template first cut by Pink Floyd on 1969's *Ummagumma*. (That said, *La leyenda del espacio* deserves recognition as Spain's answer to Joy Division's epochal masterwork, *Closer*.) Most interestingly, though, *La leyenda del espacio* is inspired by the *cante jondo*, deep song, of El Camarón and Paco de Lucia, and its closing track, "Tendra que haber un camino" ("There must be a way", dedicated to a dead friend), is sung by none other than the obviously very busy Enrique Morente…

There has been a regular traffic of musicians between Los Planetas and Lagartija Nick in recent years, with the latter sometimes kidnapping drummer Eric Jiménez (originally a co-founder of the Nicks) and guitarists Jota and Florent for their recent *Lo imprevisto* ("The unexpected", 2004) and their multi-media live project, *La guerra de los mundos* (which does indeed translate into the title of its famous dedicatee H. G. Wells' novel,

The War of the Worlds). The band is the brainchild of songwriter and musician Antonio Arias, and has something else in common with US lo-fi gods Sonic Youth in the form of bassist Lorena Enjuto, who joins Kim Gordon of Sonic Youth, Tina Weymouth of Talking Heads and Tessa Pollitt of The Slits in that small, cool but muscular elite of women bassists in hip post-punk combos. If anything, Lagartija Nick are even darker than Los Planetas, comparable perhaps to the menace evoked by Nick Cave and the Bad Seeds, or perhaps Cave's collaborations with cadaverous Berlin existentialist, Blixa Bargeld. *Omega* itself grows in stature by the year and is an essential purchase for anyone interested in contemporary Spanish culture.

JOE STRUMMER'S FINGERPRINTS

Joe Strummer leaves one last set of fingerprints on Andaluz music, although this is more accidental than causal. Early in the 2000s this writer and his partner, an OBE-toting jazz composer, witnessed one of the most extraordinary concerts in their combined eighty or so years of concert-going. The concert was an acoustic jazz trio—guitar, stand-up bass, *cajon*, the slapped rhythm box—led by the aforementioned Jerez-born guitarist, Gerardo Núñez, in front of perhaps forty people in the middle of the Plaza de Socorro square in Ronda. Jazz is in many ways the Cinderella of Spanish musical forms, although it might be said to be remarkable that it even exists here. Yet Spain's best jazz magazine, *Cuadernos de Jazz*, is one of the finest jazz publications in the world, and the big three jazz festivals—San Sebastian, Getxo, Vittoria, all of them in the Basque Country—are for good or ill plugged into the international festival circuit, which means that like Montreux and North Sea, they get the dinosaurs being trucked around the world in any particular year by powerful North American concert promoters.

Yet smaller festivals exist—in Andalucía at Almuñecar, Cádiz, Granada, Málaga, Marbella, Seville and elsewhere—that buck the trend and include indigenous talent, such as the aforementioned señores Pardo, Benavent and a lively avant-garde who mainly infest Barcelona. And in that short, modest concert in the Plaza de Socorro, Núñez provided a glimpse of genius that few others in the square that sunny late afternoon seemed to notice, or even comprehend. This has not so far been captured in any of the ten albums he has recorded, but Núñez played a set that combined the quicksilver dexterity of great flamenco guitar with a sometimes ear-popping dynamics and pugnacity that took this listener rocketing back to Strummer onstage with the Clash, perhaps even to Pennie Smith's iconic photo of Paul Simenon smashing up his guitar on the cover of *London Calling*. Nuñez, perhaps wondering why he had bothered driving to Ronda in the first place, had already fled the stage before this writer could introduce himself and asked if he'd heard the Clash...

If it has not made itself obvious already, the most remarkable thing about the interaction between all these performers, representing different generations in often wildly different genres, is how, as Morente says, they see nothing in crossing barriers of genre, age, gender, race, era or geography. This is something you will notice at concerts and in clubs, which rarely divide down tribal or generational lines, and speaks to a healthy eclecticism among musicians and listeners. It also speaks to a receptivity towards the arts that can surprise the outsider more used to the feigned boredom of a British or North American media that hides its ignorance behind world-weary cynicism. In fact this is nothing new in continental Europe, but still a rarity in, say, a Britain where phoney critical wars are fought over the Pulp versus Blur "debate", and where an artist such as Robert Wilson can find himself the subject of a backlash before he has even set foot in the country. It is just one of the many ways that Andalucía can surprise, delight and occasionally disturb the interested visitor. But then, Andalucía is the sort of place where, in one of those moments of magic realism that can happen when you least expect it, you might find yourself spending half an hour discussing art with your bank manager, or find yourself having a long chat about Deleuze and Guattari with a friend, Fran, while he is serving you over his counter in the post office, and then you find that your friend also reads classical Greek as well as French postmodern cultural theorists...

Chapter Twenty

LA FRANJA ("THE FRINGE"): EXCAVATING THE FUTURE IN ANDALUCÍA

"Moros fuera" — graffito, El Ejido, Almería, 2007

This might not at first seem to have much to do with the cultural history of Andalucía, but bear with me, and the first person singular, for a few paragraphs.

Back in the autumn of 1999, as a newly arrived guiri in Andalucía, I found myself on the train from Algeciras to Granada. The section of the journey between the stations at El Colmenar and Cañete la Real is one of the most spectacular train rides in Europe, particularly in the mountains around Ronda. The train had barely left Algeciras, however, before there was a problem. A young African man sitting a row behind me and quite obviously trying to hide the fact that he did not have a ticket by pretending to be engrossed in a cheap Walkman-type personal stereo he was wearing, was ejected quite aggressively from the train by the ticket inspector. She may have only being doing her job, but her enthusiasm for this task suggested there could have been a subtext here. The young African, barely into his twenties and dressed shabbily enough to be an illegal, was thrown off at the San Roque-La Linea station to await either the next train or the arrival of the police, who conventionally arrest, process and forcibly repatriate illegals, the *sin papeles*, "without papers".

I later realized that, had I known then what I know now, I should have simply leapt up and made an operatic production of apologizing for forgetting to buy my mate's ticket and, with the cash I probably had in my pockets—train travel in Spain is remarkably cheap—simply bought this stranger a ticket to Granada or Almería, where he was probably heading. (Only later still would I hear the as-yet untold story of the underground railroad through Andalucía, organized by Spanish and foreigners alike,

239

Excavating the future in Marbella: Christmas lights garland palm trees beneath a forest of construction site cranes in 2007

that helps sin papeles on their way from the beaches of Tarifa, through the forests of the Alcornocales, and on to destinations further east and north. Admirably, if rather rashly, author Chris Stewart has confessed in the media to aiding and abetting the Andaluz underground railroad.)

Around the same time, *Sur* newspaper (the Spanish one) published a quite startling front page photograph of a Spanish couple relaxing on a beach on the Costa de la Luz. The presence of low cliffs suggested it was perhaps in the Bolonia or Barbate area, somewhere near the garum factories of Baelo Claudia. They were sitting under a parasol on the beach, squinting out to sea, and looked as though they were discussing the weather, or where to go for lunch.

The reason the photographer had taken the photograph, however, was that the couple seemed to have either missed or were ignoring a large object on the beach a few yards away. At first glance, it looked like a dead seal. On closer inspection, it was a dead man, dressed in what was probably a burnous or djellabah.

This couple were sunbathing mere feet away from a corpse.

The photographer had obviously seen the news value in this particular composition. The drowned man was just another of the unlucky illegals who wash up on the deadly beaches of Tarifa, sometimes dumped into the surf by the people smugglers who charge them small fortunes to ferry them across el Estrecho. You did not need to be the Susan Sontag of *On Photography* to read what the photographer had read into that image. Or, indeed, why her or his picture editor bought the picture.

Africa is Already Here (Always Was...)

These two events may seem to have little to do with the cultural history of Andalucía, but in fact they speak to one of the few certainties we can entertain about its future cultural history, which is that its future will be multicultural and multiracial—whether the graffiti commentators of El Ejido like it or not. Some of that multiculturalism will be brought by wealthy northern snowbirds moving south into the sun. Some will be brought west and north by less wealthy people also hoping to take part in this modern-day economic adventure in the luckiest little corner of Europe. Whatever the graffiti artists of El Ejido and their "niggers out" (for that is the only translation of *moros fuera*) spray-can dialectic may argue, El Ejido itself in fact depends on African labour for its quite extraordinary wealth. El Ejido is not terribly comfortable with that fact, which is why in 2000 it staged its own little *Kristallnacht*.

Spend any time in Andalucía, on its costas or in its interior, in the villages and towns as well as the cities, and you will find that Africa is already here (always was…). They are working in hotels and banks and newspapers, and their children are in schools where some of them will study literature and art and become the artists of future generations. Nor really do you have to read Jared Diamond, Noam Chomsky or even Mike Davis' harrowing *Late Victorian Holocausts* to see their reason for wanting to claim their share of this lucky little corner of Europe. It was theirs before it was ours.

Andalucía's cultural future depends, of course, on how Andalucía chooses to move into the future. Or, more pertinently, how it is allowed to move into the future.

Shortly after that train journey, a fellow journalist, Spanish, claimed to have had sight of a remarkable document, a report on *La Franja*, "the fringe", the stretch of Spanish coastline between Algeciras and Empurias, just north of Barcelona, the place where those pre-Christian Greeks stepped ashore and helped invent Spain. He said that the report estimated, among other things, that by the year 2015 there could be as many as forty million people living along the fifty-mile-wide, 1000-mile-long, ribbon of La Franja. This seemed to chime with the seemingly unstoppable building craze along the several costas between Algeciras and Barcelona, at least. It also seemed to threaten to turn J. G. Ballard's Estrella de Mar into something more like *Blade Runner* al mar. And then in 2006 Andaluz novelists like Manuel Pimentel and Miguel Ruiz Trigueros started satirizing that self-same unstoppable building craze, around about the time that local authorities began tearing down some of the many illegally built housing developments along the costas. At the very least, forty million people temporarily blinded by the sun and heat represents a market that any enterprising business in the era of end-time capitalism would want to get its hands on.

The report, he said, had been produced by one of the largest corporate publicity companies in Britain, although its London offices pertly denied all knowledge of any such report. My Spanish colleague, perhaps unwittingly echoing the famous words of Mandy Rice-Davies, responded drily, "Well, they would say that, wouldn't they?"

Barring the unlikely event of the sudden appearance of the La Franja report, this is where the journalistic "facts", for what little they are worth, rest now. It is interesting, however, that my Spanish colleague should have identified this particular British corporate PR company as the source of the mythical La Franja report. However, given the company's standing in the global corporate PR world, we might be allowed at least two misgivings. The first would be that any corporate PR company would be the last source we might charitably expect to tell the truth in such circumstances. The second, more interestingly, is that any go-getting global corporate PR company worth its salt would surely be mad not to want to get a piece of the action in the biggest Spanish land-grab since the Reconquest.

Whether or not the La Franja report exists may well prove an irrelevance, not least because in 2008 the Andaluz construction boom was in meltdown, with worrying implications for the regional and perhaps national economy. There is, however, another media-inspired controversy that we should also consider, not least because Andalucía is the place where it would happen first, and that is the "Islamization" of western society. It comes as something of a relief, then, to read what those subversives at *The Economist* had to say in the autumn of 2007 about the much-touted threat of the "new Caliphate" and the concept, popular among the chattering Right, of a Europe overtaken by the "Moors", those "moros" the folks of El Ejido want "fuera":

> The imminent arrival of Eurabia can be dismissed as poor mathematics. Muslim minorities in Europe are indeed growing fast and causing political friction, but they account for less than five per cent of the total population, a tiny proportion by American standards of immigration. Even if that proportion trebles in the next 20 years, Eurabia will still be a long way off.

So if the free-marketeers and Chicago School economists of St James's Street think that, then the rest of us can sleep easy in our beds for at least the foreseeable future. (You can also read *The Economist*'s disco capitalist take on migration at even greater length in its eye-opening 5 January 2008 special edition on the subject.)

It would be too naïve to imagine that Andalucía might have a "message" for the future, beyond perhaps George Santayana's rather time-worn complaint that those who forget the past are doomed to repeat it. However, its cultural history might have left a few clues lying around among all those carelessly abandoned civilizations, lost cities, libraries and encyclopedias. It might remind us that, despite what politicians say, we did not get here first; a hominid African woman did one point eight million years before us. Despite what the same politicians say, Andalucía, like the rest of Europe, like every country in the world, has always had space for its new arrivals; it is only their policies and budgets that do not have space for the new arrivals. Moreover, if we have abdicated our economies to stateless multinational corporations, we may have to reconsider the notions of nationality and borders as little more than crowd control, a supranational version of those zigzag pens they make you queue in at airports. The fronteras of the future may exist in cyberspace, the passport replaced by the credit card—if they do not already.

Above all, the cultural history of Andalucía might remind us that we owe it to those notional Atlanteans, the warrior-king-gods of Tartessos, the Dama de Baza, the emperor Hadrian and his boyfriend, San Isidoro of Seville, the architects of Madinat al-Zahra, the librarians of Córdoba, the Cortes of Cádiz, Lorca, Machado, Jiménez and Hernández, Enrique Morente and Lorena Enjuto, not to mention a scarily clever seven-year-old Andaluza called Natalia, to keep the lights on.

Further Reading

This is a selected list of cited texts, sources and suggested readings in related areas. Some of the writers cited are currently out of print, although titles by George Borrow and others are now available at the estimable online Project Gutenberg web site, www.gutenberg.org.

Bendala Galán, Manuel, *Tartesios, iberos y celtas*. Madrid: Temas de Hoy, 2000.

Brenan, Gerald, *The Face of Spain* (1951). London: Serif, 2006.

Brenan, Gerald, *South of Granada* (1957). London: Penguin, 1963.

Brenan, Gerald, *The Spanish Labyrinth* (1943). Cambridge: Cambridge University Press, 1990.

Bonilla, Juan, *La Costa del Sol en la hora pop*. Seville: Fundación José Manuel Lara, 2007.

Bonilla, Juan, *The Nubian Prince*. New York: Picador, 2007.

Boyd, Alastair, *The Sierras of the South*. Málaga: Santana Books, 2004.

Boyd, Alastair, *The Road from Ronda*. Málaga: Santana Books, 2004.

Cernuda, Luis, *Selected Poems*. New York: Sheep Meadow Press, 1999.

Cole, Peter (trans), *The Dream of the Poem: Hebrew Poetry from Muslim and Christian Spain 950-1492*. Princeton NJ: Princeton University Press, 2007.

Cuenca Toribio, José Manuel, *Andalucia: historia de un pueblo*. Madrid: Espasa-Calpe, 1984.

Cuenca Toribio, José Manuel, *Historia general de Andalucía*. Córdoba: Editorial Almuzara, 2005.

Davis, Mike, *Ecology of Fear: Los Angeles and the Imagination of Disaster*. London: Picador, 1999.

Davis, Mike, *Late Victorian Holocausts: El Niño Famines and the Making of the Third World*. London: Verso, 2000.

Diamond, Jared, *Collapse: How Societies Choose to Fail or Succeed*. New York: Viking, 2005.

Diamond, Jared, *Guns, Germs and Steel: The Fates of Societies*. New York: Norton, 1997.

Fletcher, Richard, *Moorish Spain*. London: Weidenfeld & Nicolson, 1992.

Ford, Richard, *Gatherings from Spain* (1846). London: Pallas Athene, 2000.

Foucault, Michel, *The Order of Things*. Abingdon: Routledge Classics, 2002.

Garcia Lorca, Federico, *Selected Poems*. Tarset: Bloodaxe Books, 1992/London: Penguin, 2001.

Gibson, Ian, *Cuatro poetas en guerra*. Barcelona: Editorial Planeta, 2007.

Gibson, Ian, *Federico Garcia Lorca: A Life*. London: Pantheon, 1997.

Gibson, Ian, *Lorca's Granada: A Practical Guide*. London: Faber & Faber, 1992.

Grove, Valerie, *Laurie Lee: The Well-Loved Stranger*. London: Viking, 2000.

Hemingway, Ernest, *The Dangerous Summer* (1960). New York: Simon & Schuster, 1997.

Hernández, Miguel, *Selected Poems*. New York: White Pine Press, 1989.

Isidore of Seville, *The Etymologies* (trans. Stephen A. Barney, J. A. Beach, Oliver Berghof, W. J. Lewis). Cambridge: Cambridge University Press, 2006.

Jacobs, Michael, *Andalucía*. London: Pallas Athene, 1998.

Jiménez, Juan Ramón, *Selected Writings*. New York: Farrar, Straus and Giroux, 1999.

Kennedy, A. L., *On Bullfighting*. London: Anchor, 2001.

Lee, Laurie, *As I Walked Out One Midsummer Morning* (1969). London: Penguin, 1973.

Lee, Laurie, *A Moment of War*. London: Penguin, 1991.

Machado, Antonio *Border of a Dream: Selected Poems*. Port Townsend, Washington State: Copper Canyon Press, 2003.

Menocal, María Rosa, *Ornament of the World: How Muslims, Jews, and Christians Created a Culture of Tolerance in Medieval Spain*. New York: Little, Brown, 2002.

Paredes Grosso, José Manuel, *El Jardín de las Hespérides: los origenes de Andalucía en los mitos y leyendas de la antiguedad*. Madrid: Sucesores de Rivadeneyra, 1985.

Pimentel, Manuel, *El Librero de la Atlántida*. Córdoba: Editorial Almuzara, 2007.

Pink, Sarah, *Women and Bullfighting: Gender, Sex and the Consumption of Tradition*. Oxford: Berg, 1997.

Richardson, Paul, *Our Lady of the Sewers*. London: Little, Brown/Abacus, 1998.

Ruiz Trigueros, Miguel, *La Noche de Arcilla*. Ronda: Ediciones Alternativas, 2006.

Stewart, Chris, *Driving Over Lemons: An Optimist in Andalucía*. London: Sort Of Books, 1999.

Valis, Noël, *The Culture of Cursilería: Bad Taste, Kitsch and Class in Modern Spain*. Durham NC/London: Duke University Press, 2002.

Vernet, Juan, *Lo que Europa debe al Islam de España*. Barcelona: Circulo de
  Lectores, 1999.

Webster, Jason, *Duende: A Journey in Search of Flamenco*. London: Doubleday,
  2003.

Index of Literary & Historical Names

Index of Places & Landmarks